Political Grouping in the Czechoslovak Reform Movement

VLADIMIR V. KUSIN

Institute of Soviet and East European Studies
University of Glasgow

MACMILLAN

First published 1972 by
THE MACMILLAN PRESS LTD
London and Basingstoke
Associated companies in New York Toronto
Dublin Melbourne Johannesburg and Madras

SBN 333 13361 7

Printed in Great Britain by
WESTERN PRINTING SERVICES LTD
Bristol

TO MY PARENTS

Publishers' Note

The series of eleven volumes entitled 'Political and Social Processes in Eastern Europe' is the result of a British inter-university, inter-disciplinary comparative study, sponsored by the Social Science Research Council. Professor Ghiţa Ionescu was the organiser and co-ordinator of the research work (1968–71). The volumes are as follows:

Ghiţa Ionescu (University of Manchester): The Evolution of the Socialist State

Jane Cave (University of Birmingham), R. Amann (University of Birmingham), L. Blit (University of London), R. W. Davies (University of Birmingham), T. Podolski (Portsmouth Polytechnic), and G. Sakwa (University of Bristol): Politics and the Polish Economy

David Lane (University of Essex) and George Kolankiewicz (University of Swansea) (*editors*): Social Groups in Polish Society

Jaroslav Krejčí (University of Lancaster): Social Change and Stratification in Postwar Czechoslovakia

Vladimir V. Kusin (University of Glasgow): Political Grouping in the Czechoslovak Reform Movement

A. H. Brown (University of Oxford) and G. Wightman (University of Glasgow): The Communist Party of Czechoslovakia

J. F. N. Bradley (University of Manchester): Czechoslovak Politics 1948–68

Phyllis Auty (University of London): The Changing Role of the Yugoslav Communist Party

R. K. Kindersley (University of Oxford): The Yugoslav Federal Assembly: Relations between Executive and Legislature

F. Singleton (University of Bradford): The Yugoslav Social Groups and Institutions

D. Matko (University of Glasgow) and D. J. R. Scott (University of Glasgow): Career Patterns of Yugoslav Decision-Makers

The individual volumes have different titles and each of them is a self-contained, independent study on a separate subject.

Together they form a tripartite analysis of three given Socialist states of Eastern Europe: Czechoslovakia, Poland and Yugoslavia, as follows:

Subject of study	Poland	Czechoslovakia	Yugoslavia
The changing role of representative institutions	Jane Cave G. Sakwa	J. F. N. Bradley	R.K. Kindersley
The changing role of the Party	Jane Cave	A. H. Brown and G. Wightman	Phyllis Auty
The changing role of the groups in the interplay between the government and the economy	L. Blit, R. W. Davies, R. Amann, and T. Podolski David Lane and George Kolankiewicz	Jaroslav Krejčí Vladimir V. Kusin	F. Singleton D. Matko and D. J. R. Scott

See for a complete description of the project in the Appendix of *The Evolution of the Socialist State*, by Ghiţa Ionescu in this series.

Each book in the series will carry its own index of names and subjects. When all eleven volumes have been published a complete synoptical index to the series will be published.

Contents

Preface

While believing that the non-governmental groups and organisations in a Communist society constitute a legitimate and complete subject of independent inquiry, I would wish to draw the reader's attention to three books which complement the study of political grouping in the Czechoslovak reform movement. Dr Jaroslav Krejčí of Lancaster University has now published (Macmillan) a very factual and revealing book on *Social Change and Stratification in Postwar Czechoslovakia*. A. H. Brown of St Antony's College, Oxford, and G. Wightman of Glasgow University are co-authors of *The Communist Party in Czechoslovakia*, also to be published by Macmillan, which deals specifically with the apex of political structure. Macmillan will further publish J. F. N. Bradley's *Czechoslovak Politics 1948–68*. The present book and these three are best read concurrently.

They comprise the 'Czechoslovak' contribution to the comparative project on *Political and Social Processes in Eastern Europe*, supervised most efficiently by Professor Ghiţa Ionescu of Manchester University and the London School of Economics and Political Science and sponsored by the Social Science Research Council. I am grateful to the Council for assistance which made the final stages of material collection and writing possible. The entire series will be brought to the public by Macmillan, a deserving venture of which I enjoy expressing my sincere appreciation.

Innumerable discussions had been conducted with knowledgeable friends before this book was committed to print. I found in all of them professional interest as much as affection for the actors of the story, the Czechoslovak reformers. For both I extend my thanks to them. And incidentally, he who discerns detached description in the book should not doubt the author's personal admiration for socialism with a human face.

Full-bodied English still remains outside my reach and it has been perhaps impudent to write a book in this language. I had, however, the privilege of the typescript being ably inspected for mistakes by Mrs Catriona Soukup and Miss Jean Levitch. To them should go all the credit, while the reader's dissatisfaction with flatness of style and idiom must be laid at my door. Miss Anne Campbell and Margaret Dool applied their typing skill most carefully to the production of the final version.

Above all, my gratitude extends to my wife. For months she saw me disappear in my study at moments which most husbands keep reserved for their families. Having given me her patience and encouragement, she became in a way a co-author of this book.

Glasgow   VLADIMIR V. KUSIN
August 1971

Introduction

While it is undoubtedly true that political history cannot be reduced to the history of political parties, organisations and groups, there are situations which call for this particular angle of approach. A society claiming to be based on unity of purpose and organisation and even priding itself on its alleged capacity to overcome particular interest by inculcating into everyone a strong sense of the common good, can be better understood when its components are exposed to separate consideration. One can argue with good reason that the Czechoslovakia of the 1960s was a case history in this respect. It was a society which became increasingly aware of its own protracted malaise: both tangible things and ideas functioned badly. How to diagnose the ailment became one of the crucial questions; it had to be asked before a pain-killer was administered and the correct cure prescribed. Reform was preconditioned by method of analysis. In searching for an adequate manner of investigation, the two main probing instruments – art and social science – found the one and only official ideology wanting. They deviated from it. Art and literature became more and more critical. Philosophy questioned the concept of subservience of man's inquisitive spirit to dogma and transitory political requisites. Historiography set out to rectify the distorted image of the past from which emanated the present political postulates. Jurisprudence began to shake off the notion that legality was class determined. Science claimed for itself the right to investigate the material world without ideological guidance. Sociology was reintroduced as a method of social inquiry. Economic theory undertook a radical rethinking of the arrangements which governed production and distribution of goods and services. Practical politics made the first steps towards a realistic understanding of attitudes and processes which took shape beneath the cloak of officially imposed clichés. By 1967 all these, together with popular discontent of varying strength, coalesced to challenge the system and its leadership. The 'Prague Spring' had a body of theoretical and practical experience to draw on. For twelve years, since 1956, the reform had been maturing in the minds of men as individuals and members of groups.

One should understand this correctly: in 1967 Czechoslovakia was not on the verge of collapse, economically or otherwise. The reformers were not prompted into action by imminent doom, although in some fields relationships had been near breaking point (structure of economy; relations between Party and non-Party public, between the Czech and the Slovak political representation, between the Party leadership and the writers, and between the Party–State–police set-up and the students). Reform theories, unco-ordinated as they had to be in the absence of free interdisciplinary debate and action, were formulated as an alternative national aim of a long-term nature rather than as a plan for an immediate rescue operation. The downfall of Novotný, even though it may have been plotted in advance in rough outline as an obstacle-removing political operation, was largely accidental if measured against the expectations and aspirations of the reformist community. They were certainly not after Novotný's scalp as an end in itself when evolving their concepts. At no point did they take it for granted that a personnel reshuffle at the top would open the gate to democratic socialism. For some time in the 1960s it even seemed possible that reform could take place with Novotný's blessing. Ota Šik, for example, tried to persuade him to break away from the arbitrary course of action and to introduce more scholarly expertise into government. The dichotomy was between the national disposition and requirements of a modern society on the one hand and the existing system on the other, not between Novotný and Dubček. Had Novotný been able to read the writing on the wall in the early 1960s, he could have placed himself at the head of the reform. Instead, he steered on the collision course.

Above all the Party ideologues were afraid of giving up the barren class division concepts. For them the categories of workers, farmers and the intelligentsia blanketed any of the less general group distinctions with purportedly self-evident unity of interests. They were loathe to recognise that attitude and behaviour could be motivated by particular interests and aspirations. Ideological unity was a sacrosanct postulate. The triumphant declaration of 1960 that 'socialism in our country has become victorious' entailed a desire to draw even farther away from concrete sociological investigation and to base political decisions on the concept of an 'all-people's State'. A mere slogan was hoped to wish away the increasingly complex socio-economic and political stratification of society. In direct opposition to this wishful thinking, the majority of social scientists made the study of groups their primary target.[1] Pavel Machonin, a leading sociologist representing this trend, put it as follows: 'Contemporary societies must be understood as exceptionally complex and multidimensional social systems which ought to be subjected to scholarly investigation rather than subordinated to preconceived simplifying schemata.'[2] Zdeněk Mlynář centred his remarkable (for the time of publication) book *Stát a člověk* (*State and Man*) around the concept of the role of groups in a socialist State.[3] Michal Lakatoš's favourite theme, and hopefully an instrument whereby political decision-making could be made pluralistic, was the so-called 'civic society', i.e. the non-governmental structure of organised groups (infrastructure).[4]

Eventually, a consensus evolved among the social scientists recognising horizontal and vertical diversity between the

[1] Large groups of political scientists and sociologists joined forces to promote the study of stratification. Thus for example a conference on the social structure of a socialist society was held at Hrazany in 1964; a symposium, *Sociální struktura socialistické společnosti*, was published by Svoboda in 1966; a team of twenty-one scholars prepared a report on changes in the social structure and dynamism of socio-political developments for the Thirteenth Party Congress in 1966, published as *Změny v sociální struktuře Československa a dynamika sociálně-politického vývoje*, ed. Pavel Machonin (Prague, Svoboda, 1967); and another team, also under Machonin, conducted a large-scale analysis of social stratification in 1967, culminating with the publication of at least one volume of findings, *Československá společnost* (Bratislava, Epocha, 1969).

[2] Machonin, *Změny v sociální struktuře*, p. 6.

[3] Zdeněk Mlynář, *Stát a člověk* (Prague, Svobodné slovo, 1964).

[4] See for example Michal Lakatoš, 'Občanská společnost hledá své místo', *Kulturní noviny*, 24 February 1968.

various group interests. Horizontally, they found, group action was difficult to put on a commensurate basis. It was as often complementary (in pursuance of a common aim spanning the inherent contradiction) as it was diverse and even antagonistic. Convergence in the pre-1968 period, motivated by the desire for change as against the advocacy of the *status quo* by a greater part of the leadership, soon gave way to the more dynamic – and natural – divergence in conditions of free political debate. Vertically, the differentiation had a more lasting character even if it was generally recognised that socialism gave rise to greater mobility and less pronounced polarisation than capitalism. Vertical diversity was considered to be distributed on the following spectra: complexity (creativity) of work; range and depth of free-time interests; qualification and education; income and standard of living; share in political and economic leadership; wealth of spiritual life; and social status (prestige).[1]

On the available evidence, consisting of a fairly large body of writing before and during 1968, the Czechoslovak students of socio-economic and political groups did not, however, conclude that political processes and institutions were the direct result of an interplay of immutable vested interests. Change-seeking emerged as the principal point of reference for each group, cutting visibly across group boundaries. Thus, not all qualified workers were dedicated to identical politico-economic action (economic reform), and not all unskilled labourers threw their weight behind the system's backwater stability which guaranteed them a good wage irrespective of productivity demands. Society came to be understood as a dynamic system, finely differentiated and mobile. Social science had to sharpen its tools to examine it; the crude implements of class were demonstrably no longer suitable. Nevertheless, they still had to be taken into account, if only because they had a life of their own as a result of the primary place assigned to them in official ideology. Moreover, the reform balanced, almost right from the beginning, on the edge between the possible and the unattainable. Moscow was watching for signs of ideological impurity of which abandonment of class criteria, if only in social science, was not the least damnable. Thus, when sociological findings were to be translated into the language of

[1] Machonin, *Změny v sociální struktuře*, pp. 15–16.

practical political consideration and even decision, the quest was for what constituted the interest and/or orientation of a 'decisive majority' of a group, i.e. that section of a group which could carry the greatest weight with the whole of the group, other segments of society and Soviet ideological guardianship.

Not unexpectedly the degree of organisation (in the sense of belonging to an organisation) was high. This is a typical formal feature of every Communist society, presented as proof of wide political participation. In Czechoslovakia it coincided with an habitual mode of association already displayed by the public in pre-Communist times. By 1967 more than half of the population were members of some organisation or other. Of course, since 1948 the political set-up evolved into a single machinery, propelled from the centre through a more-or-less ingenious and certainly intricate network of transmission belts and levers. Its underlying logic was to demand execution of directives, not contribution to decision-making. Participation in control was in fact participation in fulfilment of orders. To a large extent political organisation remained divorced from socio-economic stratification and its components could not properly function as vehicles for, and channels of, political influence which the socio-economic groups might wish to exert. Hence the desire of the reformers to achieve recognition of individuals and groups as 'independent political subjects'. Zdeněk Mlynář wrote in February 1968: 'All these components have to be genuinely assured of the status of independent political subjects in order to prevent the state of affairs whereby one group substitutes another, subordinates it and regards it as no more than a transmission belt and instrument . . .'[1] Such a 'pluralism of political subjects' would hopefully constitute the first safeguard against concentration of power. Furthermore, the reformers would have liked to see 'internal pluralism' ensured within the newly independent organisations, obviously as a precaution against the hierarchic principle of 'democratic centralism'. In practice this 'internal pluralism' was variously formulated as 'safeguarding the rights of the minority', e.g. in the Communist Party, where an uncomfortable proponent of change could be fairly easily outvoted by an immobile majority,

[1] Zdeněk Mlynář, 'Naše politická soustava a dělba moci', *Rudé právo*, 13 February 1968, p. 3.

or as assertion of sectional interests, e.g. in the disintegrating Youth Union or in the continuing sub-division of unwieldy trade unions.

Opinions on what form the new system of political organisation should take remained far from unanimous. The strongest body of views, which seemed to emerge from the highly volatile exchanges of the Prague Spring, whatever its merits and demerits, favoured a cautious combination of adapted parliamentary democracy with elements of direct democracy (self-management) under the umbrella of enlightened Communist supervision. Such a three-cornered system had many good arguments speaking in its favour. Separation of legislative, executive and judicial powers, pluralistic elections, accountability of all State agencies to elected bodies, etc., were to ensure that political decisions would be taken by genuinely elected representatives of the population at large. In the spheres of production and local government the self-management principle was to apply. Workers' councils were to generate participation of producers in autonomous enterprise action. A multicameral parliament was to provide room for a flow of expertise into political decisions. Local government was to discontinue acting as the executant of central will at town and village level, and reverse its orientation towards representation of local interest and immediate responsibility to the local public for indigenous policy. Finally, the 'reality' of twenty years of development and of looming Soviet presence on the nation's horizon was to be taken into account by curtailing all newly won autonomies through the continued, even if 'modified', leading role of the Communist Party. The reformers hoped to have a sugar coat ready for this bitter pill: the National Front.

Briefly and with some simplification, the National Front can be described as permanent and mandatory coalition. As such it was welcomed by the public at large after World War II when unity of purpose and effort appeared to call for institutional manifestation, and when popular wrath as much as the interests of the legitimate parties concurred in demanding a ban on political organisations compromised by pro-Nazi collaboration or big business association. Under full Communism after 1948 the Front changed significantly and, having lost the character of political coalition with the seizure of undivided power by the

Communist Party, it soon lost all meaning other than the most formal one. It was the pre-1948 National Front that the reformers wished to revive as a forum on which political decisions were thrashed out. As the non-Communist parties had dwindled in quantity and quality since 1948 and as the major 'mass' organisations were to be incorporated into the policy-making pool, it is not difficult to see that the barring of opposition outside the National Front could only serve to perpetuate a virtual one-Party rule. 'Democracy', or whatever of it would have been made available to the Czechoslovak people, would remain largely dependent on the goodwill of the new Communist leadership. To do them justice, and to give all the credit they deserve to the reformers, the post-Novotný politicians were prepared to go a long way to demonstrate their good intentions. The Communist Party which promised to emerge from the fourteenth Congress, shaped on the new Statutes to be promulgated there, would most certainly be as far removed from its own pre-1968 image as the Yugoslav League of Communists is from the Communist Party of Yugoslavia of 1948 vintage. Consequently, the entire political set-up, which is to a large extent determined by the way the Communist Party exercises its power, would function in a novel way. Beyond this safe and general prediction it is not advisable to speculate, unless one wishes to fall victim to self-imposed value judgements.

This book proposes to tell the story of non-governmental political organisations in 1968. It leaves out the Communist Party and its subgroups (veterans, ultras, People's Militia, etc.) as well as the government apparats (army, police, National Committees, etc.), partly because at this level of detailed description the whole of the picture would be difficult to compress into one volume, and partly because other studies on the subject are in the making.[1] Above all, however, the author believes that one of the underlying interpretations of the Prague Spring must be sought in the emancipation of the 'infrastructure', i.e. precisely those organisations which were not

---

[1] See for example A. H. Brown and G. Wightman, *The Communist Party of Czechoslovakia*, typescript, to be published by Macmillan; Galia Golan, *The Czechoslovak Reform Movement* (Cambridge University Press, 1971), and *Reform Rule in Czechoslovakia*, typescript, to be published by C.U.P.

direct links in the chain of political command and whose members tried to achieve genuine autonomy. The subject of this book is thus narrowly defined. So is the method. No political theories of any range can be formulated without the developments in the governmental structure (in the wide sociological sense, i.e. including above all the Communist Party) and the outside world being taken into account. For such an exercise this book may hopefully serve as a supplier of a part of the requisite background information. Neither can far-reaching conclusions be drawn for non-Czechoslovak Communist societies; the spiritual and material milieux are much too diverse for that. This, then, is simply a description of how non-governmental groups of people thought and behaved in certain circumstances and why, according to the author, they did what they did and did not do what they might have done.

CHAPTER ONE

Workers

A consideration of the political role of the working class in the
reform movement is fraught with the danger of oversimplifica-
tion. Just about every side claimed to enjoy the workers' support. Josef Jodas, whose name epitomised stubborn conservativism in 1968, declared Novotný to be their only true champion.
At the other end of the spectrum Ivan Sviták formulated the
antagonism between the workers and the apparat. Writers of
letters and leaflets, often threatening the reformist leaders with
grave bodily harm and worse, hid their identity under the
lofty signature of 'Czech Worker' or 'Honest Toiler'. At the
same time workers from the Škoda forging shop petitioned the
National Committee, their Ministry and the government to
re-erect the statue of the first Czechoslovak President, T. G.
Masaryk, which had been pulled down in 1953. Oldřich
Švestka, editor of *Rudé právo*, worriedly rose to demand that
the working man be shielded against the consequences of
economic reforms. Ota Šik repeatedly went on the record
stressing that real benefit could accrue to the worker only from
a functioning economy based on new concepts and mechanisms.
One after another, the protagonists of reformation and counter-
reformation trooped on to the shop floor, figuratively and
literally, to compete for the most cherished support, or at the
least to win acclaim for their respective causes.

To a large extent all this behaviour was the product of an
ideologically conditioned mind. On the Communist scale of
class values pride of place goes to the workers. Once and for all
they are credited with the capacity to lead society, and no one
should dare to suggest otherwise without inviting defeat. If the
workers choose to embrace the reform, it cannot be van-
quished. If they disown it, its fate is as good as doomed. Apart
from the external factor, the way the workers would turn and

the vehemence with which they would give or deny their blessing, were apparently considered crucial by all warring factions.

The issue was, however, more rational than met the doctrinal eye. The working class was the most numerous section of the population. At the time of the 1961 census 3,361,392 persons or 52·2 per cent of the active population were registered as workers. With dependants and retired workers the proportion rose still higher (7,738,000 or 56·3 per cent of the whole population in 1961, and 8,201,000 or 58·1 per cent in 1965). In spite of emphasis in sociological studies and political thinking gradually shifting from class to group concepts, the numerical strength of the class had to be taken into account. Every policy which could be rightly or wrongly interpreted as 'anti-worker' would be by definition undemocratic, as it would go against the majority of the population.

How different this was from the Russia of 1917 and, indeed, from all the other 'people's democratic' countries of Eastern Europe! At the same time, the degree of establishment – especially in the Czech (as against the Slovak) working class – was much higher. It had originated primarily from craftsmen, rather than from pauperised peasantry. Its manufacturing experience had been both extensive and intensive, and had been handed down from generation to generation. The Czech working class had engendered its own cultural life and maintained rich contacts with the arts and with culture created outside its ranks. It had been organised politically and in trade unions for the better part of a century, but had rarely had to resort to conspiratorial or military-type organisation. Internally diversified, it was not an amorphous mass of proletarians: in the mid-1960s over 40 per cent were engaged in 'mechanised', 'complex mechanised' and 'automated' work.[1] The typical Czech worker was a machine operator, not a navvy. He had been scarred by class conflicts, but had retained for himself and his children a strong sense of national awareness; his social and national history had often walked hand in hand.

True, the Communist take-over in 1948 and subsequent

---

[1] Machonin, *Změny v sociální struktuře*, p. 28, and J. Hrabina, 'Proti deformáciam socialistickej teórie a praxe', *Nová mysl*, 2 (1969) p. 239.

developments gave birth to and sustained significant changes which affected both the composition and the modes of action of the working class. The effects were both factual and attitudinal. First, other categories were becoming workers: people from the country, demoted administrative employees, housewives, opponents of the régime. Second, a number of workers, especially the archetypal stalwarts and potential promoters of the new régime, were raised to non-worker positions, for example in the army, the police, the judicature, the Party and government (including local government), and even to the intelligentsia by way of various crash courses and half-baked educational schemes.[1] During the first five-year plan some 300,000 persons are estimated to have ceased to be workers (about 10 per cent of the total number) while 500,000 others became workers.[2] Third, together with the rest of the population, the workers had the nature of their traditional organisations changed. The Communist Party was pushed to the top of the country's political structure, the Social Democratic Party was compelled to merge with the Communist Party, the other political parties were reduced to unimportant front groups, and to the trade unions was assigned the role of acting as conveyor belts transmitting directives from above and dispensing benefits to the worthy. Fourth, industry slowly came to be plagued by general shortages, deficiencies and incompetence. Fifth, to compensate for the frustration arising from inability to influence the course of events, political and managerial, the régime created security of job tenure and remuneration. Coupled with the general tendency towards political noninvolvement and wage egalitarianism, this gave the 'working

---

[1] Special year-long courses to prepare workers without secondary education for university entrance began in 1948–9. There were 1,000 students in the first, and 2,000 in subsequent years. In addition, ministries and central authorities maintained fifty-one 'workers' schools' in 1949, and a twelve-month law course was available to train workers for posts of district and regional procurators. See for example L. Kalinová, 'Změny struktury čs. dělnické třídy na počátku socialistické výstavby', *Příspěvky k dějinám KSČ*, 5 (1966) pp. 709–35; K. Malý, 'Nad stránkami universitní matriky', *Dějiny a současnost*, 9 (1968) pp. 46–8; J. Neumannová, 'K poúnorovým proměnám kulturní politiky', *Revue dějin socialismu*, 6 (1968) pp. 817–43.

[2] Kalinová, op. cit., pp. 725–6.

masses' largely the character of 'producers of iron and steel' of whom no political action was expected, other than endorsement of the *status quo* at meetings and in the usual type of elections.

One may therefore be tempted to say that the traditional dispositions of the Czech working class and the effect of command economy and politics cancelled each other out. One-half of the population – the workers – appeared to be dedicated to inaction. Some of their characteristics militated against the continuation of what by the middle of the 1960s seemed evidently dysfunctional, while other factors made them view reformist attempts with suspicion. The reformers hoped to sway the workers one way, the conservatives another. Both were politically minded enough to realise that the kind of decision the working class would take must weigh heavily with the Soviet leadership. Hence the attention paid to the grassroots by defenders of the *status quo* and reformers alike.

Not long after January 1968 the dispute about what is and what is not beneficial to the workers became public property. When the Party Central Committee convened for the first time after Novotný's deposition, at the end of March, Josef Smrkovský saw it necessary to take issue with those who professed concern lest the new policy (by then only insufficiently crystallised) caused harm to the working man.

> Was it in the interest of the working class to be left producing, working, competing and carrying the burden of all the short-comings that exist in industry, while the results of its work were to a certain extent, and a great extent at that, turned into unsaleable stocks or exported for dumping prices? Was it in the interest of the working class to operate old machinery in bad conditions, without adequate safety measures and even without appropriate social and hygienic prerequisites?
>
> Was it in the interest of the working class to see the trade unions cease to be its own organisation, turn into an organisation of the state and side with the management? Was it in the interest of the working class to have the economic reform implemented reluctantly, not to admit to leading positions people who would know how to put production and sales on a rational economic basis and how to provide knowledgeable solutions to the complicated problems of which every enterprise had plenty? We now hear every day that workers are dissatisfied with the proposal

that they should have only one-third representation on the intended enterprise councils. This is allegedly not enough. But how were they represented to date? Who took their views into account, how did they share in controlling enterprise management, let alone in management itself? Did they have a chance to influence the appointment of leading managerial staff? Was it in the interest of the working class to give excessive preference to heavy as opposed to light industry, to neglect technical development in the consumer goods and food industries? I could go on asking whether it was in the workers' interest not to do a thing about municipal transport in Prague, about housing construction, etc., etc. The old policy was carried out in the name of the working class, true enough, but it did not bring the workers much benefit.[1]

The reformers were aware that for the sake of reform the workers must be induced to rise against the two main sources of passivity, the politico-organisational and the professional. In practical terms the two avenues that opened before them during the Prague Spring lay in reactivating the trade unions and in introducing self-management. Thus Zdeněk Mlynář, on one of the rare occasions that he addressed a working-class gathering (in the Mladá Boleslav Car Works on 16 April), spoke of 'clear-cut and effective organisational forms' which were needed, meaning precisely these two.[2])

The reformers were, in all they did, preoccupied with the institution of organisational and legislated measures, both to keep the process of reform going and to prevent anarchy. It was not easy, however, to overcome inertia and set the working class in motion. When Ludvík Vaculík went to the Škoda Works in Pilsen in March 1968 he found a workers' meeting divided into two halves: the one said nothing, the other was again divided into those who were suspicious of the new developments and those who were willing to go ahead if only instructions 'from above', i.e. from the Party or the Central Trades Union Council, were forthcoming. Some of the authentic pronouncements at this meeting may be of interest:

We need not have our own programme; the Party's programme will tell us what the trade unions should do.

[1] *Rudé právo*, 4 April 1968, p. 2.
[2] *Rudé právo*, 20 April 1968, p. 3.

Who represents the working people on the team which is compiling the Action Programme? Are workers on it?

I have the feeling that a plot against the working class is under way.

You must have more patience with us; you will learn about democracy faster than we.

I object to everything going on only in Prague, to all the democrats talking only to students and no one addressing the workers.[1]

Apart from indecisiveness and reluctance to take free action, the reform movement was further threatened by the possibility of a spontaneous explosion of wage demands. By the end of March workers in various places had realised that neither State power nor ideology were any longer unequivocally opposed to direct industrial action. They could not be, however alarming the prospect of industrial strife might be to them. To give the public freedom of expression while simultaneously denying the workers the right to withdraw their labour in pursuance of wage demands and to remedy other grievances, would be incongruous. Strike was suddenly discovered not to be a dirty word any more.[2]

This must be understood correctly. The Czechoslovak reform movement had been called to life by the intelligentsia and was led by a coalition between the intelligentsia and some change-oriented groups in the Party. Unlike similar occurrences else-

---

[1] *Literární listy*, 4 April 1968, p. 5.

[2] More dilemmas of this kind were inherent in the course taken by the Prague Spring reformers. How to implement constitutional freedom of association, and still prevent the restoration of the Social Democratic Party. How to guarantee press freedom, and still refrain from polemics with the Soviet Union. How to respond to overwhelming and unmistakable public opinion, and still retain the People's Militia. Some observers, including post-1968 Social Democratic émigrés and other groups of exiled Czechs, seem to maintain that this unwillingness of the Dubček leadership 'to step over their own shadow' constituted the cardinal problem on which the entire Czechoslovak experiment was bound to founder. I think that a reform in Eastern Europe, which above all must entail extrication from external influences, must be prepared to compromise. What may be seen as inadmissible halfheartedness by some, is in fact inevitable, especially in the initial stages of reform. Realistic self-restraint is more likely to lead to success than seemingly justifiable insistence on ideal solutions. This lesson ought to be clear now.

where (Poland), the workers were not the prime movers. The underlying causes were not only, or even primarily, economic, such as unbearable working conditions, price increases, poor standard of living, or shortages of basic foodstuffs, although of course all these were present to some extent. Essentially, however, the economic element of the reform was more sophisticated and had to do with planning, the structure of the economy, instruments of control, etc. There was consequently not much dynamite under the shop floor, although some pent-up feelings naturally could not wait to be released. Even so, full credit must go to the reformers and the workers for having kept industrial strife at the minimum and, in fact, for displaying a remarkable degree of responsible thinking. Some strikes were not about wages at all, but were motivated by concern for the well-being of the whole enterprise. The following description of some industrial action has been selected to represent what I believe was typical.

In mid-March 200 bus drivers in the Prague–Dejvice depot decided not to work more than thirty hours overtime monthly as against the average eighty hours which had been expected of them. They stated that they were unable 'to restore their labour' because their leisure was too short. The less-overtime action caused eighteen buses to remain out of service on the very first day, 18 March. The employer, the Municipal Transport Enterprise, was 2,000 workers short and unable to find more drivers. The action petered out, probably after some compensatory pay settlement.

On 26 March 800 workers struck in the *Elektropřístroj* Písek in protest against a threatened transfer of a part of their production programme to another factory and in favour of enterprise autonomy. In the course of the strike they expressed lack of confidence in the production manager of the Production Association and in the enterprise manager. To organise the action, which was taken after protracted negotiations had ended in deadlock, a strike committee came into being under the joint chairmanship of the chairmen of the factory branches of the Communist Party and the trade unions. Several other factories in Písek sent messages of support. After a strike of a mere seventy-five minutes, the general manager of the Production Association agreed to leave the disputed production programme in the factory and promised to go into the question of terminating the factory's subordination to another enterprise and to consider the implication of the workers' dislike for the two officers. Work was resumed immediately and soon proceeded 'in full swing'.

The same Production Association (*Závody silnoproudé elektrotechniky*) was affected by a still shorter protest strike in another of its factories in Teplice. Negotiations had twice broken down on the separation of the factory from a superior enterprise, but after a mere thirty-five minutes of strike action on 6 April 1968 and a workers' ultimatum that the issue should be settled in ten days, the general manager gave in. The factory was later constituted as an independent enterprise.

More than 100 workers on night shift in the Žilina (Slovakia) railway station stopped work on 5 June at 3 a.m. and were joined at 6 a.m. by the day shift. They demanded that the management of the station be recalled for 'anti-social behaviour' and incompetence. (More information on the cause of action is not available.) District secretaries of the Party and the Trade Union Council hastened to the spot. At 8 a.m. two high railway officials arrived and – in order to ensure resumption of transport – agreed to suspend several management officials pending an inquiry. Work was resumed at 9 a.m. and the strikers pledged to work an extra shift without pay to make up the losses.

Some 800 maintenance workers in the huge Třinec Ironworks elected a strike committee and announced industrial action for higher wages to begin on 3 July. More talks with trade union officials and the management were, however, held on the afternoon of 2 July when the strike committee decided not to strike because the enterprise was in bad economic shape. A recent accident had caused 5 million crowns' worth of damage. The management, while recognising that the maintenance workers' wages ought to be raised, had, for the time being, no money to do so.

A strike committee was also in action when 500 workers in four open-cast mines near Rakovník withdrew their labour on 13 August to protest against a threat to their security. Reserves of coal in their mines were nearing exhaustion and they feared redundancy. The construction of a new mine nearby had already cost 70 million crowns, but was now in danger of being discontinued as uneconomical. The strike ended on the following day with the Ministry of Building promising to take on all workers should the Ministry of Mining be forced to close down the mines. A final decision on the issue, which was more complicated than can be briefly expounded here, was to be taken by the government not later than 15 September.

Without resorting to strikes, but with the occasional work to rule, the most insistent wage and other material demands seem to have been voiced by the railwaymen in general and some of their sections in particular. This was in line with the traditional high measure of trade exclusiveness: rolling stock supervisors even suggested that they should be entitled – on account of their responsibility – to have three years added to their pensionable length of service for every two years actually served. When forty trade unionists from the Railwaymen's Union left a Deputy Prime Minister and three Ministers dissatisfied towards the end of July after they had been told that the Treasury simply did not have enough money to improve their work conditions, increase wages and modernise the railways without delay, as they demanded, a *Rudé právo* commentator wrote that many others were worse off and yet the railwaymen kept saying: 'What is that to us? We are not responsible. We want what belongs to us.' Why must they threaten action just now, when the survival of democratisation is at stake? Why not wait a few months? We can lose everything now.[1]

This was the line followed by Z. Mlynář in his above-mentioned speech in Mladá Boleslav: 'If all demands are put forward at once in an elemental fashion – including those that are justified – the working class will itself disrupt the order of things in its socialist State and play into the hands of those who do not have socialism at heart.'[2]

TRADE UNIONS

The trade union movement, with its vast established network of organisation, offered itself as an obvious channel through which working class activity should flow – reinvigorated, yet institutionalised. This, the reformers found, was more easily said than

[1] *Rudé právo*, 24 July 1968, p. 2. [2] *Rudé právo*, 20 April 1968, p. 3.

done. For one thing, the trade union organisation was too big and unwieldy. For another, in its higher echelons it was largely staffed by entrenched bureaucrats and a not insignificant number of renowned and professed conservatives. For yet another, it had been thoroughly inculcated with the Soviet-type concept of trade unions as 'a school of socialism'.

At its sixth congress (31 January–4 February 1967), the Revolutionary Trade Union Movement (ROH) had over 5 million members in more than 5,500 'basic branches' and twelve unions. It should be noted that ROH was not an exclusively working class organisation. Some 95 per cent of all wage and salary earners were organised on the 'one industry–one union' principle, where 'industry' is to be understood as a 'branch of human activity'.[1] Only freelance translators, artistes, pop singers and the like remained outside its ranks.

The list of member unions and estimated membership below gives the state of affairs in 1967. (Individual unions had been divided and merged frequently, usually following a government reorganisation. As a rule, a ministry abolished meant a trade union abolished; a ministry newly carved from a ministerial conglomerate meant a new trade union cropping up. This passive adaptation of trade union structure to government structure was in itself eloquent testimony to the true nature of trade union work.)

In 1967 there existed the Union of Workers in the Building Industry (of which both manual workers and clerical staff and designers and managerial personnel, including managers, were members, with an estimated membership of 460,000), Union of Workers in Mining and Power Generation (275,000), Union of Workers in the Chemical Industry (204,000), Union of Workers in Trade (460,000), Union of Workers in the Health Service (200,000), Union of Workers in the Consumer Goods Industry (490,000), Union of Workers in Agriculture and Forestry (430,000 – not including co-operative or private farmers, but State Farms and Tractor Stations, the timber and paper mill industry, etc.), Union of Workers in the Food Industry (200,000), Union of Workers in the Metalworking

---

[1] As of 30 June 1963 trade union membership was 92·8 per cent of the total labour force. See M. Kalenská, 'K některým právním otázkám účasti pracujících na řízení podniku', *Stát a právo*, 10 (1964) p. 81.

Industry (1,100,000 – engineering, metallurgy, ore mining), Union of Workers in Education, Science and Culture (400,000), Union of Workers in State Organs and Communal Economy (413,000), and Union of Workers in Transport and Tele-communications (534,000).[1]

Until August 1960 Slovakia had separate corresponding unions which were then abolished as part of the centralisation drive in the wake of the so-called Socialist Constitution. The set-up thus entailed 'basic branches', district committees, regional committees, central committees of the Unions, and the Central Trade Union Council with an extensive apparatus of its own and endowed with a considerable power of command.

The cumbersome hierarchic structure was exposed to criticism at a relatively early stage of the Prague Spring, although readiness to act against it continued to gather momentum for some time. The problem of independence was two-fold: of the unions *vis-à-vis* the Central Trade Union Council, and of the component sections within the unions *vis-à-vis* one another. All unions seemed united in calling for independence in relation to the council (including the right to retain a more substantial percentage of members' dues), and wished to see the centre as no more than a co-ordinating and representational 'roof' over trade-union activity.

While generally agreeing that the principle of 'one enterprise–one union' ought to be upheld, several of the large composite unions broke up. For example, the Union of Workers in Transport and Communications split into three independent unions of railwaymen, of transport and 'road economy' workers, and of telecommunications workers. The Union of Workers in Mining and Power Generation was divided into a Mineworkers' Union and a Power Generation Workers' Union. Four new unions took the place of the Union of Workers in State Organs and Communal Economy: state organs, communal economy, finance and insurance, and civilian workers of military administration. Altogether, the original twelve big unions became thirty-two. Even this could hardly be regarded as a disintegration of trade union unity. Before the war Czecho-slovakia had eighteen trade union centres (each with a number of unions) and over 700 trade union organisations operating

[1] H. Kuhn, *Handbuch der Tschechoslowakei* (Munich, 1966) pp. 266–8.

separately. Unity of organisation was, by all the signs, still considered an achievement from which there was no prevailing tendency to retreat. There is, however, no doubt that many felt that this would have to be a unity voluntarily agreed, with the Central Trade Union Council being a servant of its members, not their boss.

Inside the unions, autonomy was given to sections or 'interest groups', as the committee of the Union of Workers in Education and Science put it. These groups would be free to act as partners in negotiations with the agencies of the State, without having to delegate their powers of negotiation to the superior bodies, i.e. the union's central committee. The union demanded for itself the same right at it was giving to its sections: if problems of education and science were to be discussed with the government, why on earth should the union need the Central TUC's mediation?

Not everybody was satisfied with autonomy within a still unwieldy union. Some believed that particular interests could be well safeguarded through complete independence. The *cause celébre* in this respect was provided by the railway engine crews, who were repeatedly offered the chance to form an autonomous section in the new Railwaymen's Union but declined anything less than a fully fledged union of their own. On 29 April 1968, 'in a free election', they set up their own organisation which they called the Federation of Engine Crews, and elected a twelve-member central committee (six Czechs, six Slovaks). The federation claimed to have 23,000 members, all of whom were members of the Revolutionary Trade Union Movement as individuals. One-third were members of the Communist Party. Both the Railwaymen's Union and the Central Trade Union Council qualified this step as an infringement of the principle of unity and refused to grant the new organisation status.

The exchange of views on this problem was not abusive, but both sides remained adamant. The only public argument in favour of complete separation propounded by the federation (as far as one can gather from published and accessible material) was lack of confidence in the Railwaymen's Union, which, the engine drivers feared, would not be able to protect their interests adequately. People actually working on the locomotives, they claimed, had a position which could not be associated with all the diverse interests of other categories of workers in rail transport. The Railwaymen's Union expressed the belief that the federation would eventually find its way into the trade union movement, but said that no one would force it to do so. The Central Trade Union Council stated that it understood why trust in the united movement had been weakened in the past, but hoped that the need for unity in the democratisation process would be accepted by the dissenting engine drivers. The federation responded by saying that if it was denied the status of a trade union organisation, it would continue as 'an interest organisation'. Its uneasy existence went on until after the occupation of August 1968, when its application for official registration was turned down.[1]

Organisational questions were, of course, only one of the issues which the trade unions had to face as a result of the new conditions of the Prague Spring. Among the branches there emerged a move to rebuild trade union committees as an alternative force to the Communist Party. This tendency, a favourite object of attack by the opponents of reform became known as 'Trade Unions without Communists'. Its scope and intensity are difficult to gauge because publicity was understandably scant. A speaker at the Party Central Committee session in March–April 1968 pointed to the late start of the democratisation drive in the trade unions which left the Communists wavering. Over their heads, the rank-and-file trade unionists colluded to cross 'honest and self-sacrificing comrades' off the ballot tickets. In the *Aero* Prague factory four shop committees were elected without a single Communist. (The speaker, Vladimír Kabrna, also warned that in two unnamed factories 'we have had a concrete demand' that Social Democratic organisations should be formed.)[2] In a discussion published by *Literární listy*, a speaker from the *ČKD-Konstrukce* plant said that 'we had to try terribly hard to enforce the election of just one single Party member to our trade union committee' and hinted that the same had happened in the trade

[1] For the history of the Federation of Engine Crews see for example J. Lederer, 'Zkouška demokracie', *Reportér*, 31 (1968) p. 14, and *Rudé právo*, 21 May 1968, p. 3, 11 July 1968, p. 1, and 27 July 1968, p. 3.

[2] *Rudé právo*, 7 April 1968, p. 2.

union organisation at the headquarters of the Academy of Sciences.[1] An overall evaluation of this trend was provided two-and-a-half years after the invasion in the anti-reform pamphlet *Šli proti nám* (*They Went Against Us*, prepared by the Party Control and Auditing Commission) which admitted that non-election of Communists to trade union offices had mainly taken place after the invasion (caused then by different circumstances than those engendered by the reform movement itself) and that 10 per cent of newly elected trade union committees, often in large factories, were without a single Communist member.[2] It can safely be stated that the ousting of Communists and the overthrow of existing trade union committees were not major features of the reform process. By the beginning of June, when the stage of personal changes was largely completed, only some 250 'basic branch' and shop committees out of 12,000 resigned in toto.[3] The sweeping changes referred to by the Party Control Commission occurred in connection with the annual trade union meetings at the end of 1968 and were due as much to the effects of the invasion as to the normal process of rotation of cadres. At that time altogether 70–80 per cent of trade union functionaries were said to have been replaced.[4] During the Prague Spring the foremost concern was for a reinterpretation of the mission of trade unions in a democratic socialist society.

Before 1968, of course, the trade unions were said to be the 'school of socialism' and their primary concern was 'to organise and mobilise work initiative'. They had the most massive membership of all 'social organisations' and were always automatically quoted second only to the Communist Party in hierarchic ratings. On various occasions in the past, usually connected with periods of temporary political relaxation, they were invited to give more attention to their members' interests, but these were ritualistic pronouncements rather than real exhortations which could lead to meaningful results. Not that the trade unions were utterly useless to their members: they offered some service in the legal field and dispensed of various

---

[1] *Literární listy*, 30 May 1968, pp. 1, 3.
[2] 'Šli proti nám', *Rudé právo*, 4 February 1971, p. 3.
[3] René Frühauf in *Rudé právo*, 12 June 1968, p. 3.
[4] 'Šli proti nám', *Rudé právo*, 4 February 1971, p. 3.

recreational vouchers at nominal price; some provided shelter and funds for cultural activities and hobbies which would otherwise be difficult to finance and organise; cases of trade unions interceding for individual workers' rights were not entirely infrequent, etc. Nonetheless, the crucial point of trade union activity, bargaining for wages and better work conditions, remained largely confined to the formal procedures which would have taken place even had the trade unions not existed.

During the Prague Spring a change in this concept occurred in two distinct phases, the trade unionist and the political. The first coincided with the resignation of the chairman of the Central Trade Union Council, Miroslav Pastyřík, and two secretaries, Bedřich Kozelka and Václav Pašek, on 12 March. The resignation itself was enforced by the Communist group in the council. It opened the way to the understanding of trade unions as a protective organisation whose principal mission was to shield their members and to promote their demands in dealings with the State. By the end of March this came to be generally recognised. The new concept was undoubtedly an improvement and was progress in itself. An attempt was made to translate theory into practice and the praesidium of the Trade Union Council met twice with the cabinet (27 May and 3 June) to discuss the whole range of the standard of living.

The first joint meeting considered the following on the basis of a trade union list of demands: wage increases in industries neglected during the so-called iron concept of industrial developments, i.e. consumer goods, food, agriculture, trade, transport, telecommunications, health and education; restructuring of wage tariffs; safety at work; employed women; housing; commuting services; amendment of the labour code; health insurance; prophylactic medicine; and pensions. A joint commission was set up and instructed to propose solutions within a week (*sic!*).[1] At the second meeting the government promised to increase real wages in 1969 by 3 per cent, agreed to re-evaluate wage relationships and to reconsider the whole wage system (but refused to reintroduce part payments in kind), recommended a reform of the wage tax, pledged itself to define the managers' responsibility for work safety, undertook to improve the lot of employed women, suggested new ways of

[1] *Rudé právo*, 28 May 1968, pp. 1, 2.

financing housing and of making the construction of family houses more advantageous, agreed to improve loans to newly-weds, promised to raise health insurance funds in enterprises, promised to improve the lowest categories of pensions and adjust them to the cost of living, agreed to consider improvement of commuting services and accepted the need for an amendment of the labour code.[1]

The list was impressive; in fact much too impressive to be genuinely meaningful. It embraced practically the whole range of social problems affecting workers and non-workers alike and must be seen as an enumeration of ills prior to more concrete negotiations rather than an agenda which could be brought to successful fruition at one or two meetings.

For several months it seemed that redefinition of the purpose of the trade unions as an advocate of better living standards for the population was all that the new men in the trade union leadership were capable of and all that the reformers hoped for. Then, especially in May, the dynamic quality of the Prague Spring became more and more affected by both local and foreign fears that the reforms were going too far and that the sacrosanct working-class character of the régime was being impermissibly diluted. This fear, genuine or fabricated, found expression at the May–June session of the Party Central Committee. It was quite natural that the trade unions should have been chosen by the reformers to provide a positive answer to such misgivings. On 11 June the Party Praesidium stated that the trade unions must 'create their own policies because merely formulating demands – even if they are justified – will not be enough to ensure the satisfaction of the vital needs of the working people . . . The Communists regard the Revolutionary Trade Union Movement as one of the most important political organisations of the National Front and one of the guarantees that democracy in this country will remain socialist, benefiting the workers and all the working people'.

Karel Poláček, the Trade Union Council chairman, took up the theme, but stressed that defence of the working people's interests was still the true primary mission of the trade unions. In addition, they would seek to exert direct influence on the creation of state policies through representation in the legisla-

[1] *Rudé právo*, 4 June 1968, p. 1.

tive bodies, in state organs, in the National Economic Council and in local government.[1] Alexander Dubček himself attended a three-day national conference of trade union functionaries (18–20 June) and told them that the Party attached importance to trade union participation in the National Front so as to ensure that the Front did not turn into a mere coalition of political parties, but rather became a platform for the pursuance of political activity by all major social organisations. For that reason, neither the trade unions nor the youth and women's organisations should be permitted to split up along Party lines. The conference of delegates from primary and other organisations, which considered a newly formulated programme for the movement along these lines, marked the climax of trade union activity during the so-called Prague Spring. After initial hesitation, caused no doubt by the clumsiness of its apparatus, the movement was shaping itself to genuine trade union dimensions, while verbally accepting the political role which the Dubček reformers assigned to it.[2]

Dubček did not know then that trade-union backing for his policies would fail to be accepted by his critics as an adequate safeguard of socialism and that the first (and last) major political battle of the remoulded trade unions would only be fought in the wake of the Soviet invasion into Czechoslovakia.

ENTERPRISE COUNCILS

The Novotný leadership declared discussion of workers' self-management out of bounds. For one thing, self-management was superfluous when the existing economic and enterprise apparatus was considered adequate. For another, it was ideologically wrong and aroused dangerous pro-Yugoslav feelings. The several attempts at increased 'workers' participation in enterprise management' before the Prague Spring were confined to trade union channels, to the ill-defined right of control by the Party over enterprise economy and to the various clumsy and cumbersome 'production commissions' and conferences. Nevertheless, some sociologists circumvented the ideological prohibitions and had since 1965 managed to tackle the problem

[1] Interview in *Rudé právo*, 11 June 1968, p. 1.
[2] *Práce*, 19 June 1968, p. 1.

at least indirectly in scholarly journals and books. One of the veiled approaches went along the lines of claiming for a socialist enterprise the right to pursue the self-assertion of all its workers.[1] In another contribution, the authors recalled that Lenin had been against self-management in 1921 only because it had then been 'premature'. There had been no 'producer' as such, only small private producers and wage-earning workers. In the Czechoslovakia of the 1960s the social structure was no longer determined by class yardsticks, said the authors. Moreover, the nascent economic reform emphasised the role the enterprise was to play as a team of producers. Hence an opening for an organisation representing the team's interests in entrepreneurship.[2] Yet another writer hastened to assure the authorities that state ownership should not be transformed into group ownership, although it should be 'brought closer' to the teams of producers which were in any case 'the structural components' of the collective owner.[3]

Even in 1968 the idea gained momentum only slowly. At first the terminology (and presumably the thinking behind it) was vague. Dubček spoke at a Party meeting in the Kladno Steelworks on 2 March about 'the possibility of the workers' democratic influence on factory management'. He still may have had the trade unions in mind because almost in the same breath he was steering them towards advocacy of workers' interests. A working group of the State Commission for Management and Organisation under Professor J. Řezníček of the Party Political School had by then been deliberating on the status of a socialist enterprise for over eighteen months. Opinions in the commission were divided, it seemed, beyond re-

---

[1] D. Slejška, 'Pospolitostní struktura v modelu socialistického podniku', *Sociologický časopis*, 4 (1965) pp. 406–9. In the same issue, pp. 469–78, Slejška objectively and in detail reports on the conference of the Yugoslav Sociological Society on self-management in Split in February 1965. Slejška was then a member of the Philosophical Institute of the Academy of Sciences in Prague.

[2] Z. Mlynář and V. Pavlíček, 'Politická organizace ve vztahu k vývoji sociální struktury socialistické společnosti,' in *Sociální struktura socialistické společnosti*, ed. P. Machonin, 2nd edition. (Prague, Svoboda, 1967) p. 652.

[3] D. Slejška, 'Pracovní kolektiv ve struktuře socialistické společnosti', in *Sociální struktura socialistické společnosti*, ed. P. Machonin, 2nd ed. (Prague, Svoboda, 1967) p. 388.

conciliation or agreement. The material they put before the scientific collegium of the Academy of Sciences under Ota Šik on 25 March did not go beyond stressing the general need for 'social control' over enterprise management. Leaving large enterprises of the Škoda type aside (as the authors of the material suggested), the small enterprises – with several dozen workers – might conceivably benefit from a kind of self-management. Still greater confusion prevailed in the trade unions. One report from the middle of March spoke of 'many comrades' in the TUC who thought it correct for the working team to influence the management. This, they believed, could be done through greater powers being accorded to the trade unions.[1] M. Kimlík, a secretary of the Central Trade Union Council, later spoke about the trade unions implementing the rights of the working people in an enterprise 'through the workers' councils'.[2] No wonder that the Party's Action Programme of April remained nebulous and non-committal. It merely acknowledged the emerging need to have democratic organs in the enterprises which would enjoy certain powers *vis-à-vis* the management.

Starting from April 1968, reality and theory began to race each other: a wealth of ideas – some very wild – as to the character, composition and aims of the workers' councils were presented to the public by economic theorists and practitioners, while several dozen preparatory committees and 'initiative groups' sprang into existence without waiting for the outcome of academic debates.

The following is a survey of some of the theories:

Some, but not many, gave straightforward preference to a technocratic solution. K. Kolář from the Ministry of Heavy Industry modelled the councils on the boards of governors of limited liability companies. They would be appointed by the minister and responsible to him. As for composition, they would comprise representatives of the ministry, the bank, a higher trade union body, the Quality Inspectorate, the main customers, the servicing enterprises and possibly related associations, such as the Automobile Club for councils in the car

---

[1] Report of a meeting of the Party group in the plenum of the Central Trade Union Council on 13–14 March 1968, *Rudé právo*, 15 March 1968, p. 6.

[2] *Rudé právo*, 5 June 1968, pp. 1, 5.

industry. This type, hardly workers' councils, was unacceptable to all but the idealist technocrats, because what were at stake – and clearly postulated by the reformers – were councils that would be more than an instrument of management. In addition to materially involving the teams of producers in entrepreneurship, the reformers definitely had in mind the political awakening of the workers.

Other authors of self-management theories realised the political importance of the councils, but still could not see how it could tally with business activity. Three economists from the *Závody průmyslové chemie* in Pardubice thought that conducting business was a complicated activity which would always put 'representatives of the workers' at a disadvantage. Instead, the councils should merely keep an eye on management and be entitled to draw conclusions from the bad economic results of the enterprise, while the actual conduct of business was left to the management.

Similarly, Emil Dvořák, from the *Kaučuk* enterprise in Kralupy, visualised the council as a 'parliament' which would not co-operate with the management but would be its main opponent.

V. Jelínek, from *Průmstav* in Pardubice, would go a little further and give the council the power of electing and recalling an otherwise completely autonomous manager. To him the council would serve as an advisory and supervisory body.

Oldřich Švestka, writing as a guardian of working-class interests, warned against the danger of the councils concentrating on business to the neglect of workers' security. Why, he asked, were they called 'enterprise councils' rather than 'workers' councils'? They would obviously represent the entire team of the enterprise and were likely to have as members more technicians and clerks then actual workers. And anyway, they could guarantee social safety to the workers only after they were successful, i.e. when the enterprise's results were good. What would happen before that? He complained that neither the economists nor the sociologists had yet worked out any programme of security for the workers to apply in that intermediate period.

Ota Šik discussed enterprise councils in his speeches at the Party Central Committee session in March–April and at the general assembly of the Czechoslovak Economic Society on 20 May. The first speech was essentially managerial, while the second signalled the acceptance by the leadership of the Party of the moderately democratic political interpretation. The first was made before, the second after Šik joined the government. The first reflected uncrystallised concepts of the early stages of the Prague Spring, the second took into account two months of feverish developments and, especially, growing conservative pressure at home and from abroad. The institution of workers' councils was to counter such pressure.

At the beginning of April, Šik's enterprise would be governed by the management. The council would be no more than a 'democratically constituted (i.e. elected) controlling or supervisory organ' which, admittedly, would be superior to the management, but charged only with 'keeping an eye on the interest of the whole of society' and on the prosperity of the enterprise. If necessary, the council 'would ensure that the management was replaced'. There were no details as to who would sit on the council and how its powers were to be delineated.[1]

In the second half of May, Šik's councils (now called 'councils of the working people') would supervise and direct the management. Their powers would entail determining 'basic concepts' of the enterprise's developments, including investments, and the distribution of gross income, including profit sharing. They would postulate what the main relationships inside the enterprise were to be, and examine quarterly and annual balance sheets. They would authorise extra rewards to management officials, hire and recall the manager and decide on merger or association with other enterprises.

The composition of the council, also a matter of much disagreement, would look in Šik's May plan as follows: The 'decisive majority' of the ten to thirty members (depending on the size of the enterprise) would be elected by the employees directly from their own ranks. Independent experts, not employed in the enterprise, would comprise 10–30 per cent of the council. They would be elected by the votes of the directly elected members. If the State or a bank or other enterprises

[1] O. Šik's speech at the Party Central Committee meeting on 31 March to 5 April 1968. *Rudé právo*, 7 April 1968, p. 2.

were to invest long-term credits in the enterprise, they ought to be given a seat on the council.[1]

The reformers were aware of the political limitations of the technocratic concept of the enterprise councils and the related notion that only a third of its members should be directly elected, while another third would be appointed by various state agencies and the remaining third of seats reserved for outside experts. Robert Kalivoda for example saw the councils as above all 'one of the fundamental forms of direct democracy', whose purpose it was to prevent the economic reform from degenerating into a rule of the technocrats. The well-known (and yet anonymous) commentator of *Literární listy*, whose column appeared over the pen-name Dalimil, regarded the councils as the only guarantee against the supremacy of government bureaucrats. The political scientist Petr Pithart warned against the danger of the councils being manipulated from the top: there was no direct connection between workers' councils and political power. If political democracy was not implemented, the councils might become yet another transmission belt of the Stalinist type. On the other hand, their existence was conducive to political democracy.

The government stepped in on 6 June by issuing the 'provisional framework for the establishment and pilot operation of collective organs of democratic administration and business organs in enterprises'. The principles were to counter elemental development, although emphasis was put on their experimental nature. Also, close co-operation with the trade unions was recommended. In fact the government's 'framework' was presented for discussion to the national conference of delegates from basic trade union branches on 18 to 20 June (already mentioned earlier) and published in full on 29 June.

The 'framework' stipulated that the councils ought to be separated from the management, whose composition they would be required to endorse or reject. The council would *pass judgement* by a simple majority of those present on conceptual development of the enterprise, basic direction of investment, creation and distribution of gross income, basic measures affecting style of management and organisation, and annual

[1] O. Šik's speech at the general assembly of the Czechoslovak Economic Society on 20 May 1968. *Rudé právo*, 22 May 1968, p. 3.

balance sheets. The council would *pass decisions* by a two-thirds majority of all members of the council on appointment and recall of the manager after consultation with superior authority, and of deputy managers at the manager's suggestion; it would endorse the salary and profit share of the manager and the overall bonus to the management above a fixed sum; it would decide statutory issues, such as membership of an association, merger or division of the enterprise, etc. The council would have ten to thirty members, whose term of office would be legislated later. 'The greater part' of the council would be elected direct by the staff of the enterprise, the selection of candidates and election being organised by the trade union branch. In 'large, important or complex' enterprises, 10–30 per cent of the council would consist of 'independent experts' from outside. In enterprises 'exceptionally important from the point of view of state interests', no more than 20 per cent of the council would be appointed by the state agencies or the main customers. Where the bank had granted long-term credits, it would have the right to a seat. The same would apply to other enterprises which had invested their funds into the enterprise. No councils were envisaged for production associations, shareholder companies and state or corporation-type enterprises, such as the railways, telecommunications, forestry and water conservancy, until and unless their status was changed. Neither would there be any councils in regularly loss-incurring enterprises and those which had been earmarked for liquidation. Until the Law on Enterprise was passed, councils would have to be first authorised by the ministries, and they should start operating either on 1 July or 1 October 1968 or 1 January 1969, depending on their state of readiness.[1]

There has been criticism, particularly from post-Dubček government officials in Prague, of the alleged haste with which the councils came into existence. (Although there have also been critics who claim the opposite; according to them working-class control was impermissibly slow in coming.) On the strength of available evidence, admittedly incomplete, the amount of circumspection shown by the authorities as well as the workers was appropriate to the obtaining conditions. Practically everywhere, especially in large enterprises capable

[1] *Rudé právo*, 30 June 1968, pp. 1, 3.

of setting the pace for others, there was a preliminary stage before the actual election of the council. First, a preparatory committee would be set up under the auspices of the enterprise branches of the Communist Party and the trade unions, and with the agreement of the management. This committee would set itself the task of drafting the programme of the future council and the method of its election which would be presented for discussion to the workers. At the same time the workers and employees would be solicited to nominate candidates. Only then would the actual election take place. A period of several months was usually envisaged for the groundwork. In the *Škoda* Works in Pilsen, for example, the process began early in June, the statute of the council and the election procedure were hammered out in several weeks of open discussion and adopted on 30 July, and the council itself was elected only in September.

The *Škoda* workers' approach was in many ways an example to others. An important innovation was the stipulation, written into the *Škoda* enterprise council's statute, to the effect that members of the council should arrive at decisions independently, without accounting for them to any other social or political organisation. The actual election was described as 'truly democratic': of the 107 nominated candidates (two-thirds of whom happened to be Communists), twenty-nine were elected (the proportion of Communists remained the same). Six of the council members were workers, seventeen technicians and four 'candidates of sciences'. The first steps of the council after election were described by the *Škoda* functionaries themselves: they had to attend to personnel questions although in the long run it was the enterprise's economic perspectives which were to be given priority. A new general manager was appointed after the post had been advertised, but this was not considered the best solution. Management 'cadres' should emerge from within the enterprise itself, rather than apply for a post from outside.[1]

As far as the number of enterprise councils is concerned, which came into existence during and as a consequence of the Prague Spring, figures vary. Prime Minister Černík said that

[1] A. Komárek and V. Filip, 'Demokracii i ve výrobě', *Nová mysl*, 2 (1969) p. 148.

131 councils had been registered and some 140 preparatory committees noted as of 1 October 1968.[1] The paper *Politika* of 10 October 1968 knew about seventy councils (out of 700 enterprises) and 267 preparatory committees. A post-mortem in *Hospodářské noviny*, No. 27/1970, gave the number at 'approximately' 300 councils and 300 preparatory committees as of 30 June 1969.

The history of the enterprise councils extended well beyond the Soviet occupation and that part of it will be summarised below. During the period known as the Prague Spring only a start was made. Essentially, most reformers viewed the councils with practical eyes, hoping that they would have a wholesome effect on both the economic and the political situation. The purely political and, one might be tempted to say, visionary approach to workers' councils, which saw them spreading to replace the parliamentary mechanisms, was an exception. True enough, in their quest for a hopefully better arrangement of public affairs than the one in the West, and certainly better than the one in the East, many reformers wished to combine parliamentary and direct democracy, towards which aim the workers' council seemed to be the ideal initial step. As they were believed to add the socialist element of workers' control to economic management, the councils were hoped to evolve into a manifestly socialist safeguard of the political system. Time was, however, too short even for the theory to crystallise and be universally accepted, let alone for the practice to show whether this evolution was possible.

Not even agriculture would have remained outside this trend. In an unusual move, the so-called 'preparatory committee for democratic administration of the management of agricultural enterprises' in the Tachov district in West Bohemia, a mere week before the Soviet invasion resolved to disband the association of State Farms in Tachov, to reconstitute the individual farms as independent national enterprises, to elect workers' councils in them, to align the farms in a new association, to elect its management in a democratic fashion, and to open the new association to new members even from outside the district.[2]

[1] Radio Free Europe, *Situation Report*, 16 December 1968.
[2] *Rudé právo*, 15 August 1968, p. 5.

To a large extent the Prague Spring was the time of experiment. Many reformers readily admitted uncertainty as to the result of their concepts. In what seemed a very sensible approach, an economist suggested that different kinds of enterprise should be allowed to compete and prove their worth in terms of hard fact. As there was reluctance to enforce the enterprise councils by decree and the government's 'framework' was not presented as obligatory, this is almost certainly what would have happened. In addition to 'self-managed' enterprises with workers' councils, there would exist units of the managerial type, state (public) corporations, such as power generation and railways, so-called 'founder' enterprises (*zakladatelské podniky*) set up by 'founders', i.e. National Committees, trade unions and other social organisations (which would appoint managers and determine enterprise policies), associations and enterprises established by them, co-operatives, and private enterprises in craft and service, based on individual labour.[1]

PRESS FREEDOM COMMITTEES

At the end of April 1968 workers of Section Two in the *Moravské chemické závody* (chemical plant) in Ostrava decided to set up 'a workers' committee for the defence of the freedom of the press', the first such committee in the country. Alongside the occasional strike committees and the enterprise councils, this was another new workers' organisation to emerge outside the established pattern. The first committee was soon followed by another, in the Poruba branch of the Municipal Transport Enterprise in Ostrava. The initiative clearly belonged to the North Moravian area around Ostrava, as shown by the emergence in rapid succession during May of similar committees in the *Válcovny plechu* in Frýdek-Místek, *Hutní montáže* in Ostrava and other factories there.

This was an initiative meant to give support to the mass media which had by then found themselves under growing attack for pushing things too far and too fast and for falling

[1] R. Kocanda, 'Různé formy podnikání – reálná cesta', *Rudé právo*, 23 July 1968, p. 5. The author was on the staff of the Research Institute for National Economic Planning.

victim to anti-socialist tendencies, as contemporary terminology had it. Belatedly and rather sceptically, on 23 May
Literární listy acknowledged the initiative as a sign of support
extended by the workers to the intellectuals. While the spokesmen of the committees stated their intention to protect press
freedom until it was enacted by parliament, the writers' paper
commented that it was difficult to imagine what a committee
of this kind would do if freedom really began to be sliced off.
Nevertheless, it added that their existence was 'encouraging'.

On 24 May the praesidium of the Czechoslovak Journalists'
Union welcomed the emergence of the committees, 'especially
the fact that this decisive initiative was started in the industrial
enterprises of the Ostrava region'. *Literární listy* was quick to
change the tenor of its previous writing in the following issue.
Jiří Lederer suggested that the committees should investigate
the suppression of reporting on the reawakening of the Social
Democratic Party and on K231, the society of former political
prisoners, as well as the rumours about the impending enforce-
ment of changes in the editorial office of the *Student* newspaper.
Moreover, he expressed the view that the committees should
become a permanent institution, join forces with journalists,
writers, artists, scholars and scientists, and create a national
committee for the defence of press freedom. This then would
exist as a protector of freedom from even that kind of intervention which the law did not envisage but which still might
occur.

Lederer later volunteered to act as a co-ordinator of the
efforts to institutionalise the committees and to establish their
state-wide network, but it must be said that the movement did
not really live up to his expectations. A number of committees
sprang into existence elsewhere in the country (although no
report seems to be available on Slovakia), and a regional
association of at least formal value was set up in Frýdek-
Místek on 5 July under a twenty-seven-member committee.[1]
The committees variously styled themselves as defending 'civic
rights and freedoms', 'freedom of the press and of speech',

[1] Only in 1971 was it reported that the same district (Frýdek-Místek)
saw the publication during the first days of invasion of a clandestine pro-
Soviet and pro-invasion *Rudé právo*. Three mimeographed numbers were
issued and circulated.

'freedom of the word, conscience and personality', etc. When Eduard Goldstücker published (on 23 June) the anonymous letter threatening his life for the part he played in the reform movement, a historian suggested in *Rudé právo* that the committees should extend their aims to combat antisemitism. A group of historians appealed to the committees to protect freedom of science. The praesidium of the Journalists' Union established a section to keep in touch with the committees. One committee (in KPS Brno) included the promotion of friendly relations with the U.S.S.R. in its programme. Voices raised in opposition to the very idea of such committees were heard, for example, from a meeting of Communists 'in the army, police and People's Militia', in Olomouc (who considered the committees 'politically incorrect') and from the National Assembly deputy Vilém Nový (who rhetorically asked, 'Why such committees? Against whom?').

In all honesty, the committees cannot be regarded as more than a worthy initiative which, although promising spontaneous working class action and an alliance between workers and the intelligentsia, did not in fact go very far. No meaningful action by such committees is on record. Opposition to the curtailment of press freedom after the invasion erupted spontaneously and mainly through the existing organisations, such as the trade unions. Also, the committees were soon being formed in non-factory organisations as well, such as in academic and research institutes, an advertising agency, a hospital, secondary schools, a theatre, etc. The general atmosphere of the Prague Spring was inducive to 'all-people' action and attitude. It was practically impossible to confine an organisation to recruiting membership from only one social stratum. Neither the trade unions nor the workers' councils were exclusively working-class phenomena. This in turn provoked certain misgivings among the truly blue-collar members: 'Are we not being pushed by the intellectuals? Are we not once again being told what to do?' This is certainly not to say that organised workers' support to causes which appear to be primarily intellectual was proved in Czechoslovakia to be impossible. It did, nonetheless, turn out to be more elusive than many suspected.

POST-INVASION

The invasion of 20–21 August 1968, which initiated a series of turning points in the development of Czechoslovak reforms, was almost certainly intended to be a concerted military–political action, designed at one stroke to render the reformist community harmless and the reformist spirit ineffective, but it developed into a protracted and clumsy process of oppression, beginning with the first seven days between the military onslaught and the publication in Czechoslovakia of the incomplete version of the so-called Moscow Agreement. From this period, covered by the 'Black Book' of documents collected by the History Institute of the Academy in Sciences, we have evidence of proclamations against the occupation issued by factory workers (mostly from joint meetings and signed by all organisations active in the factory or simply by 'workers'), similar proclamations signed by various workers' trade unions (mostly the Central Trade Union Council and committees of the various Unions), and proclamations signed or co-signed by 'strike committees'. As a point of interest, disagreement with military intervention was also expressed in *Práce* of 24 August 1968 by the signatories (workers of the Auto-Praga Works) of the notorious letter to the Soviet Embassy in Prague of 16 July (which came to be known as the 'Letter of the 99') published in the Moscow *Pravda* at the time of the talks in Čierna.

The most significant testimony to the workers' attitude must, however, be seen in the clandestine holding of the Fourteenth extraordinary Party Congress in the Č.K.D. factory in Prague-Vysočany on 22 August. The delegates were simply told over Radio Prague to report to any large factory in Prague whence they would be directed to the venue of the gathering. While the meeting of a rump Party Central Committee, half-willing to start collaboration with the occupying forces, had to convene in a Party hotel protected by Soviet tanks, some 1,290 legally elected delegates to the congress conducted their business, albeit rather chaotically, practically on the shop floor under the eye of workers' vigilantes. This must be seen as a poignant reflection on the nature of things at that time. The event has been described elsewhere.[1]

[1] See for example *Panzer überrollen den Parteitag*, ed. J. Pelikán (Wien–Frankfurt–Zürich, Europa Verlag, 1969).

Both existing and *ad hoc* workers' groups proved their support for the reform movement in many other ways during those excruciating days. The delay by the railwaymen of the Soviet train carrying radio and electronic equipment has by now become a legend. It should be noted, however, that the invading troops had evidently been given orders not to occupy factories. In the context of the times, this was a masterly political move. Although some clandestine radio (and even television) stations were thus allowed to operate from factory compounds, obviously to the great annoyance of the occupiers, there was no direct clash between the Czechoslovak worker and the Soviet soldier. Such a clash, one can venture to suggest, would have been inevitable had a confrontation occurred inside the factory gates. As it happened, the workers made no attempt to provide protection for newspaper offices and social science institutions (e.g. the Academy of Sciences) which the occupiers were primarily concerned with. One can, of course, argue that this would anyway have been impossible.

It may seem that working class action remained half-hearted, and the impression is probably correct insofar as organised and determined behaviour, typical of workers' movements in comparable historical situations, is concerned. This can most likely be explained by the preceding twenty years of enforced inaction. By the same token, the organisational structure had as yet been little revivified and new leaders at factory level had as yet not emerged in adequate numbers. This, again, is not to say that the workers shied away, leaving the entire movement – at times of ascent as well as dire trouble – in the hands of the non-workers. After January 1968, and more specifically after the explosion of the Šejna affair, political reform became the concern of the nation or, as we may put it, the *populus*. There is every reason to believe that reform was desired by an overwhelming majority of the nation, just as there is every reason to include the workers in this community. As individuals they could certainly be counted as participants in every popular endeavour to bring about a change in the *status quo* or to consolidate the achievements of reform.

The dismantling of the reforms after the invasion is much less interesting than the previous emergence of new structures, groupings and attitudes. Once the decision was made by a superior power to eradicate practically every trace of the reform, the actual manner in which this was done remains relatively unimportant. Nonetheless, both the trade unions and the enterprise councils were to experience another trial of strength. We know now that it was a lost battle.

Between September and mid-December 1968 the trade union leadership, like the leaderships of all other organisations, busied itself with dividing the movement on national lines within the federalisation drive. Refraining from sweeping judgments which would anyway hardly be able to take the flow of events into account with any accuracy, I still have the impression that much of the time, energy and organisational activity which were expended on this must have been reflected in restricted action in other fields. At the same time, the trade unions were preparing themselves for their national congress scheduled for March 1969 and in this connection opponents of Soviet occupation strengthened their positions in newly elected committees at all levels. Among them, the Metalworkers' Union, over a million strong, was foremost in backing Josef Smrkovský, whose departure from the post of National Assembly chairman had been demanded by the growing lobby of 'realists', i.e. supporters of the Soviet-insisted pacification policy, under Gustáv Husák. A December resolution of the Metalworkers' Union threatened to strike should Smrkovský be forced to go. The Printers' Union even took exception to the reintroduction of censorship as late as January 1969 and exhorted its members to refuse to print whatever went against the post-January policies. In the same month the Czech (as opposed to the Slovak or Czechoslovak) all-trades union congress witnessed a clash between Prime Minister Černík and the two foremost trade union reformers, Rudolf Pacovský and Vlastimil Toman. The latter, speaking for the metalworkers, reiterated his Union's refusal to accept government and Party decisions blindly. Trade union support to the present Party leadership was qualified, and could be withdrawn, he said. The trade unions still stood for democracy, truth, humanism, freedom and socialism with a human face. Even as late as the State-wide congress in March 1969, Karel Poláček still stressed that the trade unions disliked being no more than executors of the Party's will. While recognising the Party's leading role, they wished to represent the interests of the working people. The congress adopted the Czechoslovak Trade Union Charter which postulated protection of members' interests as the mission of the unions and incorporated a number of reformist pronouncements, cautiously worded, without mentioning the right to strike. The congress further passed a resolution in support of the enterprise councils and a political resolution calling for legal guarantees of human and civil rights.

Counter-reformation moved in stages: Smrkovský was relegated under the pretext of fair Slovak representation – and the metalworkers did not strike; the printers refused to typeset the first number of the new diehard newspaper *Tribuna*, but the subsequent issues went unmolested; and not a full month after the verbally 'progressive' trade union congress, the Central Trade Union Council accepted the full subordination of the Party's Praesidium to the Soviet line in the wake of the notorious 'ice-hockey demonstrations' of 28–9 March. Over the following year more than 50,000 Czech and 13,000 Slovak trade union functionaries were purged, including Karel Poláček, Rudolf Pacovský and Vlastimil Toman.[1]

For a long time after the August invasion the fate of the enterprise councils remained uncertain. In September and October the government stalled on the issue: the whole operation should be temporarily suspended pending an investigation into the experience so far obtained. In November Černík gave way to trade union pressure and professed his government's intention to go ahead with the councils which, however, should now be formed only with the utmost prudence. In December Černík linked the question of the councils to the Law on Socialist Enterprise, then under preparation. (In fact, a draft bill of this nature had been contemplated and discussed by various committees since 1967.) The Law was expected to embrace the crucial issue of the workers' councils as well as that of enterprise autonomy, especially concerning the formation of new enterprises, their dissolution and association with others. The measure of enterprise independence was, of course,

[1] *The Czechoslovak Trade Unions 1870–1970* (Brussels, International Confederation of Free Trade Unions) 1970, p. 34.

the bone of contention between advocates of the pre-1968 alignment of the State and the economic sphere and the proponents of separation.

In the meantime the reformists were trying to save the movement by pushing on with the setting up of councils in spite of government hesitation. On 9 and 10 January a serious attempt was made to co-ordinate the existing councils at a 'consultative' meeting in Pilsen of representatives from the existing councils, preparatory committees and interested trade union branches. A member of the Sociological Institute, addressing the conference, made no bones about the hope that at least some elements of self-management could be rescued 'in order to preserve the breeding ground of democratic socialism'. The obtaining critical situation was not necessarily adverse to the idea of workers' councils, he argued. Yugoslavia had been in a grievous position after 1948 when the councils were created there, and so was Poland in 1956. 'We must make use of this historic situation and not be afraid of responsibility.'[1] J. Chaloupecký expressed the notion succinctly in the title of his article in *Listy*, 'All Power to the Workers' Councils!' The situation reminded him of that facing the Soviets in February 1917.[2]

The last quarter of 1968 and the first quarter of 1969 saw the establishment of the majority of the 300 councils and 300 preparatory committees which were said to be in existence as of 30 June 1969.[3] The public was undoubtedly in favour of them, as shown by opinion polls undertaken by the Institute of Public Opinion Research. The two polls in question (others touched on the subject as well) were conducted on a comparative basis in July 1968 and March 1969 with the following results: in favour of enterprise councils – 53 per cent (1968) and 59 per cent (1969); against – 10 per cent and 3 per cent; another view – 4 per cent and 3 per cent; don't knows – 33 per cent and 35 per cent. Supplementary questioning revealed, however, that most people were not well informed about the councils and, still more significantly, were almost equally divided in favouring consistent self-management (24 per cent),

---

[1] D. Slejška, then of the Sociological Institute, quoted by M. Lang in 'Pravda o podnikových radách', *Hospodářské noviny*, 27 (1970) p. 6.

[2] *Listy*, 20 February 1969, p. 1.

[3] M. Lang, op. cit.

a mixed self-management and managerial model (26 per cent) and a strongly managerial model with only slight elements of workers' participation (29 per cent). The rest were 'other opinions' and 'don't knows'.[1] One may well deduce that the time for maturation was short. The understanding of the economic role of the councils had not crystallised, and their political understanding remained the property of only a few intellectuals.

Hesitation, which might even have reflected the absence of clear-cut instruction from Moscow, was noticeable even during the first two months of Husák's rule. The government issued 'model statutes of experimenting enterprise councils' in June 1969 and the Party Central Committee ordered an inquiry into sixteen selected councils. (No criteria for this selection are known.) It was discovered that they had a total of 317 members, not counting those from outside the enterprise, i.e. an average of twenty (in fact ranging from eleven to twenty-nine), including sixty-six (20·8 per cent) active workers, 236 (74·5 per cent) technicians or economists and 15 (4·7 per cent) others. Some 60 per cent were members of the Party. The government found that not a single one of the sixteen worked according to a statute which was in keeping with the 'model' and subsequently decided to order their disbandment as well as of those which had come into being without the endorsement of superior (i.e. State) organs. The councils were thus finally dismantled in the second and third quarters of 1969 by decree of the Minister of Industry.[2]

In the same period the authorities had to admit that working-class support for the post-Dubček leadership came from a minority. Oldřich Švestka wrote about 'a temporary minority' of the workers comprising the 'sound core' of the Party, and cited the example of an unnamed district in which 300 people left the Party of their own will within a fortnight of Husák's ascendance to power. Seventy-five per cent of them were workers, 'good and honest', but still 'disoriented'.[3] The manager of a cement works in Brno (*Maloměřické cementárny a*

---

[1] *Šetření Ústavu pro výzkum veřejného mínění, Praha* (Prague, 1969).
[2] M. Lang, op. cit.
[3] *Tribuna*, 28 May 1969.

vápenice), which had been known as 'a Communist bastion' with every third to fourth employee a member of the Party, later described the 1968–70 process. There had been no strikes, demonstrations, recall of Communists from functions or trade union posts in 1968, but 'a number mostly of workers' left the Party. Many signed the 2,000 Words Manifesto. An enterprise council was elected in June 1969 in spite of the government's caution. The Youth Union ceased to exist and after the invasion even the All-Factory Party Committee folded up. A handful of 'the brave' were ostracised and some even physically assaulted. The trade unions abdicated their political role and reverted to issuing recreation vouchers, arranging loans, organising children's camps and excursions. A remedy was found and effected only during the 1970 purge which abolished all Party committees in the enterprise and set up a single new one. The trade union committee was also replaced by a new one and soon socialist competition got under way and output began to grow.[1]

If we accept the classification of groups into those organising sectional interests and those organising shared attitudes, we find that, among the workers, the Czechoslovak reform saw a fairly widespread reawakening of the former and an entirely inadequate formation of the latter. Defence of interests prevailed over promotion of causes. To put it differently, there was the strength (though not sufficient time) in the Czechoslovak working class to claim for itself the right to trade union organisation. At the same time, it was not quite able to live up to the reformers' expectations in the political field.

[1] *Rovnost*, 3 November 1970, p. 4.

CHAPTER TWO

Farmers

Long before Communism Czech farmers were used to being organised politically and economically. Two political parties, the Agrarians and the People's Party, vied for their votes and, to a certain extent, comprised their lobby. A vast network of co-operative enterprises was in existence. Post-war organisational channels were, however, geared to the emerging centralised political model. The United Union of Czechoslovak Farmers (*Jednotný svaz československých zemědělců*) and the *Rolnické komise* (Farmers' Commissions) were instruments of State, and eventually Party, power rather than genuine groups advocating the sectional interests of their members. Even they had to give way, however, to the single form of organisation which was enforced in two main collectivisation drives of 1949–54 and 1957–8. The Czech name devised for *kolkhozy* – the unified agricultural co-operative (*jednotné zemědělské družstvo* or JZD) – misrepresents the term 'co-operative', but can conveniently be used to distinguish collectivised from private ('individually farming') farmers and from members of the 'state sector' of agriculture, i.e. the State farms, the Machine and Tractor Stations and an assortment of procurement, dispensing and similar agencies. Of the three 'sectors' in agriculture (co-operative, private, State), the last named is subsumed under working class, although it has always been tacitly relegated to its periphery.

Some figures may be useful. The number of co-operatives has been declining since 1960 (10,816), not because members reverted to private farming, but chiefly as a result of amalgamation. On 1 January 1969 there were 6,352 co-operatives, including 4,344 in the Czech Lands and 2,008 in Slovakia. At the end of 1967 co-operative members numbered 850,984 (1,182,000 with dependent relatives), including 717,016 per-

manently working in agriculture. Including relatives, the
co-operative 'sector' comprised 8·2 per cent of the country's
population. On average there were 136 members per co-
operative. In 1967 the number of private farmers was given as
160,000 (including 119,000 in Slovakia), and as 327,000
(2·3 per cent of the population) with dependents. There were
342 State farms with 214,268 members (of whom 196,000
were 'permanently active') and 101 Machine and Tractor
Stations with 25,708 workers.[1]

One 1967 source (referring presumably to 1965) gives the
following breakdown of occupations in the co-operative 'sector':
administrative apparat and management – 55,820 persons,
crop production workers – 390,456, livestock production
workers – 229,018, tractor and combine-harvester drivers and
maintenance men – 87,796, others – 45,320. In 1963 as much
as 53·9 per cent of the co-operative labour force were women.
Only 10 per cent of co-operatives were without private plots
which, on the whole, contributed 33 per cent to the total
personal income of a co-operative farmer.[2]

Anybody could of course be a member of the non-occupa-
tional attitudinal organisations, such as the Communist Party
and, theoretically, the other political parties, or of the Youth
Union, the Peace Defenders, the Czechoslovak–Soviet Friendship Union, etc., but only workers from the State 'sector' in
agriculture enjoyed the privilege of trade union membership.[3]
Co-operative, let alone private, farmers remained without
organised expression of their sectional interests. Legally, the
issue was not quite clear: agricultural co-operatives had a two-
fold qualification of both an economic (Article 11 of the
Constitution) and a voluntary public organisation (Article 5).
In practice, however, they have never even been considered
as being the latter to any meaningful degree. Co-operative and
private farmers were, more than any other group, the object,
and not the subject, of political action. For ideological reasons,

[1] *Statistická ročenka 1969* (Prague, SNTL, 1969).
[2] Machonin, *Změny v sociální struktuře*, pp. 36–8, 40.
[3] *Rudé právo*, 19 April 1968, p. 3, gives membership of the Union of
Workers in Agriculture, Forestry and Water Conservancy at 480,000.
The union welcomed overtures to the constitution of a Co-operative Farmers' Union but did not want its own members to join it. 'Group interests'
and 'economic position' of the two categories were different.

one suspects, trade unionism was not permitted to penetrate agriculture, although this meant a certain incongruity: trade union branches existed in some non-agricultural co-operatives (craftsmen's) and, as was indicated in the previous chapter, they embraced members from among 'the intelligentsia'. The anomaly was there for all to see: the working class, the small producer-artisans and the intelligentsia had at least one and sometimes more organisations (such as a writer who was a member of both the Writers' Union and the relevant trade union in his capacity as, say, an editor in a publishing house) vying to protect their interests, while the co-operative farmers had none. Even where the co-operative determined to act as a social organisation, it could do so only at the lowest territorial level. There was no hierarchy reaching upwards, to district, regional and central levels. The political influence of co-operative farmers, and even more that of the completely isolated private farmers, was nil simply because there were no channels for its expression.

It was this situation which accounted for the strenuous efforts throughout the Prague Spring (and for the accompanying confusion, as later described) to set up a farmers' organisation. On the surface the endeavour did not seem to be different from the process whereby new and renewed organisations mushroomed in all walks of life and fields of activity. In fact the process was reversed in motivation. While most of the other new organisations resulted from successful attempts to break up an artificially imposed unity (factions in the Communist Party, multiplication of trade unions, disintegration of the Youth Union, etc.), the farmers were groping towards a united State-wide organisational structure.

The Seventh Congress of Agricultural Co-operatives on 1–3 February 1968 was the first major gathering after the deposition of A. Novotný from the post of Party First Secretary. It also gave Alexander Dubček his first opportunity to make a public speech. However, the reformist atmosphere was still only in the offing and, in spite of a marked contrast with some worn clichés of previous agricultural policy, the 1,540 delegates said and heard practically nothing about the desire to set up a new interest organisation. A commission (misnamed 'the drafting commission') was appointed under J. Karlík, a Deputy

Minister of Agriculture, to study improved economic hierarchy in agricultural management and to devise ways in which agriculture as an economic sector could best face the other industries with which it had to deal. As it turned out, the commission was in no hurry to explore new organisational avenues and never really became the prime mover in the process.

In fact, the non-agricultural public was left in the dark until the end of February about the intention to establish a new farmers' organisation. One suspects that in the first two months of the year the farmers themselves were not much more initiated. Only at the end of February on the occasion of an audience with Dubček of a hundred veteran agricultural officials, did the newspapers intimate that the participants had talked, among other things, about an interest organisation of co-operative farmers who wanted it in order to 'feel responsibility for their own production'.[1] Josef Borůvka, the popular chairman of the Dolany agricultural co-operative and a recently elevated member of the Party Praesidium (also a leading reformer and a great character), must have felt this beating about the bush unbearable, because he addressed a press conference on 5 March quite unequivocally: To continue the policy of mistrust towards the farmers and to go on arguing that their private needs run counter to the needs of society was impossible. There were two main deficiencies, notably the non-existence of an interest organisation for over a million agriculturalists and the non-fulfilment of industrial deliveries to the farming business.

While it is impossible to measure the genuine eagerness of farmers to have an organisation of their own, one can well accept the reasoning of its reformist proponents. A farmers' organisation would not be superfluous under any conditions which the reformers envisaged for the future. In fact, to any reformer's mind both the non existence of farmers' representation to date and the important place of farming in the country's economic structure, and more specifically in the effort to right one of the crucial imbalances, made the emergence of a farmers' lobby overdue.

Almost as soon as awareness of the situation became public

[1] *Rudé právo*, 1 March 1968, p. 1.

property, several concepts were seen to be at loggerheads. The picture is difficult to disentangle. The following were the key questions: Should the new organisation be 'economic' and 'social' at the same time? Should there perhaps be two organisations, one economic and the other social? Should the organisation embrace both co-operative and private farmers? Should the 'State sector' in agriculture set up an organisation of its own, even though its members had a trade union already?

At first the conceptual thinking was done almost exclusively 'from the top'. Then, on 27 March, the Agricultural Committee of the National Assembly criticised the 'drafting commission' of the Seventh Congress of Agricultural Co-operatives for delays in producing workable proposals, and appealed to the co-operative farmers (shying away from the 160,000 private farmers) to start setting up preparatory committees even if they did not really know what kind of an organisation they ought to establish. There was some response 'from the bottom' and the committee was able to meet again a month later (2 May) to discuss rank-and-file opinion. At that moment this seemed to have been running slightly in favour of a single organisation combining 'social' representation (i.e. non-economic sectional interests, including political) and economic, i.e. managerial etc., powers. There was still uncertainty: Should the State farms be members? Should membership be based on individuals or 'units', i.e. co-operatives? Should private farmers be included in special sections attached to the district councils of co-operatives (which would be set up as an intermediate step in the hierarchy of the new organisation) or should they be allowed to form a separate economic organisation? (It should be noted that a 'social', let alone 'political', association of private farmers was not even mentioned.)

J. Karlík of the 'drafting commission' told a press conference on 3 May that – notwithstanding their differing preference for two organisations or for just one – most of the farmers were allegedly united in demanding that their new association should be a member of the National Front. This was, of course, shorthand for an aspiration to influence political decision-making, because at that stage of the Prague Spring the concept of the National Front as the forum of political pluralism had already crystallised.

The political awakening of at least some farmers and their representatives seemed to have taken the central authorities by surprise after they themselves had recommended that the debate should be carried into the farming community. During the month of April a number (now unidentifiable) of preparatory committees which sprang up in response to the National Assembly Agricultural Committee's appeal declared themselves in favour of a straightforward Union of Farmers (*Svaz zemědělců*) with voluntary individual membership, which would be run on explicitly non-economic lines. It was this concept which soon came under attack as allegedly signalling a return to political Agrarianism.

In fact it had been tried before, albeit on a less conspicuous scale and under less conducive circumstances. In Slovakia a preparatory committee of a Farmers' Club (*Klub zemědělců*) had been established early in 1967. In its draft statutes it defined itself as 'a voluntary professional-interest association' and a constituent assembly was called for 19 May. Shortly before that date the authorities had second thoughts and the meeting never took place.[1]

On 6 May 1968 delegates from several local preparatory committees in the Czech Lands convened in Prague on the initiative of a committee from Prague-East (i.e. the rural area immediately adjoining the conurbation) and of the editors of *Zemědělské noviny*, the agricultural daily, who showed strong reformist tendencies throughout 1968. Apparently they received little (if any) official encouragement because a member of the central preparatory committee had to begin his article in *Rudé právo* on 20 May by 'resolutely rejecting' assumptions that his union would be 'some kind of a simile' for the infamous Agrarian Party. He claimed: 'It is our concern as well to see socialist relations in the countryside preserved; a co-operative outlook continues to be our outlook.'

In spite of such assurance, an examination of this union's proposed set-up and programme shows little to distinguish it from a political party as it is generally understood in Central European politics. The *Svaz zemědělců* would be composed on a territorial basis and membership would be strictly individual. Recruitment of members would be carried out among

[1] *Rudé právo*, 29 March 1968, p. 6.

co-operative and private farmers, workers of State farms, 'the agricultural intelligentsia' and other citizens who live in villages and country towns, especially teachers and cultural workers. They would comprise local branches of the union and there would be a district and a central level. Members could join other organisations, such as the trade unions or other interest groups. The *Svaz* would want to nominate candidates for election to the National Committees and the National Assembly. Its programme would be 'to return to the countryside the cultural and social status it had enjoyed in history'. The union would expect an economic organisation of farmers to be established separately from among completely independent agricultural enterprises.

To what extent a particular *reform* represented a *return* to pre-Communist conditions, and to what extent such a return was regressive in the sense of expressing a nostalgic clinging to the past rather than genuine remedial action, is of course open to interpretation. What appears incontrovertible is that the emergence of an agrarian organisation along the lines of the *Svaz zemědělců* was politically unacceptable to the Dubček leadership, and was tactically dubious in face of the Soviet attitude to political organisation in the countryside. The Party Praesidium did not wait long to make its preferences publicly known. On 21–2 May it secured the agreement of the Ministry of Agriculture and the Agricultural Committee of the National Assembly to a firm recommendation that a Union of Co-operative Farmers as a member of the National Front was the right kind of organisation to emerge from the embarrassing debates.

This was to be a 'social' organisation whose aim would be to protect the interests of the co-operative farmers, especially insofar as pay, labour law, social security, living conditions and 'full recognition of the merits of agricultural work' were concerned. Membership would be individual and private farmers would be allowed to join, but the co-operative farm, rather than the village, would form the basic unit. A day later (23 May) an *aktiv* of 300 chairmen of Communist Party rural branches in Brno 'spontaneously welcomed' the Party Praesidium's ruling, including the condition that an economic organisation of co-operatives should be set up separately.

Organisation along management lines ('economic') is outside the scope of this book. Let it only be noted that two competing concepts emerged, one which wished to extend the associative process begun at the end of 1967 with the establishment of District Agricultural Associations (*Okresní zemědělská sdružení*), and the other based on 'enterprises'. Another bone of contention was the inclusion or non-inclusion of the 'State sector'. Eventually the economic grouping of co-operatives did not proceed beyond the District Associations. The State farms set up on 6–7 May a preparatory committee of their own Economic Union (*Hospodářský svaz státních statků*) on a voluntary basis, proclaiming emphatically that they did not consider it a divisive element. Their spokesmen were in favour of a co-ordinating body to blanket all economic activity in agriculture. The constituent meeting in Brno on 20 August considered applications for membership from 254 Czech and eighty-nine Slovak State farms, i.e. close to 100 per cent. The union was not invested with management powers; it could only pass recommendations. The Union of Machine and Tractor Stations was also set up. Undoubtedly, foremost on the minds of the founders of all 'economic' associations was the bargaining power of agriculture *vis-à-vis* industry and the State, notably the Ministry of Agriculture and its agencies.

The slow-working 'drafting commission' which survived from the Seventh Congress of Co-operatives and never really possessed sufficient power or authority to advocate specific solutions jumped on to the bandwagon on 23 May when it endorsed the Party Praesidium's version of the future union's status. At a press conference on 28 May journalists, slightly stunned by the speed of events, were told by Josef Borůvka, who had been appointed Minister of Agriculture and Food in April, that the 'drafting commission' would bring to life a Union of Co-operative Farmers as soon as possible, in fact by the end of June. Several preparatory committees were in existence which did not see eye to eye on all issues; swift action would therefore resolve the disputes. Objections to the shortness of time for a thorough discussion of new statutes by the farmers, as well as questions about procedures designed to elect delegates were swept under the table. One must understand that by the end of May the Party leadership was acting under great pressure from the Soviet Union to counter right-wing dangers, of which the possibility of a spontaneous political organisation by the farmers was certainly not the most negligible. The offensive launched by the local anti-reformists at the Central Committee meeting at the end of May and beginning of June is well known.

The 'drafting commission' echoed the Minister on 4 June with a disclosure of some organisational details and a definite rejection of the *Svaz zemĕdĕlců* whom they, however, invited for co-operation – on the basis of the Co-operative Union. A draft programme of the prospective union was then published, proclaiming that it would be represented in the National Front, contribute to the drafting of new agricultural legislation, improve health and social insurance and promote better health and spa treatment and recreation for its members.

The constituent conference, which eventually convened in Nitra from 9 to 11 July 1968, was billed as a gathering of delegates to the Seventh Congress of Agricultural Co-operatives (*sic!*) and 'representatives of individually farming farmers'. A week before the conference a journalist sighed, 'For God's sake, let us not bring about a new organisation only according to what the leaders want it to be!' He warned that the majority of the delegates who were being elected were, in fact, chairmen of co-operative farms: 232 in the Czech Lands, as against a mere thirty-one tractor drivers, livestock attendants, milkmaids and other rank-and-file workers. (These figures are incomplete.) Only twenty-six women had been delegated by that date, in spite of the fact that they formed the majority of the agricultural work force.[1]

Still, the Nitra conference was a fully fledged affair with Svoboda, Sádovský, Husák and Borůvka in attendance. (Even this meeting regarded it repeatedly necessary 'to repudiate with all resoluteness the venomous slander that we are out to set up an opposition political party'.) Unfortunately, most of the speakers from the floor chose to raise economic grievances, and few showed enthusiasm for socio-political action. There was good reason to believe that in its present form the gathering was ill-prepared to do anything but endorse pre-processed

[1] J. Bednařík in *Rudé právo*, 3 July 1968, p. 2.

concepts.[1] This is not to say that meaningful grassroot partici-pation in future political action was excluded. For the time being it was, however, not forthcoming.

At separate Czech and Slovak sittings two national com-mittees were voted into office and their chairmen elected (Jaroslav Karhan from Henčlov, and Pavel Jonáš from Prietrž), but no agreement could be reached on whether the federal committee should have parity representation or other built-in guarantees against the superiority of the one national com-ponent over the other. After protracted and awkward bickering the election of the federal committee was postponed. The Ministry of Agriculture sought to break the deadlock on 17 July when it summoned leaders of both national unions, but the only achievement was an agreement that the two national chairmen would be alternately invited to attend government meetings. Both, however, demanded representation on the Economic Council.

The *deus* of the invasion almost literally descended from the *machina* to cut short the many conceptual conflicts. In 1969 agricultural organisations were left in a state of suspended animation. Then the counter-reformation régime struck in two directions: economic management of agriculture was returned to the State and its central agencies, and the Union of Co-operative Farmers was remoulded into a transmission-belt-type organisation. While the Economic Union of the State Farms had to discontinue its activity in March 1970 and the Union of Machine and Tractor Stations in April 1970, the Co-operative Union (which by then had 430,000 members out of the total of 570,000 members of co-operative farms; no mention was made of private farmers)[2] was entrusted at its Central Committee meeting on 22 April 1970 'henceforth to concentrate on explaining the policy of the Party in the country-side, on cementing alliance with the working class and on the politico-ideological education of co-operative farmers'. It should also strive for the fulfilment of plans, uncovering of

[1] M. Pavlík, writing in *Rudé právo* of 30 July 1968, p. 2, goes as far as to suggest that the Nitra conference often reminded him of 'a festival of wasted time', with delegates endlessly assuring themselves that a Co-operative Farmers' Union, rather than just a Farmers' Union, must be established.

[2] Radio Free Europe, *Situation Report*, 29 May 1970.

reserves and encouragement of work initiative. The only lasting achievement can thus be seen in the union's sheer existence. Someone observed that in a number of villages it remained the only social (non-Communist) organisation after the others had disintegrated or had been dispersed. The fact that not a single co-operative farm broke up during the fluid situation of 1968 is most certainly of cardinal importance. On a few occasions several officials warned against 'growing voices' purportedly demanding the return of landed property to private hands or, more frequently, compensation to previous owners for expropriation, but nothing would seem to suggest that 'democratisation' in agriculture took the form of de-collectivisation.[1] In fact, no such claim was seriously made by the post-reformation critics of the Dubček era. With the final stage of collectivisation barely ten years old, with the Polish experience on the doorstep and with the proverbially strong emotional attachment of the Czech and Slovak farmers to their land, this must count as one of the most surprising phenomena of the Prague Spring.

Several explanations offer themselves: The time may have been too short. Especially the Czech (as against the Slovak) farmer has always been known to take a long time before going into action. The element of adaptability, for which the Czech nation is known, may have been stronger than the element of tradition. At long last, Czechoslovak farming in 1966–8 appeared to have begun what promised to be a period of longer-lasting prosperity. The tumultuous disruption of political structures in the State did not coincide with economic plight and falling standards of living in the countryside. Alternatively, of course, the resilience of co-operative agriculture may be seen as a proof of popular confidence in Dubček-type socialism. A reform movement with Communist Party participation and, in some respects, under its guidance must have had a different effect on the farming population than a rebellion against the Communist Party and against practically everything it stood for (as in Poland in 1956).

[1] See for example J. Borůvka at his press conference in Prague on 23 April 1968 (*Zemědělské noviny*, 24 April 1968, p. 1) and L. Hofman's speech at a regional Party conference in České Budějovice on 3 May 1968 (*Rudé právo*, 4 May 1968, p. 3).

CHAPTER THREE

The Intelligentsia

Allowing myself the luxury of an inaccurate paradox, I am tempted to say that while Russian experience suggested that a Communist revolution could be brought about without much contribution from the country's intelligentsia, although the 'construction of socialism' necessitated it, Czechoslovak Communism seemed almost determined to prove the opposite. Meaningful definitions of the mission of the intelligentsia in post-1948 Czechoslovak society were certainly absent from the policy-shaping documents of the Party, and problems which affected the intelligentsia, such as education, culture and ideology, received pragmatic treatment tailored rather to dogma or momentary power-political needs than to genuine conceptual outlooks. After February 1948 the first major Party policy towards the intelligentsia arose from an ideological postulate which had been taken over from Soviet conditions. This was the 'creation of a new intelligentsia', a theorem which by and large had little justification in the indigenous situation. Neither the apparat of the State nor the body of white-collar and professional workers or educated specialists were immediately opposed to Communist power, and there was most certainly no large-scale sabotage or even boycott of the new régime on their part. Thus the measures taken by the Party leadership of the day against the natural arrangement and course of events in the intellectual field soon began to be felt as irritating, unjust, harmful and often plain stupid by those who would have been quite willing to try to help make the emerging system efficient.

The gradually growing alienation of the intelligentsia from the post-1948 type of Communism fed on such measures as the campaign against 'cosmopolitanism' and the accompanying political interference with science and scholarship, the enforced two-way flow of manpower in the form of transfers of politically suspect specialists and scholars 'to the production-line' and of hard-core workers and Party reliables from factories into the academic and other intellectual worlds, the introduction of bureaucratic hierarchies of supervision and planning into science, the discrimination in investment policies, the egalitarianism in pay, the reduction of scope for practical application of scientific achievements through growing inefficiency of the manufacturing industries, and – last but not least – the frequent pronouncements of distrust in, and even contempt for, 'the wavering intelligentsia'. All this could be described at great length, and one day undoubtedly will be, but for our purpose suffice it to say that the assumption that 'the intelligentsia begotten by the people will remain devoted and loyal to the people' was to prove illusory. The Soviet precept simply did not work in the conditions of a country which possessed a vastly more sophisticated and numerous intellectual potential in relation to its overall population, and whose intelligentsia became profoundly disillusioned when the Communist world of fact after 1948 turned out not to match the Communist world of vision which they had almost accepted before 1948. In fact, the history of Communist rule in Czechoslovakia has ever since 1956 been a history of strife between the intelligentsia and the leadership, rather than a sequence of economic achievements. What is now called 'the reform' was nothing other than an alternative solution to the nation's predicament worked out precisely by the intelligentsia and embraced both by the public at large and even by a part of the governing apparatus.

As a system of government, Communism in Czechoslovakia soon had to face the increasing complexity of modern social and economic management, no matter how strong were the preferences for ideological dogma. One might be tempted to say that almost against the wish of the 'old guard' the numbers and specific weight of white-collar and professional people began to grow. Ideological inertia, subscribing to the mechanical division of society into one ruling class (workers), one co-operating class (co-operative farmers), one contained class (small private producers) and one 'intermediate layer' (the intelligentsia), resulted in confusion in statistics as well as in political premises.

How numerous was the Czechoslovak intelligentsia of the 1960s and what was its structure? Czechoslovak statisticians eventually (but not consistently and regularly) devised two categories. The wider of them, *duševní pracovníci*, will be translated here as 'white-collar and professional workers', rather than the literal 'brain workers'. This blanket group included people who mostly worked with their brains, although not necessarily having the educational background prescribed for their jobs. The narrower group, *odborníci*, translated here as 'educated specialists', included persons who completed specialised secondary or higher education, although not necessarily employed in non-manual jobs. Moreover, this group specifically excluded the clergy. Certain other categories were nominally excluded as well, such as factory guards, firemen, shop assistants and messengers from the white-collar and professional group, and apprenticed experts and graduates of courses not included in the unified educational system from the educated specialists group.[1] In this way, the two groups overlapped to an extent which it is often impossible to ascertain. For example, the number of people with higher or specialised secondary training who did not work in non-manual jobs was steadily growing (from 49,922 in 1958 to 80,215 in 1966), but the size of this group could not be deduced from the available material, unless inside information from the statistical office was used.[2] As a correlative, 25 per cent (398,794 persons) of all white-collar and professional workers in 1966 had only a primary education.[3]

It seems that eventually most writers on the subject came to regard *intelligentsia* as tantamount to *white-collar and professional workers*. This category included the following groups: technicians; clerks; health workers; research workers-scientists-scholars; teachers and instructors; cultural and public-education workers; workers in law and jurisprudence; artists; telecommunication workers; management staff in trade, storage, public catering and accommodation (specifically not

[1] J. Snížek, 'K některým problémům odborné kvalifikace duševních pracovníků, *Statistika*, 8 (1967) pp. 342–7. Also *Statistická ročenka 1963* (Prague, SEVT, 1963) p. 111.
[2] Snížek, op. cit., pp. 343–4.
[3] Ibid., p. 344.

including non-management staff); and political workers. One writer[1] gave the following numbers:

White-collar and professional workers (with dependents, but without agricultural co-operative specialists)

		Per cent of the total population
1950	2,045,000	16·5
1955	2,435,000	18·6
1960 (est.)	2,593,000	18·9

White-collar and professional workers (without dependents, but with agricultural co-operative specialists)

		Per cent of all the economically active population
1958	1,197,000	19·6
1960	1,301,649	21·4
1962	1,429,843	22·8

Other sources offer a large selection of figures. A statistical compendium speaks about the intelligentsia ('represented to an overwhelming majority by clerical staff') comprising 16·4 per cent of the country's population in 1950 and 27·9 per cent in 1961.[2] A usually reliable scholar notes that the intelligentsia in 1960 accounted for almost 10 per cent of the population,[3] and a journalist – writing in 1966 – stated that it was half as numerous as the working class and 'far superior in numbers' to the co-operative farmers.[4] A sociologist wrote in 1966 that nearly 30 per cent of the population was 'active in the field of professional mental work', emphasising however that this was

[1] Z. Valenta, *Fyzická a duševní práce za socialismu* (Prague, NPL, 1965) pp. 97–8.

[2] *Hospodářský a společenský vývoj Československa* (Prague, SSÚ-SEVT, 1968) pp. 7–8.

[3] L. Dziedzinská, *Inteligence za kapitalismu a socialismu* (Prague, SNPL) 1962.

[4] V. Kotek in *Kulturní tvorba*, 45 (1966), quoted by K. Achrer, 'Lékaři jako profesionální skupina inteligence' in *Sborník prací filosofické fakulty Brněnské university*, G 13 (Brno, 1969).

not an undifferentiated mass of people.[1] Another writer put the proportion of white-collar and professional workers at 21·9 per cent of all wage and salary earners in 1961, which, as he pointed out, was far above the average similar ratio in the other socialist countries (10–17·7 per cent).[2] A sociologist envisaged the intelligentsia as comprising 20 per cent of all employed people in 1980 and 50 per cent in 2000.[3] As can easily be seen, rudimentary hard information is difficult to come by.

I have chosen two breakdowns and one global set of figures from what appear to be the least whimsical sources: a document prepared for the Thirteenth Communist Party Congress in 1966 by a team of sociologists and other scholars; a table compiled by an author who most consistently followed changes in the social structure over a number of years; and a set of figures culled from the official *Statistical Yearbook* for 1963 (not all *Statistical Yearbooks* carried figures on the intelligentsia). The figures relate to 1962 and are obviously based on the 1961 census. No newer figures are available to me at the time of writing. Gaps (such as the sum total in the first table not corresponding to the overall figure) and discrepancies (such as between the first, the second and the third tables) cannot be accounted for.

The intelligentsia in 1962[4]

Total number of working people in the country	6,244,000
Industrial workers	1,842,000
White-collar and professional workers	1,454,234
Technicians and economic personnel	594,338
including clerical personnel	187,191
Teachers at all grades	142,372*

*This figure was omitted from the table and had to be computed from a percentage.

---

[1] P. Machonin, 'Socialistická rovnost a nerovnost v naší společnosti', *Nová mysl*, 12 (1966).

[2] M. Bartoš, 'Poznámky k rozvoji školství v ČSSR', *Nová mysl*, 12 (1970) p. 1754.

[3] J. Macků, 'Über die Stellung der sozio-professionellen Gruppen der geistig Arbeitenden in der ČSSR', in *Sborník prací filosofické fakulty Brněnské university*, G 13 (Brno, 1969) p. 17.

[4] Machonin, *Změny v sociální struktuře*, p. 58.

Research and development workers   110,000
Physicians   25,823
Workers in administration, judiciary, finance,
    insurance, social organisations and unclassified   191,000
Specialists in agricultural co-operatives   24,391

The intelligentsia in 1962[1]

In technical and economic jobs   594,338
In science and research   125,000
In health and social services   193,000
In education, culture, public education and P.T.   327,000
In administration and the judiciary   107,000
In finance and insurance   29,000
In social organisations   25,000
In agricultural co-operatives   26,825

White-collar and professional workers as of 30 September 1962[2]

Total, including those with: 1,429,843
Higher education   167,640
Senior secondary specialised   391,194
Junior secondary specialised   270,249
Secondary general   111,324
Primary and other   489,436

There are 274 white-collar and professional workers per 1,000 employed people in the country.

Growth patterns can be at least partly assessed from the following percentages given by the authors of the first (Machonin) and second (Valenta) tables (see above):

Group	Machonin *1958–62* (*per cent*)	Valenta *1958–63* (*per cent*)
Technical and economic,	123·4	124·8
including clerks	114·6	—
Research and development	139·0	169·6
Teachers	104·7	—
Education, culture, etc.	—	134·7

[1] Z. Valenta, 'K problematice socialistické intelligence', *Odbory a společnost*, 2 (1966) p. 4.
[2] *Statistická ročenka ČSSR, 1963* (Prague, SEVT, 1963) p. 120.

Group	Machonin 1958–62 (per cent)	Valenta 1958–63 (per cent)
Physicians	117·0	—
Health and social care	—	119·6
Administration, judiciary, finance, insurance, social organisations and unclassified	120·0	—
Administration and judiciary	—	97·3
Finance and insurance	—	100·0
Social organisations	—	138·8
Specialists in agricultural co-operatives	221·7	243·8

Some conclusions can be drawn even from this unsatisfying set of figures. Even in the early stages of the reform process which culminated in 1968, the Czechoslovak intelligentsia was obviously a large community, second only in society to the working class. At the same time it was internally diversified and contained an excessive number of ill-prepared people (with primary education only). Divided by field of activity, the technicians and economists (including management personnel in industry, etc.) were by far the strongest single group ('the technical intelligentsia'). The second most numerous group consisted of teachers and other knowledge-dispensing persons. The bulk of the intelligentsia had a secondary education (with school-leaving examinations at the age of eighteen). Scientists and scholars were the fastest growing group, with the exception of agriculturalists, for whom the tempo was given by the fact of their small initial numbers. It should be noted that career soldiers and police were scrupulously not mentioned by the statisticians. The headings 'administration and the judiciary' in both tables are too tight to conceal them, since they must presumably include local government and ministerial staff.

In view of the high number of persons with primary schooling included in the above figures, education is possibly a better key for determining the real numbers of 'the intelligentsia', apart from its being used by the statisticians to define 'educated specialists'. According to the 1961 census the following table was compiled in relation to the population of working age and after (i.e. fifteen and over: 10,002,500 persons):

Education 1961[1]

	Absolute number	Per cent
No data given	53,779	0·6
No education	68,540	0·7
Primary	8,185,422	81·8
Secondary general	280,732	2·8
Junior secondary specialised	651,914	6·5
Senior secondary specialised	560,069	5·6
Higher, including:	202,044	2·0
Technical	78,877	0·8
Humanities	92,850	0·9
Pedagogical	17,525	0·2
Artistic	5,293	0·1

For comparison, the Institute for Research of Public Opinion was using in 1968–9 the following percentages to measure the educational composition of its representative samples: No data or no education – 0·6 per cent, primary – 76·1 per cent, incomplete secondary – 6·8 per cent, complete secondary – 13·2 per cent, higher – 3·3 per cent.[2]

The policy of a wide and rapid development of general secondary education as proclaimed in the 1960s clashed with the barriers built into the system. Graduates from general secondary schools had difficulty in finding suitable jobs; enterprises and institutions were unable to absorb even the graduates of specialised schools who had been assigned them in the plans. The main reason, it appears, was the continuing staffing of established jobs with people who did not possess adequate educational requirements, and the non-creation of a sufficient number of new openings for qualified workers (due to slow technical progress). The following two tables give an indication of how serious this problem was and to what extent it must have contributed to the growing frustration of the technical intelligentsia.

[1] *Vývoj společnosti v číslech* (Prague, SEVT, 1965) p. 205.
[2] Quoted in Z. Salzmann, *A Contribution to the Study of Value Orientations among the Czechs and Slovaks* (Amherst, University of Massachusetts, 1970) p. 30.

Qualification structure of all leading officials[1]

	Per cent
Higher education	11·9
Senior specialised	20·0
Complete secondary general	7·8
Primary or junior specialised	60·3

The author adds that 70 per cent of leading officials are below forty-five and cannot excuse themselves by saying that injustices of the pre-Communist systems prevented them from acquiring the appropriate qualifications. Also, of the total number of 657,000 with secondary and higher education in the twenty-five to fifty-nine age group, only 11·3 per cent actually held leading posts.

Compliance with prescribed qualification requirements[2]

	Per cent
Managers and deputy managers in enterprises and factories	48
Heads of departments in enterprises and factories	48
Other technical staff in departments	57
Heads of plants	42
Foremen	38
Other technical staff	49
Other economic staff (clerical)	38

Consideration of the political role of the intelligentsia in the reform movement can thus begin with the acceptance of the premise that the reformist aspirations (change orientation) were not generated from among a small aristocratic and élite group whose aims and manner of behaviour originated in the *status quo ante*. If we take as determinants both education (full secondary and higher) and the predominantly intellectual nature of work performed, the obtaining strength of the group is around 1 million (with a strong supporting group of people with junior secondary education). This figure was natural and constant in the sense of not being the sole result either of a state of affairs surviving from the *ancien régime* or of some kind of a gigantic campaign by the Communist government. In a

[1] L. Dziedzinská, *Inteligence a dnešek* (Prague, Melantrich, 1968) p. 127.
[2] Machonin, *Změny v sociální struktuře*, pp. 86–7.

country of 14 million people, or 10 million of working-age and over, the 1-million strong group not only had every right to seek political recognition for itself beyond the nebulous classification as an 'intermediate layer' or a 'wavering stratum', but also to request that its views were listened to in the running of the State and of the Party. It was not even un-Marxist to suggest that of all the socialist countries in Eastern Europe Czechoslovakia was the only one in which 'the working intelligentsia' ought to have been considered the primary ally of the working class, rather than – as in Russia – the toiling peasants.

Uneasiness in the ideological understanding of the intelligentsia's place in society came into the open fairly early in the 1960s when old clichés became patently untenable in face of the advent of the concept of scientific and technical revolution. Official pronouncements sought a remedy in a clumsy attempt to dissolve the intelligentsia into the working class. According to a resolution of the Twelfth Party Congress in 1962, the intelligentsia 'gradually loses the characteristics of a separate social layer and becomes an indivisible part of the working class and co-operative farmers'.[1] In his acclaimed (unjustly, to my mind) work *Civilisation at the Crossroads*, in which he identified the scientific and technical revolution with Communism and vice versa, Radovan Richta tried to translate this awkward nonsense into quasi-scientific Marxist jargon: for him 'specialised intelligentsia [*sic*] gradually becomes an indivisible part of the "collective worker", a qualified and growing group within the working class'.[2]

The new generation of political scientists and sociologists, some of whom prepared a well-documented paper on changes in the social structure for the Thirteenth Party Congress in 1966, could not accept this line. Neither could they, however, hope to make the Party leadership proclaim the obvious. One of them commented in private: 'As long as you need to have "a leading force" in the country for ideological purposes, you cannot hope to have the intelligentsia as a whole or some part of it, such as the scientists or the technicians, elevated to the

---

[1] *Usnesení XII. sjezdu KSČ* (Prague, SNPL, 1963) p. 24.
[2] R. Richta *et al.*, *Civilizace na rozcestí*, 3rd edition (Prague, Svoboda, 1969) p. 277.

status of leaders. While we cannot go on accepting that society simply divides into workers and farmers and that what is left is the intelligentsia, the best we can do is to create the notion of a joint leading force comprising both the workers and the intelligentsia, but consider them as separate groups.' The relevant passage in their document for the Thirteenth Congress then spoke about 'rapprochement between the workers and the intelligentsia in their function as a leading social force'.[1] In another part of the document they stated that 'especially in its creative components the intelligentsia is the main bearer of the scientific-technical and cultural revolution'.[2] That was as far as the reformers could go in the ideology-laden conditions of the day. Elsewhere one of them argued that just as the intelligentsia could not hope to achieve its mission without the workers, so the workers were unable to ensure the progressive development of society without the intelligentsia.[3]

The intensity of Czech discussions about the intelligentsia between 1964 and 1968 was, I believe, unmatched anywhere in the world. Rationally and emotionally this was felt to be one of the most awkward blank spaces on the map of contemporary society and, indeed, to be the key both to economic and administrative efficiency and to the much-needed humanisation. It was from this understanding that the unusual and in fact unprecedented solidarity of the intelligentsia emerged *vis-à-vis* the neo-Stalinist pre-1968 régime. This in turn made the intelligentsia an extremely uncomfortable element for the leadership to handle. The traditionally trained Marxists still saw the intelligentsia through the Russian eyes of 1917, notably as a small servile instrument dependent either on the bourgeoisie or on the proletariat. In politics it was expected to do nothing more than 'adjoin' to the one or the other. Only the Prague Spring was to succeed in breaking the dogma or at least the cliché. A report prepared for the Fourteenth Party Congress in 1968 pledged the Party to ensure 'an absolutely independent and autonomous position' for science. Science was

---

[1] Machonin, *Změny v sociální struktuře*, p. 55.

[2] Ibid., p. 63.

[3] P. Machonin, 'K celkové charakteristice sociální struktury socialistické společnosti', in *Sociální struktura socialistické společnosti*, ed. P. Machonin (Prague, Svoboda, 1967) p. 149.

'an equal partner and at the same time an important co-creator of policy'. The Party 'resolutely refuses to degrade science – above all social science – to an instrument for the defence and promotion of a certain political concept and of political postulates.'[1]

The pressure which the intelligentsia was capable of exerting on the Party leadership came as much from inside as from outside. It may be appropriate to conclude this section by quoting figures on Party membership among the various segments of the intelligentsia in 1968, i.e. before the purge of 1970. The figures, normally secret, appeared in the context of an article as incomplete as they are given here, and should be considered an indicator only. Of 'leading economic officials' (i.e. management, etc.), 70–80 per cent were members of the Party. The other percentages were: officials of 'social and interest organisations' – 80–90 per cent; leading officials of central institutions (Ministries, etc.) – 85–90 per cent; cultural and public education officials – 70 per cent; teachers of elementary and secondary schools (males only) – 50–55 per cent; teaching staff at universities – 60 per cent; technicians in industry and agriculture – 30–40 per cent; workers in research and development – 40–45 per cent; physicians – 25–35 per cent.[2]

WRITERS

It is difficult not to exaggerate the effect the community of writers had on the political attitudes of society and the decision making of its leaders. The various developments which took place from the Second Writers' Congress in 1956 to the Fourth Congress in 1967, the prominent part of the men of letters in the Prague Spring and the painful and disastrous suppression of the writers' community under Gustáv Husák have been described at length elsewhere.[3] For the purpose of this study

---

[1] *Panzer überrollen den Parteitag*, ed. J. Pelikán (Vienna, Europa Verlag, 1969) pp. 249–50.

[2] A. Vaněk, 'Strana a inteligence', *Učitelské noviny*, 25 June 1970, p. 12.

[3] See for example: *Aspects of Intellectual Ferment and Dissent in Czechoslovakia* (Washington, U.S. Government Printing Office, 1969); Y. Blumenfeld, *Seesaw. Cultural Life in Eastern Europe* (New York, 1968); G. Grass and P. Kohout, *Briefe über die Grenze* (Hamburg, 1968); J. Hájek, *Mýtus a realita ledna* (Prague, 1970); D. Hamšík, *Writers against Rulers* (London, 1971);

one should bear in mind both the traditional attitude of people in Czechoslovakia towards their literature and the more immediate nature of the conflict between the Novotný régime and the writers.

When Jaroslav Seifert, the poet, appealed to those assembled at the Second Writers' Congress (22–9 April 1956) to be 'the conscience' of their nation, he was not exhorting them to establish a political watchdog organisation to keep an eye on the government. In fact, the writers never constituted themselves as a political organisation. Seifert meant something more sophisticated: the concept of 'conscience', something intellectual and spiritual which rouses man to be human, humane and genuine, stood opposed to the Stalinist theorem (proclaimed at the Soviet Writers' Congress in 1934 and surviving till the present day) of the literati as 'engineers of human souls', a mission seen by many to signify the approach of a mechanical manipulator and maintenance man. From 1948 (in some cases even earlier) it was this latter role that was played by the Czechoslovak writers who subscribed to Communism.

It was not easy to shake off. As in other fields of intellectual activity (e.g. among philosophers and historians), the first stage of extrication was introverted. The emotional response of the Second Congress to Khrushchev's anti-Stalin disclosures could be kept hidden by the authorities from the general public, at least as far as the text of the speeches at the Congress were concerned. In actual creative work, suppression was more difficult and the full-scale imposition of doctrinally understood socialist realism soon proved elusive, much to the chagrin of the powers-that-be. The writers claimed for themselves the right to 'poetry of every day', i.e. deviation from the (tacitly and less so) prescribed themes towards the predicament of ordinary man, neither a red hero nor a black villain. The process can

---

V. V. Kusin, *The Intellectual Origins of the Prague Spring* (Cambridge, 1971); A. J. Liehm, *Trois Générations* (Paris, 1970); 'M', *A Year Is Eight Months* (New York, 1969); L. Mňačko, *Die Siebente Nacht* (Vienna, 1968); *Poučení z krizového vývoje ve straně a společnosti po XIII. sjezdu KSČ* (Prague, 1971); H. Schwartz, *Prague's 200 Days* (New York, 1969); I. Sviták, *The Czechoslovak Experiment* (Columbia, 1971); M. Tatu, *L'hérésie impossible* (Paris, 1968); P. Tigrid, *Le printemps de Prague* (Paris, 1968); Z. A. B. Zeman, *Prague Spring* (London, 1969). The Radio Free Europe research material and situation reports are a well-informed secondary source.

best be followed in the literary monthly *Květen*, so named (*May*) after the month in 1945 which many of its authors considered to be the beginning of their literary careers. Its first two issues in 1956 were undistinguished enough, but as soon as the Twentieth Soviet Communist Party Congress and the Second Czechoslovak Writers' Congress began to reverberate in the literary community, the emphasis shifted towards questioning illusory unity, the problem of generation gaps and the 'civilism' and 'neo-realism' (poetry of every day) which so differed from the officially postulated 'optimism of superstition and illusion' (to borrow a Czech philosopher's phrase). Josef Vohryzek, calling for the right to interpret a work of art 'from within', on its own merits, clashed with Jiří Hájek whose constructions of post-War literary developments in Czechoslovakia were modelled on the Soviet 'theory of reflection'. Is literature to be understood as 'an historically conditioned reflex of social relationships' or does it possess 'aesthetic peculiarity'?

The authorities seemed then to be willing to conclude a certain kind of peace with the writers' community, accompanied even by a measure of autonomy in matters of subject and style of writing, if only the authors did not pursue the concept of 'conscience of the nation'. This proved to be impossible. Not only were questions of subject and style less non-political than the government expected them to be, but at the beginning of the 1960s a whole range of factors combined to make the writers defy established clichés from an almost political standpoint. The Slovak cultural community was deeply offended by the virtual eradication of the last traces of national self-management and joined forces with the Husák-type 'bourgeois nationalists'. The long-promised revision of the political trials of the 1950s once again ended with the absolution of most of the current leaders and the half-hearted rehabilitation of the victims. Economic stagnation set in. Historians had by then begun to restore some pre-Communist values to their rightful place, including those usually associated with T. G. Masaryk and the men of culture in pre-War Czechoslovakia who supported him. Philosophers had more or less successfully shed the onus of being no more than the servants of the one and only ruling ideology, and Karel Kosík was writing his *Dia-*

lectics of the Concrete. Khrushchev found it necessary to continue his criticism of Stalinism at the Twenty-second Soviet Communist Party Congress and to demand, as had been customary, that the other Communist countries follow the same line.

Thus, under combined national, intellectual and economic pressure and foreign influence, the Party leadership of the day loosened its grip at the Twelfth Party Congress in 1962. Almost immediately the process of self-assertion among the writers changed from introverted into extroverted. Opposition to the understanding of literature as utilitarian social didactics turned into political criticism of the régime's handling of human values. This became apparent at the Third Congress of the Writers' Union in 1963 (22–4 May), at the conference on Franz Kafka (27–8 May), in the writing of the literary weeklies *Kultúrny život* (Bratislava) and *Literárni noviny* (Prague) and their wrestling with censorship, as well as in the publication of critical fiction, prose and verse, by, for example, Ladislav Novomeský, Ladislav Bublík (*Páteř*), Peter Karvaš (*Jizva*), Ladislav Mňačko (*Oneskorené reportáže*), Ivan Klíma, Josef Topol, Václav Havel and others. Strong support was forthcoming from the related art of film-making with the emergence of the *new wave* of Czechoslovak cinema, for which overt and covert criticism of the prevailing human condition was typical. The drama joined the reform-seeking community not much later and a clash between official views and those held by the theatrical people occurred at the Third Congress of the Theatrical and Film Artists' Union on 29–30 November 1965.

By 1967 the divergencies between a large majority of the writers and the Party leadership had crystallised. What had begun, and continued until 1963, as a search for literary assertion outside the constraints of socialist realism, became one of the major political conflicts in the country. Once again, as in the nineteenth century, the Czech writers were deputising for politicians. Writers who aspired to be their nation's human conscience assembled at their Fourth Congress from 27 to 29 June 1967 to become the political conscience of the whole country. This event, as well as the subsequent expropriation by the government of *Literárni noviny*, has been sufficiently described elsewhere.[1] Suffice it to say that, surprised as they, like others, had been by the replacement of Dubček for Novotný, the writers entered the year 1968 with the aura of being the recognised protagonists of the reformist alliance. Their union was a force to be counted with, even though it was crippled by intervention on the part of the Party leadership (no chairman, four enforced members of the praesidium, no weekly newspaper in Prague, etc.). It consisted (since April 1954) of two sections: the so-called Czech Part of the Czechoslovak Writers' Union and the Union of Slovak Writers; translators comprised a separate yet affiliated section. Membership in this organisationally anomalous union was (1967) as follows: Czech Part – 299 members, eighty-seven candidate members, 158 translators; Slovak Union – 169 members, fifty-five candidate members, sixty-seven translators.[2] Secretariats were in existence in Prague and Bratislava, and 'branches' in Brno, Ostrava, Banská Bystrica and Prešov. The union owned two publishing houses (Prague and Bratislava) and several 'creative residences' for members who wished to write in peace and quiet. Eleven newspapers, journals and magazines were being published under the union's auspices, and it also administered a Literary Foundation for which funds were made available through voluntary additions on top of tax paid on literary activities (i.e. not from the State, but from practising writers and publicists themselves). Since 1961 the union had recorded a profit and transmitted 16·5 million crowns to the State coffers from 1961 to 1967.[3]

Soon after the crucial January session of the Party Central Committee, the writers were given to understand that the new Party leadership would tolerate a repair of the breach between their union and the authorities. Their first effort, consequently, was directed at 'normalisation' of conditions in the union. The Central Committee met in Prague on 24 January 1968, gave 'full support to conclusions' from the Party plenums (December and January), unanimously elected Eduard Goldstücker

---

[1] See especially D. Hamšík, *Writers against Rulers* (London, 1971) and *IV. sjezd Svazu československých spisovatelů* (Prague, 1968).

[2] *Hospodářsko-politická rukověť, II. díl* (Prague, ČTK, 1968) p. 1028.

[3] Interview with Václav Pelikán, director of the Economic Department of the Czechoslovak Writers' Union, in *Literární listy*, 21 March 1968, p. 7.

chairman, and Miroslav Válek and Jan Procházka vice-chairmen, augmented the union's praesidium and 'decided to publish a weekly' under the title *Literární listy*. A *Rudé právo* commentator welcomed the decision: the discontinuation of the writers' paper had, after all, been only temporary and the resulting situation abnormal.[1] To an outside observer the reversal of the supreme Party body's policy towards the Writers' Union must have appeared not only remarkably swift (September 1967–January 1968), but also very smooth. The 1967 conflict with the writers had undoubtedly been symptomatic of a protracted malaise, and the Dubček-led Party Praesidium obviously found it necessary to heal the open wound first, before inquiring any further into the deep-rooted reasons of society's ill-health. One can, in fact, assume that bandaging open wounds may have been all that was at that time – January – considered necessary.

Barely a week after his election, the new Writers' Union chairman gave an interview to the Czechoslovak Press Agency. He stressed that normalisation of conditions would include the establishment of a lawful relationship between the writers and the Central Publication Authority, i.e. the censorship office.[2] This was not yet a call for the termination of censorship: 'lawful' presumably meant 'in accordance with the Press Law of 1967' whereby the censor had the right to recommend suspension of texts, but could not enforce the implementation of his recommendation against the editor's opposition, unless it was upheld by a court. The onus was on confidential Party instructions which forbade the editor-in-chief to disobey the censor's recommendation. Thus Goldstücker's pronouncement did no more than insist on the letter of the law to the exclusion of the virtually illegal practice sanctioned by the Party. At the same time, he spoke unmistakably about the refusal of the writers and their Union to refrain from commenting on political matters, as some Party bosses would want them to do. (Don't meddle in politics! Keep to literature!) The writers' desire to assist all 'progressive forces' had become greater since the January plenum, and the new *Literární listy* would not confine itself to literary matters in the narrow sense of the word.

---

[1] Miloš Vacík (-mv-) in *Rudé právo*, 25 January 1968, p. 2.
[2] *Rudé právo*, 1 February 1968, p. 5.

Bertolt Brecht, after all, had said that art was unthinkable without politics.

The Ministry of Culture's pride must have been terribly hurt by what seemed a legerdemain: the editors of the Writers' Union newspaper returned to their offices less than four months after they had been evicted by the Ministry. Even in a world used to reversals of policy this was something of a record. The sugar coat of the bitter pill looked very thin when it came in the form of a Party Praesidium statement of 25 March 1968: the comrades who had obeyed Party discipline and took it upon themselves to edit the newspaper for the Ministry when the Writers' Union had been found unsuitable to manage its own affairs ought to be protected against reproach, threat and even against prosecution. The ministerial editors dared to voice disagreement with this statement, saying that it had not been only obeisance which had brought them to the job. They had in fact desired to salvage the 'recriminated against and deserted' newspaper from 'retardatory forces'.[1] Be that as it may, after some petty sabotaging by the Ministry which righteously pretended that it was impossible to secure newsprint for the resumption of *Literární listy* since it had all been duly distributed according to last year's plans, the Writers' Union once again, as of 1 March 1968, had its newspaper. Dušan Hamšík became once again head of the editorial council. The ministerial paper, in the meantime having changed its name to *Kulturní noviny*, then uneasily continued publication (following rather unashamedly the new liberal course) until 26 April. Then the Ministry of Culture, already under a new man (Miroslav Galuška), at last stated that it did not consider it 'appropriate' to publish its own cultural paper.

With its leadership fully constituted and its traditional weekly paper back in circulation, the Writers' Union seemed ready to plunge into the political battles of the Prague Spring. It did so mainly through the newly emerging Co-ordinating Committee of Creative Unions of which more will be said later. In the meantime, some internal union problems remained to be

---

[1] *Kulturní noviny*, 26 April 1968, p. 1. The same issue of the 'ministerial' paper admits that the paper was in the red to the tune of 21,000 crowns in January 1968, 120,000 in February and 66,340 in March. The figures are monthly losses, not cumulative deficit.

settled, especially those connected with the public restoration of honour to writers persecuted for their views in the past, and with the relationship between Party and non-Party members in the union.

The first post-January meeting of Czech (as against Slovak) writers on 29 March 1968 (with 240 members and candidate members present) set up an *ad hoc* rehabilitation commission under the chairmanship of the poet Jaroslav Seifert and with Karel Ptáčník as secretary. It worked fast (very much unlike similar commissions in the Party) and aimed at concluding its deliberations by the end of May. The cases under review included four groups of writers: those who had already been rehabilitated by the courts but whose rehabilitation had not been sufficiently publicised; those who were demanding retrial and needed the union's intercession with the authorities; those who were victimised as a result of the stand they had taken at the writers' conference in 1959 (especially managers of the Writers' Union Publishing House, a secretary of the union and those associated with the *Květen* magazine); and all others.

At the same meeting Alexander Kliment announced the establishment within the union of a 'loose association' of writers who were not members of the Communist Party – *Kruh nezávislých spisovatelů*. Fifty-eight non-Communist authors and translators signed the constituent statement, emphasising that their aim was not to break up unity.

The absurd consequences of the division of the writers' community into Party and non-Party people had been long known. Instead of natural grouping by style, artistic creed or simple human friendship, the bond that had been ordained gave Party members the prerogative – often, as many felt, tiresome and always ludicrous – to decide every issue facing the union before the non-Party writers were allowed to utter a word on it. Though frequently circumvented and ridiculed before 1968, the rule was obviously now regarded important enough to be disavowed completely and openly. Hence the non-Party writers' countermove; they too would meet beforehand to consider the agenda of a prospective joint meeting with their Communist colleagues. In a way one could regard the *Kruh* as the second Party, confined to the writers' organisation, except that it did not – of course – work this way. For one thing, the barrier between Communist and non-Communist had long been felt in the union to be artificial and had frequently been simply disregarded. There were no Communist secrets and the organisational rigmarole was generally considered stupid. To have a non-Communist organisation juxtaposed to the Communist would perpetuate the artificial division precisely at a time when the overall tendency indicated the removal of ideologically drawn boundaries. Also, the writers reacted badly to organisational grouping. Nevertheless, the good intentions of Kliment, Havel, Kopta and the other founders of the *Kruh* cannot be doubted. They elected the playwright Václav Havel their chairman and a seven-member committee. Among their statements, they spoke in favour of a general political rehabilitation, i.e. the automatic quashing of all political sentences passed after February 1948, with the State prosecuting anew where legally justified. They further expressed non-confidence in Jan Pilař, director of the Writers' Union Publishing House.[1] Their statement of 6 June gave a summary of their programme: coexistence of Communism and non-Communism and of Marxism and non-Marxism, pluralism of political organisations and of publication opportunities, independence of the writer in particular and of culture in general, rehabilitation of reason, ethics and work, participation of non-Party writers in the editorial boards of periodicals, publishing houses and cultural institutions, and reconstruction of the Writers' Union to make it more independent, democratic and non-bureaucratic.[2] Finally, the *Kruh nezávislých spisovatelů* met jointly with representatives of the Communist organisation in the Writers' Union on 17 July 1968 to prepare the scheduled extraordinary congress of the union and to debate the union's future structure. The very fact of this joint meeting corroborates the trend which was bringing reform-minded Communists and non-Communists closer together rather than separating them.

At the end of March 1968 the Writers' Union initiated a

---

[1] *Literární listy*, 16 May 1968, pp. 6–7. Pilař defended himself in the subsequent issue of 23 May 1968.

[2] *Literární listy*, 4 July 1968, pp. 3, 7.

series of political debates held in the Union's headquarters under the aegis of an informal Club of Critical Thought (*Klub kritického myšlení*). The chairmanship was in the hands of Karel Kosík, the philosopher, Miroslav Holub, the physician and poet, and Milan Kundera, the writer. While it is possible to interpret the existence of this club as an attempt to extend the Writers' Union's influence in the political field, the practical achievements were small. Barely half-a-dozen sessions were held (on such subjects as political pluralism and self-management) and then the majority of participants (usually numbering twenty to fifty) agreed that this was largely an exercise in self-education, upon which it simply petered out. There seemed to be little time and energy left to bring the considerable intellectual potential of the club to bear upon the practical political scene.

Yet another plan to generate political influence from within the Writers' Union was hatched in March and first mentioned at the meeting of the Czech Part of the Union's Central Committee in Prague on 29 March. This was the idea of starting an independent daily paper, to be called *Lidové noviny* (the name of a quality paper of pre-War and immediately post-War fame), which would incorporate *Literární listy* as its Sunday Supplement. In April the full Central Committee of the union met in Brno and gave its blessing to the project, appointing at the same time Karel Kosík as chairman of the new paper's 'Board of Governors'. A fortnight later the plans matured still further: the board would be entirely independent – a vice-chairman of the Writers' Union said – and although the union would act as the publisher, there would be no subordination in matters of policy. The board would select the editor-in-chief and personnel, altogether some seventy people, of whom thirty-five would be editorial staff. The paper would start with eight pages daily and there would be a foreign-language version once a month, summarising the main features. *Literární listy* would retain its present staff and expand to twenty-five to thirty pages every Sunday. The first number of *Lidové noviny* would appear in October, possibly on the occasion of the fiftieth anniversary of independent Czechoslovakia. Later in May A. J. Liehm, the publicist, was appointed editor-in-chief, and Ludvík Veselý was appointed the director of the new paper.

Even if *Lidové noviny* was not to be, the project can easily be considered one of the major initiatives which would have made the Writers' Union politically still more powerful than it was. *Literární listy*, with its circulation steadily rising throughout the Prague Spring (from about 150,000 before closure in 1967 to about 250,000), enjoyed an immense popularity and was given great credit for its advocacy of liberalisation by a large segment of the public, certainly by the 1-million strong group of 'the intelligentsia' (according to the statisticians' reckoning). Much of this credit would undoubtedly be transferred to the daily paper which by definition could be even more political. There is every reason to believe that the paper would have been of a high professional standard, arising from the erudition and sophistication of the designated staff. (Several appointments had been made or agreed on.)

Finally, to complete the summary of moves which made, or were designed to make, the Writers' Union a political factor, an increasing number of writers and journalists associated with the union went to address workers' meetings in factories, mostly at the organisers' invitation. The frequency or indeed the number of meetings or speakers cannot be established without recourse to inaccessible archives. Judging from the far from complete and often cursory reports in the press, these encounters did not produce any striking manifestations of unity. Neither, however, did they seem to precipitate animosity. More often than not, the reform-oriented press stressed the subscription by the workers' spokesmen to the various views expressed by the writers. Some steps were made to put writer-worker co-operation on a more permanent and institutionalised basis, but once again, practical results did not quite match ideological expectations.[1]

---

[1] A joint meeting was, for example, held on 28 March 1968 between the Works Committee of the Communist Party in the Praga Factory (the same factory from which later a declaration of pro-Moscow loyalty was sent to the Soviet Embassy by ninety-nine workers) and the Communist Committee in the Writers' Union. They agreed to co-operate and delegated some members to draft joint proposals in this respect. Later, in May, *Literární listy* arranged a debate with workers from the ČKD Works: of the nine workers who turned up in the editorial office, eight were non-Party. One of them commented: 'We had difficulty in finding a conservative Party member in the factory. Just you try to find a conservative Party man nowa-

In March 1968 a major dispute erupted in the Slovak Writers' Union with the resignation of the venerable poet Laco Novomeský, Miroslav Válek and Vojtech Mihálik from the editorial council of *Kultúrny život*, the union's weekly paper. Their version of the story, as told at the end of April to the Czechoslovak Press Agency, saw the Slovak writers' community essentially divided by differing attitudes to the Israeli–Arab conflict. While others were biased in this respect, the three resigning authors did not want to be. *Kultúrny život* was nationalistic and did not reflect the politico-cultural views of the elected bodies of the union. The paper advocated democratisation first and federalisation second, while the three believed in the reverse priority. They would not be a party to the process whereby extremist forces maimed and undermined the Slovak writers' community.[1]

The row continued at the Slovak writers' conference in Bratislava on 30 April at which the entire editorial council of *Kultúrny život* was recalled and the union's committee abdicated. There followed a proposal that the conference should declare itself a fully fledged congress but, having studied the union's statutes in the interval, the praesidium found the proposal unconstitutional and the abdication was withdrawn. There was recrimination about whether the Slovak writers had or had not tripped up their Czech colleagues at the Fourth Congress in 1967 and whether they were now doing it once again. Some suggested that the Slovak writers had been co-operating with the Dubček–Husák–Bilak group against Novotný and had therefore been unable, for tactical reasons, to openly support the Czechs. Válek, Mihálik and Matuška accused the Czech writers of masterminding the 1967 Congress from behind the scenes without letting the Slovak writers in on their plans. The Slovaks had been partly exhausted by previous struggles and partly unwilling to provoke a Novotný-led anti-Slovak pogrom. Further discussion revealed that Novomeský and his friends had other grounds for leaving *Kultúrny život* than those given in the ČTK statement, notably because the paper 'had given space to non-Communist views'. This concerned an article by

days!' On the other side, the *Literární listy* delegation comprised six Communists and one non-Party member of staff.

[1] *Rudé právo*, 27 April 1968, p. 5.

the Bishop of Nitra, Dr Necsei, and the non-Communist publicist Vladimír Maňák. Novomeský saw the Communist Party as being gunned at by the democrats. He did not want to be a party to the liquidation of socialism. Some speakers suggested that not everybody was a Party member and that those who were not should also be entitled to have their views published. This did not seem to cut much ice with the dissenters.

With the benefit of hindsight there seems little doubt that the rift in the Slovak Writers' Union of March and April 1968 represented the embryonic formation of what later came to be known as the Husák line. (Novomeský was Husák's personal friend, and the three dissenters soon began to write for *Predvoj*, later renamed *Nové slovo*, almost a house organ of the Husák faction.) The stand adopted by Novomeský *et al.* was then and subsequently criticised as an obsession with federalisation at the expense of democratisation. This reading of their position should be, to my mind, reversed, even if it still remains correct. They were, above all, frightened by the apparent collapse of the traditional concept of the leading role of the Party and by the gaining of momentum by the various notions of political pluralism. As a shorthand for newly emergent ideas about the arrangement of political life, 'democratisation' must have been seen by them as a danger. Under 'democratisation' it was possible to disagree with the Party's (and Soviet) interpretation of the Israeli–Arab conflict. Under 'democratisation' the Slovak nation could be allowed to discuss the form and staffing of federalisation before it was decreed by the existing supreme organs of power. Under 'democratisation' the Slovak community of writers might not speak with one voice, but tolerate expression of group and even individual interests and views. All these anxieties were remarkably similar to the post-invasion Husák type 'moderate conservativism', before the 'ultra-conversatives' swayed it their way. It was certainly the same type of thinking which, borrowing from the author of the *Good Soldier Schweik*, one could call 'moderate progress within the framework of the law'. The law, of course, came from Stalin's mould in the 1930s.

The slow strangulation of the Writers' Union after the invasion and the institution of government by a coalition of moderate and extreme conservatives is again sufficiently well known. One observer said that the union died on its feet, not its knees. When Goldstücker absented himself to Britain, the first meeting of the Czech part of the Writers' Union Central Committee elected Jaroslav Seifert acting chairman on 31 October 1968. The committee also expressed itself unequivocally: there had been no counter-revolution to justify an invasion; socialism with a human face remained the union's goal; compromise with, and capitulation before, the alien force were wrong. To stress continuity, the union would, on 7 November, once again start to publish its paper, now to be called simply *Listy*. (*Literární listy* – rather prematurely – declared its unwillingness to continue publication in face of the so-called Moscow Agreement and Protocol of 26 August 1968.) With the dust appearing to settle a little in the period of stunned bitterness after the Treaty on the indefinite stationing of Soviet troops in the country, defiance took different forms. Václav Havel, speaking on the radio on 3 December, suggested that the best thing might be to pretend that no invasion had happened. The *Kruh nezávislých spisovatelů*, he said, had changed nothing in its programme. This stand, perhaps better than anything else, demonstrated the amount of political naïveté in even otherwise adroit minds.

The preview came from Slovakia of how the political weapons (newspapers, organisation) which the writers possessed would be eaten away. *Kultúrny život*, the writers' weekly, was suspended at the beginning of September 1968 and the Slovak Office for Press and Information (the embryonic post-invasion censorship bureau) insisted on removing some of the prominent reformists from the staff before 'registering' the paper for resumed publication. The writers responded by calling an *aktiv* on 13 December and declared that if a permit was not speedily forthcoming they would start publishing the paper, now to be called *Literární život*, without regard to the Press Office. Almost immediately – on 17 December – the Novomeský group, now committed to the Husák policy of 'realism' through collaboration with the occupying authorities, made yet another attempt to sway the Slovak Writers' Union in its direction. At the Union Central Committee session, nine out of the thirteen members of the Praesidium (Novomeský, Válek, Šmatlák,

Mihálik, Mináč, Matuška, Horov, Kot and Žary) resigned in protest against the above-mentioned *aktiv*'s disobedience of the authorities. The arising deadlock (there was no clear-cut support for the Novomeský policy in the plenum of the Central Committee) was temporarily patched up by the election of Ivan Kupec as compromise acting chairman of the Union to replace M. Válek. (Válek, who is said to be Valeriyan Zorin's son-in-law, later became Slovak Minister of Culture.) The bickering about *Literárny život* continued: neither D. Tatarka nor Š. Drug, successively nominated as editors, were found acceptable by the Press Office. Eventually the registration was granted on 2 April 1969, but only one number was published, on 17 April, and on the same day the paper was suspended for two months because it 'did not observe the agreed policy'. This was virtually the end of organised democratic activity in the Slovak Writers' Union. On 11 June 1969 the congress of the union elected as chairman a member of the Novomeský group, Vojtech Mihálik. For all practical purposes, the union has accepted without question the policy of the new Party leadership ever since.

Meanwhile, the Czech section still published *Listy* (until April 1969) and made use of whatever opportunities remained open to it for the expression of a political stand, mainly through the Co-ordinating Committee of Cultural Unions. With the deposition of Dubček, the union realised that at least a temporary halt of public activity was inevitable and attempted to salvage its organisation. The division of the various organisations into Czech and Slovak, in pursuance of the federalisation scheme, offered an opportunity of holding a congress which had anyway been overdue. At the same time, both the Dubček leadership until April 1969 and, naturally, the 'realist' Husák régime afterwards, were afraid lest this congress should once again become what writers' gathering had always been since 1956, namely a politically disturbing event. After several postponements, the Czech congress took place in Prague on 10 June and the Slovak on 11 June 1969 in Bratislava. By then it was clear that the Czech writers could not hope to do more than cut their losses and preserve for themselves an organisational basis. It was on the understanding that political statements would not be made at all that the authorities allowed the congress to take place. In Prague, 326 members, candidate members and translators elected Jaroslav Seifert to replace Goldstücker as chairman. Jiří Brabec and Karel Ptáčník became vice-chairmen. Seifert stated the need for creative freedom and assured the Party leadership that the writers did not wish to interfere with politics, while hoping that their literary work would continue to be accepted and recognised. A number of reformist exponents of the Prague Spring were retained on the Central Committee.

In connection with the full-scale purge of reformists in 1970, the post-Dubček Party was no longer satisfied with a neutralised Writers' Union: what it needed was a co-operating organisation. As the existing union refused to expel reformists, recant and swear an oath of active allegiance to the old-new government policy, a dismantling of the union's apparat was ordered in October 1970 and its material assets were impounded. A new Writers' Union was at long last called into being late in 1970, comprising mostly officers of the various cultural departments in the Party and government machinery. (Twenty-seven signatories attached their names to a preparatory committee statement of 18 December 1970.) No writer can become a member 'whose political stance differs from that of the present leadership of the Party and the State'.[1] As there has been no rush to join the new union, this condition seems almost superfluous. At the time of writing (mid-1971), the new union is still to hold its constituent congress and has yet to do more than talk about the publication of a monthly journal.

CREATIVE UNIONS

The Writers' Union, singled out for separate consideration because of its prominence in the public eye and the weight it carried in the reform movement as a result of its history of conflict with the Establishment, was but one of several intellectual associations known under the generic name of Creative Unions (*tvůrčí svazy*). The literal translation, clumsy as it must sound in English, is chosen here for want of a better term: both Art Unions and Cultural Unions would imply that a

[1] *Zemědělské noviny*, 5 January 1971, p. 3.

narrower, or wider, meaning is intended. The customary organisational pattern of a Communist society provides for the organisations of intellectuals, writers, theatrical people, fine artists, composers, architects, film and television makers and journalists, to be run on the usual transmission belt lines. The intellectual nature of their members' work tends, however, to make these organisations transcend the limits of 'sectional' interests and evolve a strong attitudinal character. Nowhere more so than in Czechoslovakia. The Czech intellectual, if one is permitted to deliberate along intangible lines, has always been a political animal *par excellence*. He deputised for the aristocracy when it had been all but wiped out, he deputised for the bourgeoisie when it turned cowardly and he was ready to deputise for political opposition under Communism. There has traditionally been little of the ivory tower atmosphere both among creative intellectuals and scholars. By the same token, the relationship between, say, a painter and a writer or an actor and a composer has been more than a chance appurtenance to the brotherhood of refined mind and taste. Culture, to cut a long story short, has always been felt as a political as well as a professional bond.

In a way, this seemed to be congruent with the Communist understanding of culture as an instrument of politics. From being a tool to seize political power, culture became after February 1948 one of the implements for preserving and stabilising power. However, for an intellectual it was eventually not the combination of culture and politics which went against the grain, but rather this constant relegation to the role of mere instruments. In opposition to the primitive bequeathing of optimistic dicta, he evolved the concept of culture as 'a sum total of activity by all the creative forces in the nation'[1] in which the intellectuals would act as the 'conscience' of the nation rather than being the 'engineers' of its soul. Does culture need socialism at all? Would it not be better off without it? These questions, logically arising from the rejection of enforced didacticism, were discussed, for example, by A. J. Liehm at the Fourth Writers' Congress and at a conference of film and television artists in March 1968. The answer was realistic: our

[1] *IV. sjezd Svazu československých spisovatelů* (*Protokol*) (Prague, Čs. spisovatel, 1968), p. 103.

society is already different from capitalism and we ought to make an effort not to let it change into a simile of a Western-type consumer society. Culture is the religion of modern man and we should not abdicate its higher forms. Socialism must arrange things for culture, rather than control it. A truly socialist State must not regard culture as a necessity or a luxury, but as a necessary luxury. Of course it is an expensive commit-ment, but the nation's life depends on it. Britain has had her navy, America her cosmic flights, France her atomic bomb. Czechoslovakia can have none of these, but she can have culture. A project of this nature must not be measured by the yardsticks of a commercial market, because through culture and art society can become aware of itself, its own qualities and defects.[1]

Thus, while advocating and acting for an overall reform of the political system, the artists and men of culture were simul-taneously promoting their own interests. This they found possible to do through the organisations at their disposal as soon as they had wrested control over them from the centre of power, as was the case of the writers and the film-makers even before 1968, or as soon as control slackened as a result of changes in the Communist concept of centralism after January.[2]

The membership of the unions in 1968 was as follows: architects – 1,920; theatrical artists – 1,734, film and television artists – 433 and 121 candidates; journalists – 4,000; com-posers – 860; writers – 468 and 142 candidates; fine artists – 3,380 (including candidates and 'registered' members).[3] All were 'selective' organisations, i.e. membership was not open to everybody but depended on compliance with certain condi-tions or qualifications. Each published at least two newspapers or periodicals and, through them no less than through their

[1] *Rudé právo*, 2 April 1968, p. 5.

[2] The Ideological Commission of the Party, still with J. Hendrych in the chair, held two meetings on 8 and 15 February 1968 to discuss the impend-ing changes in Party policies. The press release sounded very humble: 'The Ideological Commission has expressed the conviction and the confi-dence that Communist artists as well as all the other leading workers in the field of art and culture are capable of responsibly and independently carrying out the cultural policy of the Party in state, social and interest institutions.' *Rudé právo*, 17 February 1968, p. 1.

[3] *Hospodářsko-politická rukověť, II. díl* (Prague, ČTK, 1968) pp. 1004–5.

creative work, exercised considerable public influence far surpassing the actual number of members.

In the early stages of the Prague Spring all the unions had to devote time and energy to internal conditions and to basic formulations of policy. There were also some unresolved antagonisms between the Writers' Union and the Journalists' Union, arising from the latter's stand in 1967. At its Fifth Congress in the autumn of 1967, the Journalists' Union obediently followed the Novotný leadership in condemning the writers for their Fourth Congress and wholeheartedly endorsed the decision to transfer the Writers' Union newspaper to the Ministry of Culture. For several months after January the writers refused to talk to or co-operate with the Journalists' Union until its less than half-a-year-old attitude was officially and publicly reversed. This only happened after personal changes in the leadership of the Journalists' Union. The first meeting between representatives of the two unions only took place as late as 26 April.

With this exception the tendency to present a united front *vis-à-vis* the power centre (whose capacity for reformist action appeared by no means unequivocal in the initial stage of the Prague Spring) was gaining momentum in all unions. A joint statement was, for example, issued on 23 February to mark the twentieth anniversary of the full seizure of power by the Communist Party in 1948. It was signed by representatives of the Writers' Union, the Film and Television Artists' Union, the Theatrical Artists' Union, the Fine Artists' Union, the Composers' Union and the Architects' Union.[1] Early in March *Rudé právo*, the Communist Party daily, invited chairmen or chief secretaries of the six unions (with the journalists pointedly still left out) to a round-table discussion on the unions' policies which was then published in two lengthy instalments.[2] On 23 March the Central Committee of the Architects' Union expressed the desire for unity very clearly: 'We are aware of the negative consequences of the creative unions' mutual

[1] This statement differed from the usual laudatory pronouncements. It gave support to the 'humanist aims of socialism' and saw a new possibility of implementing 'the true legacy of February', i.e. harmony between the ideal and the practice of revolution. *Literární listy*, 1 March 1968, p. 2.

[2] *Rudé právo*, 17 March 1968, p. 3 and 19 March 1968, p. 5.

isolation in recent years. We are in favour of forming a cultural front which henceforth will act under any conditions as only its most progressive part has acted in the recent past.'[1]

Which were the main postulates of the common policy of the unions? They can be summarised under several headings. First, the unions wished to have freedom of action restored to them. This included an end to subordination to the Ministry of Culture and, more implicitly than explicitly, to the appropriate department in the Party Central Committee. The unions wished to be free to organise themselves as they deemed fit, i.e. in accordance with the nature of the work of, say, the fine artist who is as a rule a solitary worker, even if bound by similarity of style to a loose grouping, or of the theatrical actor who is (in the traditional Czechoslovak context) tied to a theatre and consequently doubles as an artist and an employee. In the political sense, to the extent to which every expression of man's self-assertive quality becomes a politicum in a Communist society, the coveted freedom included choice of content, form and means of communication, i.e. extrication from the ideological arrangement whereby prohibition of the one and prescription of the other goes hand in hand. In short, the unions were unanimously opposed to political censorship.

The second set of common beliefs, as reflected in the various pronouncements by the unions, had to do with participation. They wished to have a say not only in their own affairs, but as representatives of a not unimportant section of society in the running of the *res publica*. This desire, a part of the overall participation explosion which characterised the Prague Spring, led them to demand that they should contribute to the formulation of the cultural policies of the State and, through representation in the policy-making National Front (in its newly understood role), to the shaping of the country's political life.

Finally, as the third common denominator, they jointly called for the restoration of human and, more specifically, political rights and values which they saw to be missing in the pre-1968 situation. This included judicial and administrative rehabilitation of victims of prosecution and persecution, ratification of the Pact of Human Rights, free travel, and end to discrimination on political grounds (Party membership), etc.

[1] *Rudé právo*, 23 March 1968, p. 3.

In the second half of March the idea of putting the emerging unity of views on to some kind of an organisational basis gained momentum and by the end of April Co-ordinating Committees of Creative Unions (*Koordinační výbory tvůrčích svazů*) had been practically established in Prague, Bratislava, Brno and Ostrava. It should be noted that this process met with the approval and even support of the Party leadership. The one thing which the new Party leaders were afraid of was disintegration of the existing structures. Even if they were unable to prevent the Youth Union from dissolving itself in a number of separate organisations, they encouraged its reunification at least in the form of an aggregative structure, namely the Federation of Youth and Children's Organisations. By the same token they welcomed the associative trend among the intellectuals more than they would a collapse of the existing unions. What the culturalists saw as a natural inclination towards unity of organisation where unity of opinion obviously prevailed, the centre of power accepted on orthodox ideological grounds.

Even before the constitution of the Co-ordinating Committees, on 15 March, the ideological department in the Party Secretariat invited Party groups from the unions to send delegates to a conference at which (with others) they were informed about the main features of the Party's Action Programme – more than a fortnight before it was promulgated. Party groups from the unions used the opportunity of being present at this gathering to set up an *ad hoc* joint commission and charged it to sum up the different unions' comment on the Party programme. Although this early move concerned only Communist members of the unions and it can be assumed that at this juncture the Party leadership would have wanted to keep its contacts with the Creative Unions on this level, the division between Communist and non-Communist soon proved too artificial and clumsy to maintain. Most of the subsequent action was between the Co-ordinating Committee, representing the unions as a whole, and the authorities.

The Co-ordinating Committee was not, as its name testified, the usual apex of a monolithic organisation. Its existence revealed certain makeshift characteristics. The member-unions, for example, agreed to delegate to the committee representatives endowed with full powers to make authoritative decisions at short notice, but the committee refused to be considered superior to the committees of the various unions. Its decisions had the character of recommendations and could be promulgated only if adopted unanimously by delegates of all member-unions. No one union was superior to any other. Neither was there any subordination of the provincial Co-ordinating Committees to the Prague Co-ordinating Committee. Sessions of the Prague Co-ordinating Committee were held alternately 'on the territory' of the various member-unions. Administration was to be entrusted to a different union every year, with the Film and Television Artists' Union acting in this capacity in 1968. (This partly explains why it was this union which, after the invasion, was subjected to the sharpest attacks next to the writers and journalists.) In short, the organisational principle behind the Co-ordinating Committees was not democratic centralism.

Nor were the unions' delegates to the committee always the same, although for important sessions the chairmen or chief secretaries were usually present. The committee's secretary (L. Pacovský of the Film and Television Artists' Union) gave the following names as most frequently represented: writers – Goldstücker, Procházka, J. S. Kupka, Maršíček; composers – V. Neumann, Mácha; fine artists – Hoffmeister, Kočí; architects – Gočár, Kuča, Ztratil; theatrical artists – Balvín, Kolár; journalists – Ruml, Šíp, Lederer; film and television artists – Helge, Novák, Pacovský.[1]

The seven constituent unions (including journalists, after a personnel change and embarkation on reformist policy) were later joined by another, the Union of Scientific Workers (*Svaz vědeckých pracovníků*), which had not existed before the Prague Spring. An appeal to set up such a union was issued by the staff of the Faculty of Philosophy at Charles University on 21 March 1968. Its purpose was to be in a joint endeavour to free research, universities and science of all regimentation, as well as in demanding legal guarantees of academic rights, such as had been accorded to higher learning prior to the arrival of Communism. Rather unexpectedly, the Commission of Scientific Workers attached to the Central Trade Union Council hastened to establish a rival preparatory committee on

[1] L. Pacovský, 'Tvůrci a politika', *Reportér*, 33 (1968) pp. 27–8.

26 March and protested against the spontaneous and allegedly non-representative nature of the group which responded to the Philosophical Faculty proclamation. The latter replied that it was typical of preparatory committees (was it not?) to spring into being spontaneously, and that they had anyway no intention of dabbling in trade unionism. Theirs was to be a 'creative' union. It was this 'spontaneous' committee which sent a representative (Dr M. Holub) to the Co-ordinating Committee of Creative Unions.

With some 12,000 qualified scientists and scholars in the country, the founding of a 'creative' organisation appeared to be well justified. Not that there had been no organisational outlets: one of the existing trade unions associated 'workers in education, science and culture'; the so-called Socialist Academy (modelled on the lines of the Soviet *Obshchestvo-Znanie*) promoted dissemination of political and scientific knowledge; and the Czechoslovak Scientific and Technical Society (*Československá vědecko-technická společnost*) was active among technicians. Nevertheless, against the background of the Prague Spring, inducive as it was to the assertion of various groups in policy making, many felt that neither simple trade unionism nor popularisation of science or preoccupation with technical innovation gave the 'creative' scientist and scholar adequate scope for expression of attitude and action. By then it had been more or less generally recognised that 'scientific and technical revolution' was the order of the day and that the scientist and the scholar had a certain special responsibility. (It was to this aspect of the Pugwash movement that Czechoslovak scientists responded fairly actively in the 1960s.)

When the two warring factions eventually arrived at a *modus vivendi* in Brno on 22 May 1968 (and elected a joint committee with Academician O. Wichterle as chairman), the policy of the new union was formulated as follows: The union will be a 'creative and selective' organisation enabling the scientists (the Czech term *vědec* includes scholars) to express and promote their attitudes to public life and to the development and organisation of science itself. The union will stand for freedom of thought and adhere to the charter of the World Federation of Scientists. It will advocate 'scientific ethics' and the quest for truth. While associating scientists and scholars from the humanities, natural sciences and technical fields, it will seek co-operation with the other branches of spiritual culture. Membership will be individual and based on personal application. Both professional and moral criteria will be applied to prospective members. The union will hold a congress and democratically elect its governing bodies.

At the outset the Co-ordinating Committee agreed to pursue its activity along two lines, the economic and trade unionist on the one hand, and the political on the other. While not entirely ignoring the former (taxation of works of art, cultural foundations, State prizes, decorations and honorary titles), it soon found itself preoccupied with the latter. In retrospect one can perhaps say that it mainly played the part of a watchdog over the progress and regress of political reform. It gave strong encouragement to political reformists in the form of public pronouncements often backed up by signatures of people who were held in general esteem. It was undoubtedly influential not only because it represented the intellectual cream of society, but also because it had easy access to the mass media (through the Journalists' Union) and thus could alert the public to practices which even the new power centre would have preferred to keep confidential.

Thus an open letter signed by 134 men of culture had been published on 27 March, after the Dresden meeting and after Novotný's resignation but before the election of a new President. The signatories assured the Party Central Committee of support and expressed the belief that responsibility for this country rested with its leadership, even if it might seem necessary to explain the true nature of things to the other socialist States. As far as the new President and Prime Minister, Minister of the Interior and Minister of National Defence were concerned, the signatories considered it self-evident that only those men ought to be elected to these posts who were committed to the democratisation process. Ideally, the new President (Svoboda's name had been only whispered by then) should be connected with the working class, but close to the intelligentsia – or vice versa. We feel obliged, they said, on the strength of our commitment to reform in the past to respond to signals which might herald stagnation or even a political reversal.

At the end of April the 'Czech part' of the Creative Unions

jointly demanded the convocation of an extraordinary Party Congress to replace 'discredited members' of the existing Central Committee. *Rudé právo* replied somewhat sourly that 'all over the world it is natural' that only members of a party can call for its special congress. Someone retorted that nowhere outside the Communist world did one party assume all responsibility for non-party people as well as for its own members.

In the middle of June, after the mass media had been under fire at the Party Central Committee session and elsewhere for advocacy of anti-Party, anti-Soviet and anti-socialist views, the Co-ordinating Committee (of the Czech parts of the unions, as was explicitly stated) publicly objected. The mass media reflected the real state of affairs and could not avoid echoing all existing trends. And anyway, why did 'the conservative forces' not speak up? For fear of discrediting themselves in open debate, the 'conservatives' sought to discredit the press. Every attack on the mass media was an attack on the freedom of speech and on socialist democracy.[1]

Later in the same month, a day after the publication of, and furore over, the *2,000 Words Manifesto*, the Co-ordinating Committee gave its reading of the situation to the Press Agency. Once again, the committee said, those responsible for the deficiencies of the past were mustering their strength. They were distributing illegal printed matter, sending out anonymous threats and resorting to demagogy when forced to speak up. They took the *2,000 Words* as a pretext for provoking hysteria, a state of nervousness and pressure on the reformist elements in the Party. Hysteria and nervousness were the breeding ground of violence – the only means with which the power monopoly of the old guard could be restored.[2]

At the beginning of August a letter was sent to Dubček on behalf of the Co-ordinating Committee expressing concern over the handling of the affair of General V. Prchlík, who had mildly criticised some aspects of the style of command in the Warsaw Pact and was subsequently, under Soviet pressure, removed from his job in the Party Secretariat. The department he had been heading was abolished simultaneously.[3]

[1] *Rudé právo*, 13 June 1968, p. 5.
[2] *Rudé právo*, 29 June 1968, p. 2.
[3] *Rudé právo*, 9 August 1968, p. 2.

Apart from issuing statements, of which the above-mentioned have been chosen as an example, the Co-ordinating Committee strove throughout its existence for a meaningful representation in the National Front. The committee spokesmen told F. Kriegel, chairman of the Front, that they would not want to take part in a formal organisation, but that they believed that the Front was being transformed into a genuine policy-forming body. Dr Miroslav Holub, unanimously elected by the committee, was delegated to the Praesidium of the National Front to be the 'cultural field's single representative' there. Each of the Creative Unions then claimed the right to send a delegate to the wider Central Committee of the Front. It should be noted that Holub was not a member of any Party. This, the committee admitted, influenced his choice: 'We would like to win over as many of our non-Party colleagues as possible precisely for political work in these [i.e. National Front] organs.'[1] The Co-ordinating Committee expressed the desire to participate in the selection of candidates for election to parliament and hoped to be invited to send delegates to the parliamentary Commission for Culture, Education and Science. (Co-operation within the National Front, still largely following the well-beaten track of rubber-stamping Party decisions, was not smooth. When the Party Praesidium panicked over the *2,000 Words*, the National Front Central Committee followed suit with a condemnation which it had adopted in the absence of delegates from the Co-ordinating Committee.)

Even though the Co-ordinating Committee was a non-Communist body to the extent that it spoke for the Creative Unions as a whole rather than just the Party members in them, a certain number of the men of culture and art who were not affiliated to any Party felt under-represented. The trend towards a non-Party semi-organisation, as observed in the constitution of the *Kruh nezávislých spisovatelů* (Group of Independent Writers), found reflection in the other unions as well. At a joint meeting on 6 June, the following such organisations were represented: Group of Independent Writers (*Kruh nezávislých spisovatelů*), Group of Non-Party Members in the Composers' Union (*Kruh nestraníků při Svazu skladatelů*), the preparatory committee of the Group of Independent Fine Artists (*Kruh*

[1] L. Pacovský, op. cit.

nezávislých výtvarných umělců) and the preparatory committee of the Club of Independent Film and Television Artists (*Klub nezávislých filmových a televizních umělců*). They agreed to hold regular conferences, exchange information and co-ordinate activity. In the long run, so they stated, the possibility of founding an Association of Independent Culture (*Sdružení nezávislé kultury*) ought to be examined as 'a community of politically unorganised artists and men of culture which would promote the basic principles of cultural independence'.[1] Disquieted by the multiplying attacks on the freedom of speech, they appealed to their 'colleague-Party members' to take relevant action, possibly to hold 'a large meeting' devoted to this problem. Not long afterwards the Group of Independent Architects (*Kruh nezávislých architektů*) was founded and joined the other non-Party groups.

The call for meetings organised by the Communist men of culture to discuss press freedom came a little belatedly. In fact, the day before it was issued, on 5 June, 163 culturalist members of the Party held an *aktiv* in Prague and constituted themselves into a *de facto* 'cultural commission' of the Party. (The Party had no cultural commission, although it had an ideological one.) Delegates of all Creative Unions (mostly chairmen) set up a twenty-five-member 'leadership' of the *aktiv* and decided to be 'permanently in session' until the holding of the Fourteenth Party Congress. The *aktiv* expressed support for the election of new 'progressive' people into the prospective Party Central Committee (to be voted into office at the Congress) and demanded that henceforth it should be the artists themselves, associated in the cultural commission, who should be responsible for the Party's cultural policy, rather than the apparatchiki in the Department for Culture in the Central Committee's Secretariat. This signalled the emergence of yet another 'cultural' pressure group which, enjoying unmistakable popular support both for its policy and for the prominent names represented on it, had to be taken into account by the Party leadership. This became obvious when Dubček had to rely on the general public more than at any previous time, notably after the Warsaw meeting of the Five, their open letter and the Czechoslovak Communist Party's reply. The 'leadership' of the

[1] *Literární listy*, 13 June 1968, p. 2.

aktiv recommended on 22 June that the network of cultural and social establishments ought to be put to use to organise public meetings and lectures to explain the Czechoslovak position *vis-à-vis* Soviet pressure and to rally public support behind Dubček in a way which traditional Communism understands best, i.e. in resolutions and public pronouncements. On 30 July nearly one hundred cultural workers, Communists and non-Communists, gathered at short notice in the Party headquarters to hear a report by high Party officials (Císař, Slavík) on the current talks at Čierna. Their message of solidarity, dispatched to the Czech leaders in Čierna, could be brief because there were no doubts about their stand: 'We think of you, think of us.' This slogan immediately became public property.[1]

Like most organisations, the Co-ordinating Committee set out to salvage at least some qualities of the Prague Spring after the invasion. They undoubtedly shared the fairly widely spread belief of the day that the 'new reality' need not necessarily mean a full-scale retreat into pre-reform style of government. The resolution which the Co-ordinating Committee adopted at a gathering in the *Slovanský dům* in Prague on 22 November 1968 indicated the directions in which they considered an independent action still possible: the leaders of the nation ought to abide by the will of the people as much as they could; the law of the country should be respected; the cultural organisations should be consulted before measures concerning the intelligentsia were taken; foreign travel should be kept open; the movement of workers' councils ought to be supported; a government commission ought to be set up to investigate who had invited the interventionists; and an acknowledgement for their work should be given to the directors of radio and television (Z. Hejzlar and J. Pelikán) who by then were among the few summarily dismissed reformists. The meeting also elected a four-member delegation to call on Dr F. Kriegel, the ousted member of the Party Praesidium and chairman of the National Front, in order to convey to him

---

[1] The Department of Culture in the Party Secretariat had to assure the public on the following day (*Rudé právo*, 1 August 1968, p. 2) that the *aktiv* had not been given any extra information on the Čierna talks, generally shrouded in secrecy.

feelings of solidarity. The resolution was more than the Party leaders could tolerate, and a press conference was not allowed. Dubček did, however, meet a delegation of the Creative Unions and asked them to change certain formulations in the resolution and to drop some points altogether, notably the acknowledgement to Hejzlar and Pelikán and the inquiry into a possible call for invasion by Czechoslovak diehards. The unions had to meet again (on 25–6 November) to amend the resolution. On this occasion, the member-unions were joined by the new Union of Musicians and Artistes and the Trade Union of Art and Culture Workers.[1]

The November meeting and resolution was the last positive pressure-group type of action on the part of the Co-ordinating Committee. The Husák leadership, even in the embryonic form in which it came to power in the middle of April 1969, had a completely different understanding of 'reality'. Its policy entailed eradication of reformism and banishment of exponents of reform from public life, not only adjustment of reformist policies to foreign pressure. This was a qualitative, not only quantitative, change, to borrow from Marxist terminology. The heat was on almost immediately and when the Co-ordinating Committee held its next meeting, less than five weeks after the replacement of Husák for Dubček (22 May), its resolution could be no more than an expression of defiance. From then on, the committee was in no position to 'demand' a certain type of action from the Party and government. Its resolution was defensive and ethical: 'They can silence us, but they will never compel us to say what we do not believe in . . . They can deprive us of freedom of speech, but they can never take away from us freedom of spirit.'[2] Needless to say the statement could not be published. On 28 May the Praesidium of the National Front decided to discontinue all contacts with the Co-ordinating Committee, claiming that there was no need to deal with a 'roof' organisation of the cultural community and that henceforth all dealings would be with the unions separately. At a stroke, the struggle for united organisational representation of the intellectuals – ideologically in keeping as it was with the Communist postulates – came to an end. What

---

[1] Radio Free Europe, *Situation Report*, 26 and 28 November 1968.
[2] Radio Free Europe, *Situation Report*, 30 May 1968.

would have been considered sacrilege and revisionism in the trade union movement (dismantling of the Central Trade Union Council), was applied to the intellectuals without any ideological qualms.

The process did not stop there. Early in 1970 the Union of Scientific Workers was barred from National Front membership and thus effectively dissolved. In the course of 1970 the other unions were pushed out of action and eventually, in December 1970, new organisations were set up in their stead, comprising only those willing to sign an oath of obeisance to the Party leadership of the day.

MASS MEDIA

With the exception of publicists writing largely for the cultural (literary, etc.) press, very few journalists could boast a reformist past comparable to that of the writers, philosophers, historians, political scientists and economists. Even though professional standards had undoubtedly increased since 1963 as had the amount of unadulterated information proffered to the reader, the supply of the usual breed of laudatory journalist did not seem to be drying up. Criticism expressed in private by many was unevenly matched by the public courage of a few. To do the newsmen justice, censorship on political writing was tight. However, there is no public record of the 4,000-strong Journalists' Union showing even remotely the same spirit as the Writers' Union, the Theatrical Artists' Union, the Film and Television Workers' Union, the several semi-organised groups of historians, the Socialist Academy, the various scholarly institutions, etc. And yet, the very rapid acceptance by the journalists of the post-January course proves that they were no less change-oriented than the public at large.[1]

At first it looked as if just another twist of policy was to be applauded, and the Journalists' Union was in fact the first to send a unanimous letter to Dubček from its Central Committee

---

[1] The development calls for a psychological study. Are journalists under Communist conditions disposed to a relatively rapid transformation into staunch advocates of a free press? Or was the Czechoslovak situation unique as a result of the slow gradualism with which the notion of reform evolved for twelve years from 1956 to 1968? A comparison with Polish journalists in 1956, 1968 and 1970–1 might be elucidating.

meeting on 16 January promising full support of all newspapermen 'to the conclusions of the October and January plenums'.
With the usual diligence a two-day seminar of editors-in-chief
was arranged in conjunction with the Party's Ideological
Department on 18–19 January, and 105 participants had the
ousting of Novotný explained by no other than Jiří Hendrych,
for long the former First Secretary's ideological mouthpiece.

The routine was however soon disrupted by rebellion on the
part of individual journalists and groups associated with some
editorial offices. Influenced undoubtedly by the cultural publicists, they began to press their union's leadership for renuncia-
tion of recent servility, especially the resolutions of the Fifth
Congress of the Journalists' Union in October 1967, in which
the Writers' Union was condemned for political opposition
and the confiscation of *Literární noviny* by the Ministry of Culture
endorsed. Initiative in this respect was first expressed by the
Head Office of Political Broadcasting in Prague Radio. Also
demanded by rank-and-file journalists was an amendment of
the existing Press Law (in force since 1 January 1967) which
legalised censorship in the form of the Central Publication
Authority (*Ústřední publikační správa*). Finally, a radical group
of Prague journalists pressed for the establishment within the
union of an autonomous Prague Branch, arguing that just
about half of all Czechoslovak journalists (2,000) worked in the
capital and ought to have the same organisational autonomy
enjoyed by their colleagues in the provinces.

The union's Praesidium under Adolf Hradecký was visibly
embarrassed and stalled, although it did not dare to immediately reject any of the proposals. At its meeting on 29 February
it only agreed to speed up (with no deadlines given) the convocation of the union's Central Committee. It was also willing
to meet the representatives of the Writers' Union and 'regretted'
that their willingness was not reciprocated. (The writers let
it be known that they would not be party to any negotiations
until the resolution of the Journalists' Congress of 1967 was
revoked.) As the political tide of the Prague Spring was
accelerating, expressions of non-confidence in the leadership of
the Journalists' Union grew in strength. On 8 March – the
same day the Slovak Journalists' Central Committee recommended that the postulates of the Fifth Congress be revoked –

the Educational Commission of the union attacked the Praesidium for sluggish action, and on 14 March a club of free-lance journalists (*Klub nezávislých novinářů*) constituted itself and joined in the call for a new union policy. By then a number of journalists' 'chapters' as well as 'sections' of newsmen writing on education, youth and agriculture had gone on record demanding a revision of the Fifth Congress and an election of a new Central Committee.

A few days before Novotný's resignation, the full Central Committee of the Journalists' Union met in Brno on 19–20 March, accepted the resignation of the union's Praesidium and in a secret ballot elected a new one. Its seventeen members were to function only till the Congress of the union, which it was agreed to hold later in the year. A. Hradecký was not replaced by a new chairman (he was, however, elected to the new Praesidium); this was left for the Congress to do. In the meantime, Dr B. Marčák, editor-in-chief of the Brno Party paper *Rovnost*, was made acting chairman. Nonetheless, pressure continued and A. Hradecký and L. Kapitola, former editor-in-chief of the Socialist Party daily *Svobodné slovo*, stepped down from the new Praesidium on 29 March. Hradecký also resigned as editor-in-chief of the union's weekly *Reportér* and was replaced by Stanislav Budín, a veteran journalist who had been dismissed as editor of *Rudé právo* and expelled from the Communist Party in 1936 when the then leader of Czechoslovak Communism, Klement Gottwald, had been ordered by the Communist Internationale to rectify a rightist deviation in the Popular Front policy. (Budín never again became a Party member.)

The 'co-ordinating group of Prague journalists' in the meantime went ahead with its plans to set up an autonomous branch in the capital and campaigned for the early holding of an extraordinary Congress which would work out a new programme of the union, consider its reorganisation and elect new leading bodies. In less than a week (the second week in March) 1,018 members, i.e. over a half of the journalists active in Prague, signed a petition to this effect and were soon joined by provincial branches. Thus more than one-third of the members, as stipulated by the union's statutes, were calling for a Congress.

The Prague conference on 1 April 1968 (attended by 900 journalists according to one source, and 870 according to another)[1] was the first openly political meeting of journalists. In addition to the by now sweeping demand for a Congress, it asked for the transformation of the union into 'an autonomous and independent organisation to protect all professional, financial and social interests of newspapermen'. It also demanded legislation to abolish censorship, which at that time 'did not operate, but still existed', and called for the establishment of a parliamentary Committee for the Mass Media. The meeting even suggested that the government should resign, especially the Ministers of Foreign Affairs and National Defence. This demand was not as radical as it sounded because by then a government reorganisation had been discussed (not publicly) by the Party Central Committee and the new Action Programme of the Party, about to be promulgated, would obviously necessitate the working out of a similar document along governmental lines.

A twenty-member committee of the Prague branch was elected at the meeting on 1 April which, in turn, on 3 April elected Jiří Ruml as its chairman and set up commissions for rehabilitation, for the preparation of a new Press Law, for the preparation of an extraordinary Congress of the union, for the drafting of new union statutes, and for checking the mandates of Prague journalists who were members of the Union's Central Committee. The Prague journalists' committee dissociated itself without much hesitation from the condemnation of writers at the Journalists' Congress in 1967 and immediately held an informative talk on co-operation with representatives of the Writers' Union. It further decided to press for the holding of the union's extraordinary Congress as early as June. While no statutory provisions were apparently infringed, the swift action of the Prague journalists was little short of a revolutionary takeover of power within the union. From the meeting of 1 April it was they, rather than the transitory Praesidium elected in Brno, who called the tune to union action. Their policy was radically liberal and reformist as was their writing.

The 350 delegates to the extraordinary Journalists' Congress (including 100 from Slovakia) assembled in Prague on 21 June.

[1] *Literární listy*, 18 April 1968, p. 2, and *Novinář*, 3 (1971) p. 83.

It should be noted that G. Husák was the chief Party and government guest on the first, and A. Dubček on the second, day of the Congress. The Congress was explicitly political. Vlado Kašpar, editor of *Signál*, said: 'Journalists have become the co-creators of the policy of this country, and consequently are co-responsible for the direction it takes.'[1] The Congress adopted new statutes in which the union was defined as a voluntary, social, creative and trade unionist organisation. (The chairman of the Central Trade Union Council protested in a letter to the Congress against the union's assuming trade union rights. This amounted to breaking up the unity of the labour movement, he said. His remonstration was not heeded.) Also passed by the Congress was a resolution quashing the conservative statements of the previous Congress in 1967, a political resolution in favour of unequivocal pursuance of democratisation in the country's political life, and a resolution insisting on the discontinuation of prepublication censorship by way of adequate legislation. On its third day the Congress split into separate Czech and Slovak Congresses to permit the constitution of independent national unions. Vlado Kašpar and Svetozár Štúr were respectively elected chairmen of the Czech and Slovak Journalists' Unions. The two Central Committees established a federal body, the Czechoslovak Journalists' Centre (*Ústředí novinářů ČSSR*), at a joint meeting in Bratislava on 27 June and elected V. Kašpar federal chairman. S. Štúr became first deputy chairman, and F. Kaucký secretary-general.

Thus the new organisational set-up was complete after a clean break with the past, and the union was poised to pursue its newly formulated policy. In a way, this amounted to little more than a formal confirmation of the tendency already followed at least from mid-March by the growing majority of reformist journalists, especially in the Prague branch of the union. The men who represented journalists in the Co-ordinating Committee of Creative Unions (J. Ruml, E. Šíp, J. Lederer) were already even before the Congress staunch supporters of the 'new course'. The various clubs and sections within the union (associating newsmen covering particular fields) as well as some 'chapters' in editorial offices or publishing

[1] *Rudé právo*, 22 June 1968, p. 1.

houses had been swayed towards democratisation long before the Congress. In some instances this meant a parting of the ways with the publisher who would not be as radical. In this respect, the case of *Rudé právo* was particularly interesting, even if not entirely typical because of the paper's special position.

In the second half of March the staff of *Rudé právo* agreed to demand that the newspaper should be considered 'the organ of the whole of the Party', and not just of the Central Committee. (This in itself was a subtle form of heresy, reflecting the growing distrust in conservative members who still held posts in the Central Committee. If the paper was to represent the Party 'as a whole', it would have to express above all the opinions of the emerging majority of critics and proponents of reform from within the Party ranks, much more than the fading voices of the defenders of the *status quo*. It would no longer just convey Central Committee directives and explain immutable theorems formulated by the oracles. Some members of the staff would proudly say that it was their aim to make the paper more into an *Iskra* than a *Pravda*.) Further, the *Rudé právo* journalists would want to contribute independently to the shaping and implementation of Party policies, rather than be subject to regimentation by individual apparatchiki or departments in the Secretariat. Their responsibility would be to the plenum of the Central Committee (implying that this would be the new committee elected at the future Congress) not just to functionaries in the Secretariat.[1] At this stage Oldřich Švestka, the editor-in-chief, went with his staff and received their unanimous confidence. Not much later, almost coinciding with the first signs of Soviet displeasure over Czechoslovak developments at the Dresden meeting, the *modus vivendi* in the editorial office became seriously disturbed: some members of the staff left, others rebelled more or less openly, at first over the dispute whether the paper should give publicity to the rank-and-file call for the early holding of an extraordinary Congress. Švestka had to give way because he was caught in a crossfire between his own staff and the reform-minded members of the Party Praesidium who were his superiors. He even sought to present himself as a champion of reform and an ally of progressive writers under Novotný's rule (see his two articles 'Jak to bylo?',

---

[1] *Rudé právo*, 20 March 1968, p. 1.

18 and 19 June). The cup of discontent overflowed and nine members of the *Rudé právo* cultural section, including its head, Miloš Vacík, published a scorching criticism of their editor-in-chief in *Literární listy* on 11 July. By then Švestka was cautioning reformers against the introduction of workers' councils which, he found, would in fact be detrimental to the working class. He finally ceased to be editor-in-chief of *Rudé právo* after the invasion, but even with him in the chair (and often against him) the paper acquired a distinctly reformist character during the Prague Spring, unprecedented in the history of Communist journalism.

Other newspapers found themselves in a similar, though not identical, predicament. Was *Mladá fronta* to be an 'organ of the Youth Union Central Committee', i.e. a paper for the young, or should it become a paper of the young? Was *Zemědělské noviny* to continue to act as the spokesman of the Ministry of Agriculture, or should it primarily reflect the views of farmers and agriculturalists? Elsewhere, chief editors who had been too closely linked with the dogmatic past were sent packing, e.g. in *Svobodné slovo* and *Lidová demokracie*, the dailies of the Socialist Party and the People's Party. Everywhere the journalists began to recognise their strength as both explorers and co-creators of genuine public opinion, as against their previous mission of promoters of policies from above. Quite obviously the one thing which made this possible was the discontinuation of censorship.

Censorship in Czechoslovakia was both institutional and non-institutional. The censor's office, at first called the Main Authority of Press Supervision (*Hlavní správa tiskového dohledu*) and from 1967 the Central Publication Authority (*Ústřední publikační správa*), was typically subordinated to the Ministry of the Interior. It acted directly, with most periodicals other than dailies shipping page-proofs to its headquarters in Bartolomějská Street, and indirectly through censors who occupied their own cubicles in the editorial offices of the dailies and associated publications. Editors themselves were censors, willy-nilly clipping the wings of their writers to fit the established practice. The entire operation was conducted in the twilight between the obvious and the incomprehensible. There was no clear-cut manual or statute, although occasionally confidential Party directives spelled out the duties of the editors *vis-à-vis* the censors, mostly in general terms giving the benefit of doubt to the latter. More often the censors would refuse to discuss the reasons which lay behind their decisions. Where the editors did not want to take the ruling lying down, such as in *Literární noviny*, the obtaining atmosphere was one of constant tension and nervousness. Wednesdays and Thursdays in *Literární noviny* were dubbed 'talking-to-the-censors-days'. Hamšík[1] quotes from an official source which gave the number of major interventions by the censors in his paper: 1963 – 25, 1964 – 124, 1965 – 85, 1966 – 57, 1967 (to close-down in September) – 141. All but one were motivated by the editors' sinning against 'other interests of society'. This referred to the curious division of offensive material (often no more than a sentence, phrase or word) into that which allegedly betrayed State secrets and that which harmed society 'in another way'. The formulation obviously invited arbitrary and opportunist interpretation.

All kinds of the printed and spoken word (not to mention visual representation)[2] were censored, and belles-lettres got more than its fair share. Censorship was in fact the common denominator, amalgamating the reformist strivings of journalists, literati, other artists and even scholars who suffered from the impossibility of publishing their own findings as much as from having foreign non-Communist sources of knowledge all but denied them. In 1953, for example, two indexes of *libri prohibiti* were (secretly) issued and never formally revoked. They were the 'Principles to Determine the Main Categories of Defective and Obsolete Literature' (*Zásady k určení hlavních kategorií vadné a zastaralé literatury*) which listed as obnoxious the complete works of some 300 authors, including C. Gide, B. Russell, J. P. Sartre, G. Greene, M. Aymé and others, and the 'Auxiliary Lists of Books to Supplement the Principles to Determine the Main Categories of Defective and Obsolete Literature' (*Pomocné seznamy knih k zásadám určujícím hlavní kategorie vadné a zastaralé literatury*) with nearly 700 separate books by such authors as E. Hemingway, A. Christie, A. Malraux, H. G. Wells and others. These books were automati-

---

[1] D. Hamšík, *Spisovatelé a moc* (Prague, Čs. spisovatel, 1969) p. 172.

[2] A government Commission for Visual Representation (*Vládní komise pro zpodobování*) was in existence, whose duty it was to supervise works of fine art which included State symbols and portraits of statesmen.

cally excluded from libraries. All new literature from abroad had to pass through the censor's office where it was either cleared or earmarked for 'special stock' kept at selected libraries for persons with special ideological clearance (these books received one hexagonal stamp), or consigned to disappear altogether (two hexagonal stamps). Hundreds of incredibly ludicrous stories have been told about books vanishing from private parcels without the addressees ever being told, only to turn up under lock and key in 'special stock' library vaults. The whole system was sufficiently elastic to permit temporary relaxation, followed by periods of dire chicanery.

The first step to relax censorship after January 1968 was taken by the Party Praesidium (with Novotný still a member) at its meeting on 4 March. In 1971 the official condemnation of the reform movement flatly stated, making it of course sound like a grave offence, that the Praesidium had 'abolished censorship' on that day. What the Praesidium really did was less conspicuous: it revoked its own decision of August 1966 which had made it incumbent on the editor-in-chief to obey the censor's orders, and it asked the government to put someone other than the Minister of the Interior in charge of censorship. This was, of course, the very uncertain time when the hatching of genuine reform still remained in a precarious balance. Some cloak-and-dagger (though more cloak than dagger) stories about military intervention in support of Novotný emerged, tension between reformists and conservatives grew because of the evident mishandling of the escape of General Šejna by some highly placed personalities, the cultural policy of the Party, of which the question of censorship was an integral and significant part, had to be rectified in the wake of the deep rift of 1967, and so on. In short, the reform-minded top Party officials had to secure public support for themselves against the post-January conservative backlash. There is no reason to presume, however, that the complete removal of censorship was intended at this juncture. More probably, the reformist majority in the Party Praesidium wished to revert to the letter of the Press Law of 1967 with some liberal amendments: this would preserve the Central Publication Authority's power to recommend suspension of objectionable material while giving the editors the genuine right of appeal against the decision and possibly even the right to go ahead with publication at the risk of subsequent court action. The Ministry of Culture and Information was instructed to solicit proposals as to which amendments to the Press Law the various interested parties considered necessary. At a leisurely pace, the Ministry appealed on 12 March to the Creative Unions and the National Assembly committees to 'evaluate experiences from the implementation of the Press Law' and submit the relevant proposals which would then be processed and put before the government in due form. It all looked a long-term programme indeed.

Then the pace visibly accelerated and within a week the overall demand was for nothing less than for full abolition of political censorship. In many respects, this was a crucial week in mid-March: Novotný's abdication was the order of the day, the trade union leaders resigned, two Party cells in the Ministry of the Interior expressed dissatisfaction with the Ministry's top functionaries, the Slovak National Council dismissed its President and pressed for constitutional powers in Slovakia, the Praesidium of the National Assembly passed a vote of non-confidence in the Minister of the Interior and the Prosecutor General and both were dismissed from office, the liberal Č. Císař was put in charge of Party policies in culture, education and science, the first round of district Party conferences gave support (even if not as unequivocal as the second round a week later) to the 'new course', and Colonel-General V. Janko shot himself amid persistent rumours of an abortive armed attempt to salvage Novotný the previous December. Thus the demand for the complete discontinuation of censorship, while being the natural product of the cultural community's endeavour, came into the open as a corollary of a series of political developments, rather than as a defiant postulate disregarding political realities.

The statement by 'Communists in the headquarters of the Central Publication Authority', published on 16 March, will forever remain one of the fascinating documents of the Prague Spring. The censors themselves demanded the abolition of censorship, bravely disregarding possible redundancies in their own ranks.[1] It will also be remembered that they were without

---

[1] The statement said that the censors 'are of the opinion that preventive political censorship ought to be at present abolished, and suggested that

delay joined in their call by the Government Committee for Culture and Information, a little-used body, whose chairman was the then Minister of Culture and Information, Karel Hoffmann, later to be known as a staunch hardliner and a party to the Soviet invasion.[1]

More easily said than done. The Party Praesidium was treading uncertain ground: Novotný's resignation on 22 March was followed by the Dresden meeting on 23–4 March and the first open Soviet charges against the reform. With the special instructions to the Central Publication Authority and the editors already revoked, the Party leaders must have thought that legislation, of necessity an act of great publicity value, would not be the wisest step to make at this point. For another three months censorship remained in a state of suspended animation. It was not exercised, but its machinery and legal basis remained intact. Journalists and the other Creative Unions felt irritated by this half-heartedness and repeatedly demanded legislative action. If it is impossible to rewrite the entire Press Law immediately, they argued, why not quash censorship by a partial amendment and prepare a brand new Press Law at a later date? Eventually, the leaders gave way and, in another of the paradoxical situations so loved by history, it was the government meeting on 13 June, presided over by Deputy Prime Minister Gustáv Husák, which approved the wording of the Bill declaring censorship impermissible. Censorship was explicitly understood as the interference of the State with freedom of the word and of visual representation and with their dissemination through the mass media. The statute of the Central Publication Authority was suspended and editors-in-chief made responsible for not divulging State secrets.

There was a last-minute difficulty in the National Assembly when it came to debate the Bill at its twenty-fourth plenary

---

censorship should henceforth be guided only by the constitution and the law of our country'. *Rudé pravo*, 16 March 1968, p. 2.

[1] This statement said among other things, 'In order to promote culture and information on a wholesome basis, the principle of the freedom of expression should be ensured by the abolition of censorship through legislative action . . .' *Rudé právo*, 19 March 1968, p. 3.

session on 25 June. Some members showed a worried concern (as they had never previously shown in many more worrisome situations) lest the freedom of the press was 'misused' by reckless journalists. A. Švec suggested that next to the abolition of censorship the Assembly should write into the amended Press Law a provision whereby such misuse would be punishable by a fine of up to 100,000 crowns. In this way, he argued, the integrity of the individual would be protected against attacks in the press. The session had to adjourn and after some frantic debates in the committees (and corridors) reconvened on 26 June. Švec accepted the explanation of the Constitutional and Legal, and Cultural Committees (chairmen V. Knapp and A. Poledňák) to the effect that the rights of the individual ought indeed to be protected more than the present legislation stipulated, but that it was not necessary to hitch this on to the simple postulate terminating censorship. The Bill was then put to a vote and passed, with thirty members voting against and seventeen abstaining. The new legislation was supplemented on 29 July by two ordinances on State secrets: one was issued by the Ministry of the Interior listing on thirty-five pages items of information which constituted State secrets, and the other came from the Ministry of National Defence specifying on eleven pages military items about which it was permitted to write.

Two further questions have to be considered in connection with the role of the mass media during the Prague Spring. Did the journalists (or the information media) constitute a political pressure group (or, as some would have it, a 'weapon of counter-revolution')?[1] Why was the situation so noticeably lopsided and why did the conservatives lose practically all holds over the mass media?

None of the more usual definitions of 'group', 'pressure group', 'political group' or 'lobby' entirely fits the activity of Czechoslovak journalists in 1968. The Journalists' Union could not be fully identified with the mass media. While the former undoubtedly constituted an organisation trying to

---

[1] One should note that in Communist parlance, especially the post-invasion evaluations of the reform movement, the term 'pressure group' (*nátlaková skupina*) is meant automatically to have pejorative connotations.

influence the policy of the government in a chosen direction without being itself prepared to undertake the direct government of the country, the latter served as a channel for the transmission of ideas from the much wider mass of citizenry to the government. Within the mass media, mutually disagreeing and even antagonistic 'attitude groups' established a coalition in the pursuit of a common cause, i.e. the reform. In this sense one can consider the mass media a 'promotional group', although the one basic common cause naturally blanketed a host of diverse and divergent causes pertinent to the various 'attitude groups' within it.

The one-sidedness (with the whole of the press, radio and television in the country advocating a single common cause) had existed before, at the time when censorship virtually obliterated all other causes. The Prague Spring situation was however different not only because it pointed in the other direction but because it evolved spontaneously. As such it was unique. The absence of an adversary or dissenter (in relation to the basic cause) is at once difficult and easy to explain. An explanation has to be sought in the intangible psychological sphere more than in the directly political. The desire for change was simply so overwhelming and the release of pent-up feelings so sudden that the constitution of a conservative group in the mass media was out of the question. Even the most likely domains of conservativism, like *Rudé právo*, the ministerial *Literární (Kulturní) noviny*, the organ of the Czechoslovak–Soviet Friendship Union *Svět sovětů*, the Party apparat journal *Život strany* and others, either speedily converted themselves or at least willingly abdicated dyed-in-the-wool policies. There was little administrative action whereby conservatives were forced to give way to reformists: several editors-in-chief were made to resign, including directors of radio and television, but others stayed until after the invasion in spite of conservative leanings (Švestka, Sulek); *Kulturní noviny* was closed down, but not before all the editors had turned their coats and proclaimed themselves as standing in the van of progress; a plan was approved by the Party Praesidium in July to replace *Život strany* by a more flexible *Tribuna*, but the change never materialised and after the invasion the former paper remained in existence while the latter was founded as a mouthpiece of pro-invasion elements in the Czech Party Bureau; *Svět sovětů* (The World of the Soviets) changed its name into *Svět socialismu* (The World of Socialism), but it did so at its own will, etc. It has been suggested, among others in the report which the conservative members of the Party Praesidium prepared for the crucial Praesidium meeting on 20 August, as well as in evaluations of a later date, that the editorial staffs emancipated themselves from the influence of their publishers to an extent unmatched anywhere in the world. Even if the publishers (which in a number of instances must have meant 'the State') wanted to oppose the radical reformist trend, so the argument went, the journalists would not obey.[1] The reasoning is lame; cases of journalistic disobedience were few and far between. Insofar as information on such a delicate issue is at all available (no factual evidence has so far been offered by the critics of the Prague Spring) it included the dispute between Švestka and the *Rudé právo* staff, the dissociation of *Mladá fronta* newsmen from the hopelessly discredited leadership of the Youth Union, the similar case of *Práce*, which gave support to the emergent new trade union leadership, and the several provincial Party papers, especially the Ostrava *Nová svoboda*, which openly clashed with conservative speakers (and even Party Secretary A. Indra) at regional Party conferences. In all these instances the transformation of the 'publishers' in question into reform-oriented organisations (Party, Youth Union, trade unions) was well under way even without help from the newspapers. For many journalists it must have been a moral issue: whether to side with the obviously outgoing, discredited and isolated handful of functionaries, or with the overwhelming majority which was in the process of forming a new leadership. On the more general plane, this applied to monopoly mass media as well, notably radio, television and the State press agency. The government, acting as the owner-publisher, professed its reformist policy (especially the Černík government, formed at the beginning of April) which entailed freedom of thought and speech as well as free access to information. It was this policy

---

[1] See for example 'Zpráva o současné politické situaci v ČSSR a pod-mínkách činnosti KSČ', issued on 20 August 1968 for the Party Praesidium, first published in *Rudé právo*, 2 July 1969.

that the radio, press and – in its way – the press agency pursued. For the more gazette-type dissemination of official information, the government contemplated the launching of a special daily paper.

Thus the almost unanimous association of journalists with the policy of reform was above all the result of non-symmetrical political conditions. If the mass media stayed with the defenders of the *status quo ante*, the obtaining relation of forces would be unnatural, artificial, ideologically imposed. And yet, the fact remains that the conservatives of all shades were left without so much as a single newspaper and without adequate representation in broadcasting. An absolutely normal situation would call for the existence of a *Literární noviny* in reverse. In this sense the post-invasion conditions were paradoxically better balanced, discounting of course the growing administrative constraints inflicted on the reformist press. (In purely speculative terms the conservative *Tribuna*, the Soviet-sponsored *Zprávy* and Radio *Vltava* broadcasting from East Germany would seem adequate outlets for the half-a-million or so of counter-reformers, provided again that coercion did not enter into the picture.) As it was, we must regard the disappearance of the conservative press as one of the unresolved problems of the Prague Spring. Once again the time-span of the experiment was too short to permit more than theoretical extrapolation. As the reformers demonstrably did not aim at introducing a dictatorship but a democracy (albeit with limitations), it is more than likely that the reformed régime would later tolerate expression of cautious and possibly even radical conservativism. Unfortunately the dust was not allowed to settle.

Many observers agree that the popularity of the mass media reached an all-time record during the Prague Spring and was unmatched anywhere in the world. In Prague alone, with its 1 million inhabitants, 557,192 copies of daily papers were sold on 20 March 1968.[1] The following figures briefly illustrate the point:[2]

[1] K. Bartošek, 'Revoluce proti byrokratismu?', in *Rudé právo*, 31 July 1968, p. 3.
[2] Compiled from *Statistická ročenka* 1969 and 1970.

Item	1967	1968
Number of newspapers and periodicals published	1,204	1,403
Number of copies sold	1,866,930	1,974,055
(incl. political press)	1,379,218	1,456,759
Hours of sound broadcasting (incl. foreign service)	75,154	73,742
Hours of political sound broadcasting and news on central stations	6,568	7,869
Hours of television on air	3,161	3,253

An evaluation of the content is an extremely accident-prone exercise, and one is liable to accusations of bias. Trying to be as detached as possible, we find the content falling into four main categories: criticism of the past, discussion of the present, discussion of the future and news and information. A telegraph-style enumeration of subjects may be more illuminating than lengthy description.

1   *Criticism of the past*
(a) Theoretical criticism of the Communist system and deliberations on the Czech and Slovak national predicament.
(b) Specific criticism of pre-1968 policies and their implementation.
   i. Exposure of miscarriage of justice, unlawful practices and crime, especially those committed by the police.
   ii. Criticism of action arising from monopoly of power, especially Party-political, at all levels.
   iii. Censure of economic policies and faults of the pre-1968 economic system.

2   *Discussion of the present*
(a) Expression of support for the 'new course'.
   i. In general terms.
   ii. In connection with specific steps.
   iii. In relation to external pressure, including polemics with foreign critique and comment.
(b) Criticism of the new leadership.
   i. For secretiveness.
   ii. For procrastination and half-heartedness.
   iii. For going too far.
(c) Specific discussion of economic, political, cultural action.
   i. Proposals.
   ii. Warning against certain types of action.

    (*d*) Personnel questions.
        i. Criticism of personalities up to pressure for resignation or dismissal.
      ii. Commendation of personalities up to proposals for elevation into important positions.

3 *Discussion of the future*
    (*a*) Deliberation on the qualities of the system which was to emerge from the reform.
        i. Theoretical.
      ii. Consideration of specific guarantees to be built into this system in order to prevent relapse.
    (*b*) Long-term extrapolation of consequences arising from the would-be reformed system.

4. *News and information*

The emphasis shifted from general and vague formulations of democratic desires to more specific criticism and proposals, and from veiled dissatisfaction with unnamed function-holders to open expression of non-confidence. As time progressed, the style of newspaper writing changed as well, from the cryptic and ambiguous (as conditioned by years of censorship), to the cautious and timid, to the bold and candid. In most cases the professional and linguistic standards were unusually high, incomparable to the bulk of the press in pre-1968 years.

What, then, are our conclusions? The critics of reform repeatedly castigated the mass media for meddling in affairs which they should leave alone, i.e. the leading role of the Party understood as a monopoly of decision-making. The reformists, on the other hand, tended to overrate the specific weight of the media, perhaps understandably so in the absence of other sufficiently well-established channels of organised political action.[1] Both sides evidently viewed the role of the

[1] For example: *Rudé právo*, 21 April 1968, p. 1, reported a press conference at which J. Smrkovský 'appealed to the journalists to re-evaluate their role in society and to become a specific social category which will contribute to the shaping of the legal system and the development of our democratic and socialist society. The point is that you should also become partners of the National Assembly and, in this way, co-creators of the project of social control.' The report prepared for the Fourteenth Congress in 1968 called the mass media 'an institution of social control over power and government'. *Panzer überrollen den Parteitag*, ed. J. Pelikán (Europa Verlag, 1970) p. 241.

press in society through the prism of traditional Communism which considers it 'a weapon of the working class' and 'an organiser of the masses'. From the distance of three years, with many emotional contours mercifully blurred, one could perhaps best qualify the mass media of the Prague Spring as a somewhat onesided and highly critical factor of communication between the masses and the government, and between the various attitudinal groups of the reform-seeking community; as a vertical channel it evolved into a pressure group for the promotion of a cause which was common to the great majority of both its makers and its users, albeit insufficiently crystallised in detail; as a horizontal channel it offered a good opportunity for the exchange of views, but for reasons not quite under its control it did not embrace the full spectrum of the public.

To describe the heyday of the Czechoslovak mass media during the invasion week is outside the scope of this book.[1] Suffice it to say that experience confirms the conclusion about the almost total indentification of the masses with the reformist orientation of the media and vice versa. (If we wished to play on words, we could suggest that 'mass media' acquired the meaning, 'media of the masses'.)[2] The Communist understanding of the media seemed to be corroborated: they did often become a collective organiser and instrument of struggle. A similar development is unlikely to take place – should a similar situation be repeated elsewhere – without the journalists previously identifying themselves with the reform cause and without the acceptance of a free press among the masses.

Action against the journalists and the mass media, first by the invaders and the hard-pressed Party and government

[1] Almost every book on the invasion has something to say on this subject.

[2] In public opinion poll No. 68–15 conducted by the Prague Institute of Public Opinion Research from 14 to 16 September 1968, a representative sample of 1,882 persons (1,860 respondents) was asked, among other things, 'What is your opinion of the activity of those journalists who after 21 August did not stop broadcasting and publishing news?' The following answers (in per cent) were given:

	Very positive	Positive	No opinion	Negative	Very negative
All	77·4	17·2	4·6	0·6	0·2
Czech Lands	80·9	14·3	4·0	0·6	0·2
Slovakia	69·0	24·3	6·0	0·5	0·2

leadership and later, vehemently, by the Husák régime, followed expected paths: military seizure of editorial offices, reinstitution of censorship, suspension of more than two dozen outspoken newspapers and periodicals, purges of hundreds of journalists and their replacement by loyal or at least submissive followers of the old-new course, formation of the hard-core of a new journalistic force which subscribed to the policy of the day without questions, and the final take-over of the mass media for service to the new Party and State leadership.

SCHOLARS AND SCIENTISTS

The grouping of scholars and scientists, mostly originating before 1968 and even prior to the Second World War, was originally not 'political' or 'pressure', although it was influential. The element of organisation varied and there was a considerable amount of overlapping, with several outlets open to most. There is no doubt that in 1968 the influence particularly of social scientists on public affairs, including policy-making, grew considerably beyond the pre-1968 level. The desire to replace the unimaginative and haphazard policies of the Novotný era with more 'scientific' approaches was widely proclaimed and recognised. The modest beginnings of this process date back to 1963–4, when the Party leadership, largely under the impact of poor economic performance, half-heartedly agreed to commission *ad hoc* teams of experts to work on background material for policy decisions. Some specialists did not even wait for commission, made use of a propitious moment and got together to volunteer analyses and proposals. In this way the first drafts of the economic reform were worked out by economists (under Ota Šik) from the Economic Institute of the Academy of Sciences, the Czechoslovak Economic Society and a working group in the State Committee for Management and Organisation. Similarly, a number of historians, economists and political scientists (under Milan Hübl) were asked to study some aspects of the political trials of the 1950s, notably the charges of so-called Slovak bourgeois nationalism, to document a long-delayed rehabilitation.[1] An inter-disciplinary

[1] This was the Working Committee of the Barnabitky Commission, set up to reconsider the case of the so-called Slovak bourgeois nationalism in

team was set up (under Radovan Richta) to examine the effects of the scientific and technical revolution on Communism and vice versa.[1] Sociologists, vigorously making up for lost time during the period in which their science had been regarded as 'bourgeois', prepared (under Pavel Machonin) a study for the Thirteenth Party Congress on changes in the country's social structure and the resulting political implications.[2] More or less the same team stayed together for the launching of the most ambitious sociological survey up to that date, an inquiry into socio-economic and political stratification by means of a field-study among over 12,000 male family heads.[3] A group of political scientists and jurists (under Zdeněk Mlynář) virtually elicited for themselves a commission from the Party to propose what political changes in the system ought to be implemented to match the hoped-for economic reform.[4] There were other groups, in various stages of constitution, which felt the need for unconventional team work in their respective fields.

Czechoslovak scholarship has traditionally been both well organised and inducive to team action. Practically every scientist would have the opportunity to assert himself through a number of channels. He would be active at a usually well established place of work (in 1968, 56 per cent of all scholars and scientists worked at schools of higher learning, 26 per cent in ministerial institutes and industry and 18 per cent in the Academy of Sciences). He could promote his views through the so-called scientific collegia of the Academy of Sciences (twenty in the Czechoslovak and seventeen in the Slovak Academies of Sciences). He could join one of the professional societies, many

---

1963, the first such body to consist of economists, historians and jurists, and not just political officials. See for example *Das Unterdrückte Dossier*, ed. Jiří Pelikán (Europa Verlag, 1970) pp. 257–9 and 341–3. The English edition, *The Czechoslovak Political Trials 1950–54* (Macdonald, 1971), has only one reference because a document has been left out.

[1] See *Civilizace na rozcestí*, ed. Radovan Richta (Prague, Svoboda, 1966).

[2] See *Změny v sociální struktuře Československa a dynamika sociálně-politického vývoje*, ed. P. Machonin (Prague, Svoboda, 1967).

[3] See *Československá společnost*, ed. P. Machonin (Bratislava, Epocha, 1970).

[4] The only available summary of the work of this team (in addition to numerous discussions of its individual conclusions) appeared in two articles by Zdeněk Mlynář, 'K demokratické politické organizaci společnosti', in *Nová mysl*, 5 (1968) and 'Právo, právní věda a náš politický vývoj', in *Právník*, 5 (1968).

of them traditional (in 1965, eighteen such societies existed for the natural sciences and thirteen for the humanities, attached loosely to the Academy of Sciences; others existed separately). He would, if he so wished, work through the two institutions largely devoted to popularisation of science and scholarship (the Socialist Academy and the Czechoslovak Scientific-Technical Society). And he would contribute to the several dozen scientific and scholarly journals. In addition, scope for political work, not necessarily always divorced from scholarly preoccupation, especially in the social sciences, could be found in other public organisations, including the Party. Thus several scholars were members of the Party Central Committee. Karel Kosík, the philosopher, was active in the Writers' Union. Zdeněk Mlynář, the jurist, eventually became Party Secretary and even a member of the Politburo. Ota Šik was appointed Deputy Prime Minister in April 1968. Several scholars regularly contributed to the Party monthly *Nová mysl* and even served on its editorial board. Some political scientists joined the Institute of Political Sciences attached to the Party Central Committee. Theoretical economists worked for the State Planning Commission. The trade unions had scholars on the staff of their research institute. In 1968 the Union of Scientific Workers was set up and given representation on the Co-ordinating Committee of Creative Unions. In short, there was no organisational barrier to prevent a scholar or scientist from entering into vigorous horizontal communication with his colleagues, and even vertical political influence was made easier by the official recognition (albeit hesitant and inconsistent) that science ought to be listened to if the machinery of the State was not to falter.

Essentially, the scholar's 'political' aspiration was no less freedom-oriented than that of a writer or journalist. Freedom of research was on the agenda since 1956 and freedom to publish not much later. The endeavours for freedom took various forms. Abstention from, or outright opposition to, the various semi-literate 'Party Decisions on Philosophy' and the like was common. Collective solidarity was shown to chastised colleagues (as in the case of the dismissed editor of *Dějiny a současnost*, Zdeněk Šikl, in 1965).[1] Grouping designed to give

[1] In the Spring of 1965 the Ideological Department of the Party Central

greater weight to scholars working on subjects considered taboo or ticklish led to the mushrooming of sections in established organisations (as in the case of historians devoted to the most recent history of socialism in Czechoslovakia).[1] Conferences were held on subjects which could not avoid having critical connotations for neo-Stalinist policies (as in the case of the conference on Franz Kafka in 1963[2] or the conference on the Czechoslovak road to socialism in 1965),[3] and so on. Also

Committee (under Pavel Auersperg) ordered the replacement of the editor and changes in the editorial office of *Dějiny a současnost* for 'gross political mistakes'. These included the publication of a memoir article by a former member of the Protectorate Government, an article on the American Revolution without critical comment and on the Russian Revolution with a critical comment, an anniversary article on the Slovak poet and 'bourgeois nationalist' Laco Novomeský and the non-publication of any article on the birthday of Antonín Novotný, and giving space to 'criticised authors' Ivan Sviták and Milan Hübl. The majority of the editorial board expressed solidarity with the editor and resigned. Next to the writers, the historians were in fact the most frequently and harshly attacked segment of the intellectual community. The Novotný leadership was particularly irritated by their aspiration to become 'the memory of the nation', parallel to the writers' claim to be 'the conscience of the nation'. As, accidentally, the ideological onslaughts usually occurred in the Spring, the historians talked about the 'Spring shooting season'.

[1] Historians specialising in the post-1945 period tried to protect themselves by setting up a semi-institutional Commission for the History of Socialism, similar to the already existing Committee of Historians of the National Liberation Struggle (Second World War). The idea of the commission emerged in 1964, but proposals were repeatedly turned down by the Ideological Department of the Party. It was not until December 1966 that the commission came into existence.

[2] See for example *Franz Kafka. Sborník projevů na Liblické konferenci 1963* (Prague, ČSAV, 1963); Eduard Goldstücker, *Na téma Franz Kafka* (Prague, Čs. spisovatel, 1964); also discussed in Vladimir V. Kusin, *The Intellectual Origins of the Prague Spring* (Cambridge University Press, 1971) pp. 63–8.

[3] This conference, remarkable in many aspects, took place at Liblice from 16 to 19 March 1965 in the presence of 102 Czechoslovak and nineteen foreign historians. The subjects under discussion included peculiarity of Czechoslovak transition to socialism, the pre-February 1948 understanding of the National Front, the mixed economy element in socialism, etc. Special mention should be made of Karel Bartošek's concept of the Czechoslovak road to socialism as a long-term process since 1918. The participants' names read like a list of protagonists of the Prague Spring: Bartošek, Křen, Kaplan, Hübl, Opat, Janeček, Mlynář, Goldmann, Šedivý. See for example J. Belda, 'Konference historiků k 20. výročí osvobození ČSR', *Příspěvky k dějinám KSČ*, 3 (1965) pp. 450–5.

noticeable was a shift away from ideological preoccupation to genuine research. Many Departments of Marxism–Leninism at the universities, first set up to indoctrinate students as much as to guard ideological purity, evolved into centres of genuine political science and sociology. So did the Institute (it had three names during its twelve-year history) which came into being to further the education of the largely young staffs of these departments.[1] The Institute of the History of the Czechoslovak Communist Party, another case in point, gradually ceased to be a watchdog of political and ideological merit in Czechoslovak historiography, and its staff produced some valuable works of critical insight in Party history. Serious historical research was going on in the Military History Institute and, at least in embryonic form, some earnest sociological work was undertaken in the two Military Academies in Prague and Brno. A not insignificant support for the economic reform and for budding political science came from some departments in the Party Political School. Many of the political scientists, whose activity had long been unrecognised (don't we have

[1] The establishment of the Departments of Marxism can in fact be interpreted as an attempt to combine university teaching and Party education, i.e. science and ideology. The dual character persisted until their dissolution in the wake of the invasion. In 1964 the departments had 1,041 staff, including 137 associate professors and professors, of whom 646 simultaneously held unpaid functions in the Party. It was never quite clear whether the departments ought to be fully subordinated to the Party apparat or the Ministry of Education. Their members were alternately criticised for liberalism and intellectualism (by the Party) and for unscholarly propagandism (by teachers from other departments). From 1964 the trend towards sociology and political science (rather than propaganda) gradually asserted itself. The Institute for Further Education of Teachers of Departments of Marxism-Leninism (*Ústav pro další vzdělávání učitelů kateder marxismu-leninismu*) was founded on 1 December 1957 and attached to Charles University. On 1 January 1960 it became known as the Institute for Teaching and Research at Departments of Marxism-Leninism (*Ústav pro výuku a vědeckou práci kateder marxismu-leninismu*) and on 1 January 1964 it was again renamed *Ústav marxismu-leninismu pro vysoké školy* (Institute of Marxism-Leninism for Universities). In 1967 it had a staff of forty-nine and two branches in Brno and Bratislava. Under Pavel Machonin, the sociologist, it was instrumental in bringing about a reorientation of the departments in favour of research. See for example Kladiva in *Nová mysl*, 9 (1964), Morkes in *Příspěvky k dějinám KSČ*, 6 (1967) and Machonin in *Revue dějin socialismu*, 1 (1968).

Marxism?), emerged from the Institute of State and Law and the Institute for International Politics and Economics which was subordinated to the Foreign Ministry.

Practically not a single social science institution, for whichever purpose it might have been originally established and by whichever political body it might have been controlled, remained unaffected by the growing awareness of a need for political reform in the country even before 1968. This in itself distinguished the Czechoslovak situation from that of Poland and Hungary in 1956, and again that of the Poland of 1968–70. At the end of Novotný's rule, it was not the case of a conservative social science institution fighting a reformist one. The vast majority of scholars in all institutions were oriented towards reform both in their own respective fields and in the political set-up. (A certain exception could be observed among the economists. The State Planning Commission and the Prague School of Economics as well as the 'practical economists' of the managerial type included a high percentage of opponents of reform or dissenters from some of its major aspects.) In addition to standing for freedom of research which, they demanded, ought to apply to non-Marxist approaches as well, the community of scholars were united in calling for a change in the system which presupposed 'direction' or 'control' (*řízení*) over science by the centre of political power. Thus they avidly accepted the Prague Spring which promised both. The Dubček leadership could, from the very beginning, count on unprecedented expertise, such as the previous régime was partly denied and partly refused to accept. With its accent on greater freedom and on the cessation of crude political intrusion into human life and work, the 'socialism with a human face' was above all well suited to the intellectual and scientific community. And, in reverse, it was precisely the reformist transformation of social sciences before 1968 which made the formulation of democratic socialism in Czechoslovak conditions possible. The symbiosis boded well for the future: few régimes had ever been able to rely on such formidable theoretical support. Nevertheless, miracles were once again proved not to happen. The one commodity of which Czechoslovak social science was in short supply was sufficient time for open crystallisation of ideas. All the ingredients of a new system were there: an economic arrangement combining framework planning with the market, a theory of unconventional political pluralism shaped around the consensus about the need for guarantees against an abuse of power, a nationality solution of the federative type, a participatory economic-cum-political system of workers' councils, a system of civil rights linked to a high measure of vertical identification of the populace with its national state, a cultural policy protecting the public from the two *diktats* of power and commercialisation. Unfortunately, more time was needed to translate the generally prevailing opinions into workable majority solutions of a more detailed nature.

The extent of the consensus can be seen from the large-scale eradication of social science (and creative intellectualism in general) after the ascendance of counter-reformation in April 1969. At the time of writing, three years after the invasion, creative social science in Czechoslovakia is still dead. Even if its slow resurrection can be safely predicted, the scope of suppression, larger than in any other field of activity apart from practical politics, journalism and foreign travel, is in direct proportion to its upsurge before and during the Prague Spring.

Professional groups of social scientists formulated straightforward political demands only rarely and indirectly during the Prague Spring. This was undoubtedly so because their members could express their views through other, more directly political, organisations, such as the Party or the Creative Unions. When professional gatherings convened, they showed concern primarily for the unhampered development of their disciplines. For example, at its two meetings on 29 February and 28 March 1968, the Scientific Collegium of Philosophy and Sociology of the Academy of Sciences debated the understanding of philosophy and sociology 'in their diversity', which must include 'non-Marxist thought'. This, they believed, ought to be reflected not only in such activities as teaching and publishing, but also in the Constitution and other legal norms which hitherto had justified the existence of a single 'State philosophy'. Historians from university departments, assembled in Poděbrady from 1 to 5 April 1968 for a seminar to discuss fifty years of Czechoslovakia, issued a statement which combined the political and the professional: the new political system about to be created should not be a replica of either 1967 or pre-1948 or pre-1938; as one of its preconditions, completely new organs protecting the interests and security of the State (i.e. police) must be established; at the same time compromised supervisors of historiographic institutions ought to be dismissed no less than discredited politicians. On 10 April the Scientific Collegium of History expressed itself against 'the so-called direct Party control over social sciences' and asked for greater independence to be granted to the individual social science institutions. On 2 May a conference on the philosophy and methodology of science was held at Černá and suggested that full freedom should be given to all philosophical schools, branches and disciplines, that the so-called 'direction and planning' of philosophy from the power centre should be put to an end and that those Party decisions which forbade the employment of non-Party people in social science departments at the universities should be revoked. A gathering of historians at the Philosophical Faculty of Charles University passed a resolution on 26 June demanding legal guarantees of freedom of research and an end to discrimination against scholars on non-scientific criteria.

The two organisations devoted to the popularisation of science were the Socialist Academy (*Socialistická akademie*) and the Czechoslovak Scientific-Technical Society (*Československá vědecko-technická společnost*). Both were organised on the lines of democratic centralism, with full hierarchic structures, the former being nominally independent while the latter was attached to the Central Trade Union Council. Precisely because of their national networks and experience in holding lectures, they proved of some value at a time when the element of direct democracy, i.e. public gatherings, became an important political instrument.

This was particularly true about the Socialist Academy. It had already existed before the War as the Communist Party's organ of political enlightenment. Revived in 1946, it was transformed in 1952 to fit the image of the Soviet *Obshchestvo Znanie* and renamed the Society for the Dissemination of Political and Scientific Knowledge. Popularly known as the Long-name Society, it offered an additional income to underpaid scholars for lecturing on a host of subjects, such as atheism, economy, agriculture, natural sciences, international affairs, technology, art, Marxism and sanitation. In 1965 it resumed its old name, but not before its chief secretary, Robert Horák, had been purged for ideological errors, including refusal to take to task the editor of one of the Society's journals, *Dějiny a současnost*. The new boss came straight from the Ideological Department in the Party Secretariat. The Academy had around 40,000 members,[1] but it was not an exacting duty to be a member and formalities were on the whole minimal. In 1968 the Academy appointed Horák chief secretary again and reinstated the original staff of *Dějiny a současnost* which had resigned in 1965 as a sign of solidarity with their editor Zdeněk Šikl. At the same time a certain effort was made to proclaim the Socialist Academy 'the spokesman and advocate of the interests of all Czechoslovak intelligentsia as a social group' and to reshape it into a major political organisation. The Academy's chairman, Ivan Málek, claimed that it was the only organisation in which all segments of the intelligentsia found representation and that fully fledged functioning within the National Front was thus not only imperative but also possible.[2] It would appear that this aspiration was not quite matched by the members' enthusiasm. Although a certain gap in the existing State-wide organisational set-up remained open as far as the lower echelons of the intelligentsia were concerned, there was little desire to fill it in precisely the way the Socialist Academy was offering. After all, the academy existed for another purpose and was tailored to popularise scientific knowledge rather than to act as a sectional interest organisation. Apart from proclamations, carried mostly by the fervour of the Academy's leadership, nothing much therefore happened. After the invasion and enthronement of the Husák régime, the Socialist Academy eventually fell apart and was replaced in 1971 by a new body, once again charged to organise propaganda lectures and seminars.

The Scientific-Technical Society claimed in 1963 to have

---

[1] *Hospodářsko-politická rukověť*, Part II (Prague, ČTK, 1968) p. 1004, or Heinrich Kuhn, *Handbuch der Tschechoslowakei* (Munich, Robert Lerche, 1966) p. 237.

[2] *Rudé právo*, 18 April 1968, p. 2. This article gives the number of members as 34,000.

160,000 members in 3,600 branches.[1] It had existed since 1958 as a loose offshoot of the trade union structure. Its aim was to associate 'technicians, scientists and innovators' for the purpose of enhancing their qualification, facilitating their contribution to technical progress and spreading technical and scientific propaganda. In 1968 the society, like the Socialist Academy, replaced its enforced chairman, V. Koukol, by Miroslav Šmok, who had previously been in charge (1962–6). The main endeavour in 1968 seemed to be to achieve independence from the trade union movement (generally considered an unwieldy and largely bureaucratic organisation) and possibly to regroup the society so that it might act as an interest organisation of the technical intelligentsia. There is no evidence of this effort having proceeded beyond the proclamation stage. In a letter to *Rudé právo*, five technicians from Prague said that the first phase of the renascent process (as they put it) had mainly concerned conceptual and political matters in which social scientists were more competent than technicians. With the accelerated implementation of the economic reform as the order of the day, the practical economists and technical experts would henceforth have more to say even on questions of wider importance.[2] The five technicians were right, although the traditionally low level of social criticism among the technical intelligentsia did not quite fade away under the impact of political tumult. One can think of at least three characteristics which promised to link up this socio-economic sub-group with the envisaged economic advancement. Its age structure was relatively young and consequently it was more vehemently opposed to dogmatic incompetence than an established group would be. Its numbers were rapidly increasing, which led to a growing self-awareness of the social weight it could carry. Professionally and socially it was closely connected with the economic structure and economic performance of the country and therefore directly exposed to the salutary congruence or the ill-effects of both. It seems more than likely that some kind of politico-professional organisation of the technical intelligentsia would have come into existence had the planned progress of reform not been halted.

---

[1] Kuhn, op. cit., p. 273, gives the number of members as 160,000 in 1963. *Rudé právo*, 24 May 1968, p. 2, says 'over 150,000'.

[2] *Rudé právo*, 13 May 1968, p. 6.

CHAPTER FOUR

Youth and Students

YOUTH

Czechoslovakia is not an exceptionally young society and her young people do not derive particular social or political weight from numerical predominance. Nevertheless, a bias towards the young age groups is noticeable from statistical records. As of 31 December 1967 the order of five-year groups according to size was as follows:

1.	15–19	11.	45–9
2.	10–14	12.	60–4
3.	20–4	13.	50–4
4.	5–9	14.	65–9
5.	40–4	15.	70–4
6.	35–9	16.	75–9
7.	25–9	17.	0–1
8.	1–4	18.	80–4
9.	55–9	19.	85 and over[1]
10.	30–4		

The late adolescent and early adulthood groups rank first and third; all below thirty groups (excepting small children) are to be found in the first seven; the late thirties and early forties groups are the strongest middle-age segment.

The strength of what are often referred to as the young, the intermediate and the old groups is for our purpose best measured in relation to three political points in time relevant to the reform in general and the Prague Spring in particular; notably the Communist takeover in February 1948, the Nazi

---

[1] Computed from *Statistická ročenka ČSSR 1969* (Prague, SNTL, 1970) p. 85. See also 'Odhad věkového složení obyvatelstva', in *Demografie*, 2 (1970) p. 166.

Occupation and War from 1939 to 1945 and the heyday of the First Republic in 1929 which was also the time of Gottwald's coming to power in the Communist Party. Let us once again use data for 31 December 1967 to cull three groups from the total population:

The young group. People who in 1948 had not been older than nineteen and consequently did not take a meaningful part in the seizure of power; they had never been old enough to know any other than the Communist system of their own adult experience; at the start of the Prague Spring they were twenty–thirty-nine years old; they numbered 3,913,497.

The intermediate group. People who in 1939–45 had been at least twelve–seventeen years old and therefore experienced Munich, the Nazi Occupation and the War in their formative years, and the 1945–8 interlude and the Communist takeover and rule as adults; at the start of the Prague Spring they were forty–fifty-four years old; they numbered 2,487,893.

The veteran group. People who in 1929 had been at least seventeen years old and therefore experienced all the recent political history as adults; at the start of the Prague Spring they were fifty-five–seventy-four years old (older groups, i.e. seventy-five and over, are not counted here); they numbered 2,749,169.[1]

Applying yet another criterion, that of 'generation', we can compare the numerical strength of the 'young' (twenty–thirty-four years old on 31 December 1967), the 'middle-aged' (thirty-five–forty-nine) and the 'old' (fifty–seventy-four). Apart from the usual pitalls of this division, we deliberately choose not to select three equal time-spans in order to match the figures against the watershed experiences of February 1948, War and Liberation, and the First Republic.

The 'young' (twenty–thirty-four). No adult experience of pre-Communist régimes: 2,940,447.

The 'middle-aged' (thirty-five–forty-nine). War in childhood and adolescence, 1945–8 in formative years and early adulthood, Communism in their prime: 2,768,056.

The 'old' (fifty–seventy-four). First-hand adult experience of four régimes: 3,422,156.[2]

As is usual, political conclusions drawn from demographic

---

[1] Ibid.   [2] Ibid.

figures must be heavily qualified and circumstantial. The only two points which to my mind can be deduced from the above patterns are self-evident: the Czechoslovak reform movement in general and the Prague Spring in particular were not the result of an overwhelming number of young people in the population, although the specific weight of a first-generation Communist youth (first ever in Czechoslovak history, the 'post-1945 generation') must have been increasingly felt.

It was this generation that the Czechoslovak Youth Union (*ČSM-Československý svaz mládeže*, so named since 1949; before that date the two national unions were SČM and SSM) was created to organise, educate and control. Coupled with the Young Pioneers it covered age groups from six to twenty-six (six–fifteen and sixteen–twenty-six), i.e. some 5 million people. Youth Union membership was for long given as a steady 1 million; however, a 1968 source said that ČSM members represented the following percentages of the corresponding age groups: 1961 – 54 per cent, 1962 – 52·5 per cent, 1963 – 42·4 per cent, 1964 – 43·7 per cent, 1965 – 35·3 per cent, 1966 – 32·0 per cent, 1967 – 26·0 per cent.[1] Official reluctance to subject membership trends to accurate public scrutiny was undoubtedly due to the generally, if tacitly, acknowledged fact that the bulk of the members had joined the ČSM for formal reasons only. Once in possession of the membership card, often a proviso if not a guarantee of a good job or place at a university, they slipped into inaction very easily.

Unlike the Komsomol, the ČSM was not meant to serve as an ante-room to the Party. Even though periods of relative ideological lenience in the union's life alternated with rigid 'direct rule' by the Party, the ČSM was always expected to act as a 'mass' organisation, keeping an eye on and vouching for all young people. Similar to other organisations of this type it often fell between two stools. Striving to weld together the duties of a Communist unitary and single-purpose organisation with the relative liberties of an interest group catering for the diverse tastes of the 'masses', it succeeded in neither. It alternately invoked the displeasure of the Party bosses and drew a

[1] The figure for 1961 appeared in K. Mácha-J. Máchová, *Lidé a socialismus* (Prague, Svobodné slovo, 1964) p. 30. Figures for 1962–7 were quoted in *Literární listy*, 7 March 1968, p. 6.

blank from its members. It was unable to promote the cause of
Communism as required without losing its members' co-
operation, and it was equally unable to advocate the interests of
the younger generation without falling out with the Party
leadership.

It became too large and bureaucratic. The ideologically
postulated singularity of goal was thought to necessitate rigid
centralism which precluded any spontaneous action so typical
of young people. All activities not directly connected with
'constructive work' and 'politico-ideological education' were
viewed with suspicion and discouraged.

Corroded from within and increasingly pushed to the periphery of action and thought by the progress of reformist
thinking, the Youth Union had become a sick man by 1967.
If there was an organisation with clay feet in Czechoslovakia,
the ČSM must have been considered a front runner for the
title. The students, secondary and university, had long withdrawn their loyalty. Interest among young workers and farmers
had never been overwhelming. Only functionaries remained, a
top-heavy army of career organisers whose inner drive ranged
from zero to frustrated dogmatism. Take away the notion that
Youth Union endorsement is needed to get a youngster into a
senior secondary school and thence to the university – and
the whole empty pyramid was bound to collapse. This is
precisely what happened during the Prague Spring.

So ready to explode was the situation that the rebellion
reached the Youth Union Central Committee sooner than
many other organisations, notably in the middle of February
1968. The leadership tried to stall, but could not entirely
suppress the pent-up feelings. The first post-January session
(in České Budějovice) could not be satisfactorily wound up but
had to be adjourned and pressure from below continued. In
mid-March reformists among the Communist members of the
ČSM central apparat gained a majority and publicly disavowed
the old-guard leadership. No organisational form can simply
be imposed on the young people, they declared. The youth
should have an organisation which it has freely and democratically chosen. For this purpose an extraordinary Congress of the
union ought to be convened as soon as possible, the present
functionaries should be 'assessed' and victims of previous

persecution, including Boy Scouts, rehabilitated. Once more the die-hard Praesidium tried to save its skin and stated that it was not against discussing a reorganisation of the union. The Communist cell retorted by saying that an entirely new relationship between youth and society should be sought, rather than taking the concept of a unitary organisation, albeit 'reorganised', for granted. Two days later (on 21 March) the Youth Union Praesidium found the pressure too strong to bear and four of its members, including chairman Miroslav Zavadil, tendered their resignation.

In a way this was a remarkable encounter, not untypical of the Prague Spring. A Communist group in a formally non-Communist organisation took to arms on behalf of reform against the leaders of this same organisation who, however, were also members of the Party. It looked fratricidal, but in fact the Communist reformers were promoting a cause which had been long overdue and which was now open to contest as a result of a process which originated essentially outside the pyramid of power. Had it not been for January, the very people who castigated Zavadil and his colleagues for half-heartedness in March would have almost certainly gone on bowing to him.

Several courses were now open to the critics of the Youth Union. Some wanted to see separate and fully independent organisations emerge in its stead. Others agreed but suggested that it would be wrong to dissipate the strength arising from even the slightest degree of unity and co-ordination which could be put to good use in favour of reform. Yet others hoped that the ČSM could be salvaged in a reorganised form whereby autonomy would be granted to age and social groups within the traditional hierarchy of 'democratic centralism'. The latter alternative proved impracticable, if only because by then the very name of the Youth Union had become the epitome of dogmatism. In fact the three-day session of the Youth Union Central Committee from 25 to 27 March itself publicly proclaimed that it did not insist on preserving the union; it disbanded its secretariat and Praesidium and elected a temporary new leadership under Zbyněk Vokrouhlický. The first of the three alternatives, separate organisations without a centre, appeared too revolutionary; only students continued to uphold it. 'Federalisation', as the second solution became known, offered the reformists a welcome escape hatch: they could deal a *coup de grâce* to the ČSM and still retain an organisation which would preserve the appearance of unity. Moreover, it went without saying that the new Youth Federation would remain a member of the National Front and thus within the radius of direct Communist influence.[1]

And that is what happened, even though not before the Soviet invasion. The eight months of the Prague Spring were a gestation period from which ten youth organisations resulted. They were: the Union of University Students, the Czechoslovak Pioneers, the Boy Scouts, the Union of Military Youth, the Campers' Union (*Tábornická unie*, professing kinship with Woodcraft and other open-air activities), the Council of Agricultural and Village Youth, the Council of Secondary Students and Apprentices, the Union of Youth Clubs, the Union of Workers' Youth and the Union of Polish Youth.

The case of the Boy Scouts (*Junák*)[2] merits special attention. The movement had been popular in Czechoslovakia before and immediately after the War. In 1945 the Boy Scouts had 144,922 members[3] and were the second largest youth organisation after the Youth Union (SČM). With the strong post-war trend towards unity, *Junák* agreed in September 1945 to become a collective member of the SČM, retaining extensive

---

[1] Ota Šik recommended to the Party Central Committee session in March–April 1968 not to insist on the unity of the youth organisation, but suggested that a federative structure might be advantageous. '. . . every disintegration weakens the promotion of certain common interests; in this respect a united federation has its advantages for the younger generation', *Rudé právo*, 7 April 1968, p. 2. After some exploratory noises from sporadic groups of young members of the non-Communist political parties about the possibility of constituting youth branches affiliated to the Czech Socialists and the People's Party, the Communist Party Praesidium 'unequivocally recommended' at the end of May that an end should be put to this kind of thing. 'The young people must themselves make decisions in their organisations.' The Praesidium was in favour of a federation which would enhance young people's influence in the National Front. *Rudé právo*, 24 May 1968, p. 1.

[2] The term *Junák* is generic and includes Girl Guides.

[3] Membership rose to 177,589 in 1946 and dropped to 135,819 in 1947. See F. Morkes, 'Příspěvek k úloze a postavení junácké organisace v Československu po roce 1945', *Příspěvky k dějinám KSČ*, 4 (1967) pp. 565–82.

autonomy. As the subjugation of the Youth Union to the Communist Party grew considerably even before full seizure of power, there was increasing friction. A purge committee was appointed in February 1948 to oust 'reactionary elements' from the Boy Scouts organisation, and in April of the same year a *modus vivendi* seemed to have been found whereby *Junák* would become the children's organisation for seven–fifteen year-olds, subordinated to the SČM. The international Communist youth conference, held on Hungarian initiative in Budapest in August 1948, then castigated scouting as an agency of imperialism within the children's movement. The Young Pioneer type of organisation was proclaimed the only permissible one. From then on *Junák* was gradually contained and finally dispersed and banned as from 1 January 1951. A number of Boy Scout leaders were victimised and even sent to jail.

There was some confusion at the outset of the Prague Spring about the Boy Scouts: the Union for Co-operation with the Army (*Svazarm*) decided to form a Boy Scout branch, and the Central Pioneer Council invited old Scouts to join and co-operate with them. To genuine followers of the Boy Scout idea (there is some indication that certain bonds of emotion survived the twenty years of prohibition under the aegis of other organisations) both initiatives must have appeared false. In spite of warnings that twenty years of inaction rendered the old organisational forms obsolete, the Boy Scout movement was officially relaunched on 29 March 1968. The organisers described their programme as filling the gaps in the education of the young to a love of nature, morality, honesty and independence. They proclaimed their willingness to co-operate with other youth and children's organisations and to enter a federated structure. Almost overnight, without any full-time officials, the Boy Scout movement was reborn and began to pursue its non-political aims. (I have no data on its numerical strength, but first-hand experience testifies to the amazing vigour of the idea and its promoters.)

The first congress of Boy Scouts took place in November 1968, after the invasion. Antonín Sum was elected Chief Scout; he had been one of Jan Masaryk's private secretaries, sentenced to twenty-two years' imprisonment and rehabilitated in May

1968. In September 1970, *Junák* was once again forcibly merged with the Young Pioneers. A number of Boy Scout detachments were said not to have succumbed, but rather hidden away or even destroyed their organisation's property.[1]

Federalisation of the Youth Union, marking the official end of a centralised structure, was accomplished on 19–20 December 1968 at the constituent congress of what was to be the short-lived Association of Children's and Youth Organisations of the Czech Socialist Republic (*Sdružení dětských a mládežnických organisací ČSR*). The ten constituent organisations (see above) were given an assurance of full independence, with the National Council discharging only co-ordinating functions. The association did not regard itself as spokesman for the entire younger generation (a key concept in the pre-1968 ČSM) but only for its members. On this issue it clashed with L. Štrougal, speaking on behalf of the Czech Lands Communist Party Bureau, but neither side wished to pursue the controversy any further at that time. Time played into the hands of centralisers: the association was not matched by a counterpart in Slovakia, where post-invasion 'normalisation' delayed the holding of a constituent congress until 4 February 1969. Then the emerging organisation kept the old name Union of Slovak Youth (*Sväz slovenskej mládeže*) and its six new components were styled 'collective members'. They were the Pioneers, the Boy Scouts, the Union of Village and Urban Youth, the Union of Workers' Youth, the Union of Secondary Students and Apprentices, and the Union of Slovak Students. A federal council, embracing both the Czech and the Slovak organisations, only came into being in March 1969, shortly before the deposition of Dubček.

On 7 March 1969 some 250–300 persons congregated in an obscure hotel in Prague, refused entry to observers from the Youth Association and to journalists, and founded the Union of the Young (*Svaz mladých*), later (in September) renamed the Leninist Union of the Young. Circumstantial evidence suggests that the Party die-hards, especially those connected with Štrougal's Czech Party Bureau, encouraged and possibly even instigated this act which they saw as the emergence of a group around which the recentralised Youth Union of the future could

---

[1] *Jihočeská pravda*, 8 October 1970, quoted by Radio Free Europe *Situation Report*, 20 November 1970.

rally. By September 1970 counter-reformation had progressed sufficiently to allow the Leninist Union of the Young voluntarily to disband itself and form the hard core of the new Socialist Union of Youth of the Czechoslovak Socialist Republic – *Socialistický svaz mládeže ČSSR (SSM)*. (At that time the Leninist Union had 11,042 members. In Slovakia this union was founded in September 1969 and merged with the Socialist Union in April 1970. Its membership numbered 8,000.)[1] The leaders of the old-new SSM formulated the basic tenets of their organisation as active support for Communist Party policies, confidence in the Communist Party, advocacy of Marxism–Leninism, especially its teaching on the class struggle, promotion of proletarian internationalism and socialist patriotism, especially love for the USSR, and regulation of the relations between society and youth.[2] The wheel thus turned full circle, and the youth organisation was back to square one, in its pre-reform stage.

STUDENTS

Students have the dual nature of a group which can be subsumed both under 'youth' and 'intelligentsia'. On both counts they inclined towards reform. In 1967–8 university students numbered 95,872 Czechoslovak daytime, 3,464 foreign daytime and 38,161 extra-mural. (For comparison, the 1957–8 figures were 52,568, 1,414 and 23,773. University staffs included 3,361 professors and associate professors, and 12,258 other teaching personnel in 1967–8, as against 1,633 and 6,940 in 1957–8).[3] This represented a sizeable community; young, concentrated in several urban centres which were politically important, committed to freedom of research and speech, traditionally affected by the democratic Czech way of pursuing scholarship, and close to such motivating factors of reform as social science, literature, art and technical and economic progress.

Some figures may help illustrate the conditions pertinent to

---

[1] Radio Free Europe *Situation Report*, 20 November 1970.

[2] J. Varholík and O. Čmolík, 'Jaká bude mládež-takový bude stát', *Nová mysl*, 6 (1970) pp. 787–97.

[3] *Statistická ročenka ČSSR 1969* (Prague, SNTL, 1970) p. 483.

the student community. The following table shows the division of the community by specialisation in 1967–8 (only Czechoslovak daytime students are included):[1]

Natural sciences	3,572	Civil Engineering	7,346
Mining and geology	784	Transport and	
Metallurgy	1,169	communications	2,166
Engineering	12,087	Agriculture and forestry	11,094
Electrical		Economics and	
engineering	8,421	management	5,268
Chemistry	3,574	Health (medicine)	12,613
Food technology	593	Social sciences	4,978
Consumer goods		Education (teaching)	19,472
industry	1,387	Arts	1,348

The data, which do not include students of establishments administered by the Ministry of Defence and the Communist Party, neither students of theology, show a natural bias towards science and technology; the other three main groups of specialisation are teachers' training, social science (including economics) and art, and medicine.

Thirty-five institutes of higher learning were in existence in 1968. They included ten technical institutes, seven humanities, two economics, four agricultural, six arts (i.e. music, theatre, film, television, fine art, applied art), and six theological. As far as territorial deployment was concerned, Prague was by far the largest concentration with 27,624 students, followed by Bratislava with 18,099, and Brno and other Southern Moravian centres with 15,029. The next group included Eastern Slovakia (Košice, Prešov), Northern Moravia (Olomouc, Ostrava), Western Slovakia (Žilina, Nitra) and Central Slovakia (Banská Bystrica), each with 5,500 to 6,600 students. Then came Western Bohemia (Pilsen), Eastern (Pardubice, Hradec Králové) and Northern (Ústí, Liberec) with 2,400–2,700 students each, and Southern Bohemia (České Budějovice) with 1,700.[2]

The social origin of students, a highly important factor in any Communist society, is not easy to ascertain. One writer produced the following data, unfortunately ending with 1963–4:[3]

[1] Ibid., p. 488.   [2] Ibid., pp. 484–7, and p. 482.
[3] M. Chlupáč, 'Student a jeho výchozí sociální pozice', *Nová mysl*, 12 (1966).

School-year	Workers' families	Farmers' families	Others
1949–50	27·6	9·9	62·5
1950–1	34·4	9·7	55·9
1951–2	31·6	10·1	58·3
1954–5	28·1	8·9	63·0
1955–6	29·1	13·4	57·5
1957–8	34·4	12·6	53·0
1960–1	34·5	9·0	56·5
1963–4	37·9	8·3	53·8

Dr J. Hájek, when still Minister of Education, said that 39 per cent of students came from working-class backgrounds in 1967–8. He also mentioned the fact that 60 per cent of all students were accommodated in halls of residence (as against the usual 20–30 per cent in the Western countries),[1] which is a

[1] *Literární noviny*, 20 January 1968, p. 1. The Communist seizure of power in 1948 affected the social and political composition of the student community; many fled abroad while others were summarily dismissed. Nevertheless, the Party was not satisfied. Rudolf Slánský said in November 1948: 'We shall mercilessly purge secondary schools and universities of reactionary students and see to it that the overwhelming majority of students come from working-class families.' His pronouncement foreshadowed large-scale purges in 1949 when quotas of students to be expelled were assigned to the individual faculties in advance. Some data, long treated as secret, are now available. They concern universities only in Prague, where 7,565 students, or 28·1 per cent of the total, were dismissed. It seems pertinent to put the following figures on record:

Faculty	No. of students	No. of expelled	Did not report for interview
Law	3,330	1,151	350
Medicine	4,440	751	205
Philosophy	3,610	439	495
Natural sciences	1,710	159	107
Pedagogy	691	68	19
Pharmacology	351	68	10
Engineering	2,945	696	62
Civil engineering	747	154	50
Chemistry	1,703	293	25
Agriculture	1,283	424	50
Political science	1,393	507	220
Economics	3,037	783	706
Applied art	603	46	7
Arts	148	10	6
Fine Art	318	27	18

See J. Hanzal, 'Studijní prověrky na vysokých školách', *Dějiny a současnost,*

useful indication of the degree of concentration, so conducive to group action.

As far as Party membership is concerned, we have data for Prague students only; the percentage of Communist students steadily decreased from 11 per cent in 1958, 10 per cent in 1960 and 8·2 per cent in 1963 to 5·2 per cent in 1967.[1]

Although political discontent among the students found its way into such sporadic public occasions as the May Festivities (*Majáles*) in 1956 and spontaneous May Day gatherings in the late 1950s and early 1960s, the butt of their dissatisfaction was for a relatively long time directed against the curtailment of academic freedom and the general incompetence of educational administration. Targets of criticism included the practice of *libri prohibiti*, frequent reorganisations of university curricula, poor conditions in hostels and canteens, shortage of teaching and learning aids, rigidity of study regulations and examination procedures, absence of self-government in student establishments, etc. No positive formulation of a student programme is known to have been attempted until 1964.[2] Even so, after the tumultuous debates in the wake of Khrushchev's denunciation of Stalin in 1956, the Party leadership viewed the student community with uneasiness and suspicion. District committees of the Party which had a university on their territory were repeatedly instructed to look after it with greater vigilance and regularity. More easily said than done; the Party secretariats were largely staffed with functionaries who did not possess the requisite qualifications for high-level ideological surveillance. That is why special University Committees of the Communist Party, and subsequently the Youth Union, were founded in Prague, Brno and Bratislava in 1963. Responsibility for Party supervision was taken away from the regular apparat (at district level) and entrusted to the new bodies in which it was hoped to concentrate the necessary brainpower. As it turned out, this reorganisation eventually worked the other way. By

---

6 (1969) p. 30. (Students not reporting for interviews automatically disqualified themselves and were as good as expelled.)

[1] F. Povolný, 'Studenti a polednový vývoj, *Nová mysl*, 4 (1969).

[2] The article 'Strana a my' (The Party and Us) in *Buchar* (1964) is generally considered the first argued presentation of the students' political commitment to have been published in the context of the reform movement.

the mid-1960s the degree of change-orientation in the intellectual community had gathered enough strength to influence the students. In their turn, they were gradually able to influence the Party Committees which had been originally set up to bring them to heel. The independence of student action was facilitated rather than impaired by the existence of the special University Committees. An alliance between groups of reform-minded students and the Party Committees developed into an influential lobby connected with the power-wielding section of the Party apparat.

Several surveys conducted in the first half of the 1960s clearly indicated that apathy and indifference, arising from innumerable frustrations, characterised student attitudes to public participation.[1] The first signs of a change appeared in 1964 among a group of students of the Engineering Faculty of the Prague Technical University (ČVUT) who were publishing the paper *Buchar*. Not much later they were joined by similar groups from the Faculty of Nuclear Physics, and the Philosophical, Law and Natural Science Faculties of Charles University. The rallying cry was the demand for student autonomy, i.e. extrication from the constraining organisational clichés of the Youth Union and from Party tutelage. Academic Councils of Students (ARS – *Akademická rada studentů*) emerged at some faculties as the first attempt at by-passing the Youth Union hierarchy. Sufficient pressure was generated to make the Youth Union University Council convoke the first national conference of university students in December 1965. There the students of engineering presented for debate the framework of a new student organisation based on the federalisation of the Youth Union (on socio-economic, age-division and group interest lines). As a member of this federation, the student community would enjoy sufficient autonomy to ask for representation in local government. It would also claim for itself the right to criticise the government and to conduct a dialogue with the holders of political power. The defenders of the

[1] Some of these surveys were described by Z. Raiman, 'Vysokoškolská mládež ve světle jedné ankety', *Nová mysl*, 9 (1965), F. Povolný, 'Studenti a polednový vývoj', *Nová mysl*, 4 (1969) and A. Matějovský, 'Studentské hnutí v ČSSR-mýtus nebo skutečnost?', *Politika*, 4 (1969).

status quo in the Party and the Youth Union parried this attempt which, nonetheless, became immensely popular among the student rank and file. The authorities grew more and more apprehensive and took advantage of the venting of discontent at the 1966 *Majáles* Festivities to prohibit another student conference. At the same time dissident student spokesmen were dispersed, some sent down and conscripted, others disciplined. Independence of the student organisation and the related issue of the federalisation of the Youth Union were declared out of the question.

The Fifth Youth Union Congress in May 1967 offered another opportunity for the federalisation issue to be publicly discussed, and a number of students hoped to win over other delegates. Nevertheless, a Youth Union congress proved not to be a suitable forum for genuine deliberation on key issues, and the proposal to relax the union's centralism was predictably turned down. The students felt that they had done everything they could to achieve the coveted autonomy while still remaining within the Youth Union; from then on they began to speak up for an entirely separate organisation. Things moved fast in 1967. The alliance between students, writers and social scientists grew stronger under the impact of the Israeli–Arab war and the Writers' Congress. By autumn the students were in the front ranks of the reformist community (having covered the road from indifference to militancy in two years) and it became clear to many that a single spark could now ignite the explosive charge.

After a long time of preference on both sides for talk and the printed word, the clash between the police and students on 31 October 1967 brought the flow of events to boiling point. What happened is by now common knowledge: students from the Strahov dormitory in Prague protested against repeated breakdowns in the electricity supply, marched past the Castle with lit candles, chanted 'We Want Light', and ran into strong police detachments hastily summoned by security and Party officials scared stiff lest the demonstration called for political, rather than actual, illumination and aware that the Party Central Committee was by chance meeting at that very time in the Castle. The police brutally drove the demonstrators back to where they had come from and even invaded their dormitory. Vicious as the police behaviour undoubtedly was, the significance lay elsewhere than in the amount of physical violence. For an absolute majority of the students this clash represented a final rift with the authorities, a kind of climax to all the striving for a greater say in their own affairs. Many students felt that this was almost war, and they could not see themselves retreating, just as the writers could not after their Congress. For a while they endowed the Strahov Dormitory Committee (KRAS – *Kolejní rada Strahov*) with supreme powers of representation, but the Party and Youth Union University Committees soon joined the students and support was forthcoming from the cultural community, freshly mutilated as it was by the expropriation of *Literární noviny* and reprisals against several writers.

When the Prague Spring began, the students had already put all their cards on the table. They would want to have a separate organisation. They would support the reform movement and, indeed, spearhead its endeavour for freedom of action and thought. They would claim for themselves the right to have a say in public matters.

It was definitely the parting of the ways for the students and the Youth Union: Academic Student Councils (ARS) were introduced throughout the community as early as January 1968, and the students set up their independent Union (SVS – *Svaz vysokoškolských studentů Čech a Moravy*) on 22–3 March in Brno. The preparatory committee worked out draft statutes, an organisational structure and a programme. According to them, the faculty would be the basic organisational unit. The University Centres in the main towns would form the second tier and the structure would be topped by a Student Parliament, i.e. a gathering of delegates from all faculties. The programme included the following: promotion of humanitarian aims 'as laid down by socialism', advocacy of the social, cultural and professional interests of the student community, representation of the community at home and abroad, enhancement of its political and social prestige, restoration of the concept of 'academic honour' and co-operation with Slovak students and other youth groups.

There was some opposition to complete separation. A number of students (and others) suggested that membership of a united (if not unitary) organisation of the younger generation would give the students a greater say in public matters. The impact of their attitudes and action might be dissipated if they formed an exclusive organisation. Dubček touched on this problem when addressing the municipal Communist conference in Prague on 26 April: '. . . the more united and diligent the youth organisation is, the more effective it can become as a political force which must be taken into account . . .'[1] At the same time he thought the students would have to decide this issue themselves; no imposition of official views would be attempted. Nevertheless, throughout the Prague Spring the students remained outside the Youth Union (to the disintegration of which they had contributed a lion's share) and even outside the National Front. They said they would like to wait and see whether the new concept of the National Front worked before joining. It must be noted that the new Students' Union did not secure official registration (i.e. government sanction required by law) until September 1968[2] and that its activity was consequently supposed not to go beyond the preparations for its proper establishment.

The range of students action was fairly diverse. Prospective university entrants from Brno demanded the abolition of admission interviews, the *numerus clausus* and the 'cadre references'. The Minister of Education (V. Kadlec) regretted that this was not possible because the universities were short of places, but promised that the faculties would be free to conduct interviews as they pleased and dispense with them where possible. Moravian students and scholars pressed for the reopening of the Faculty of Law in Brno. Students of the Faculty of Philosophy in Prague wrote a letter of solidarity to Polish students on 12 March after the Warsaw demonstrations, but let it be known that no public protest meetings against the treatment of their Polish colleagues were intended in view of the delicate Czechoslovak situation. Support was given to the

---

[1] *Rudé právo*, 27 April 1968, p. 2.

[2] Two 1970 sources say that registration was granted to the reformist students' union after the 'personal intervention' of the then Party Secretary Zdeněk Mlynář. See Josef Ondrouch, 'K vývoji studentského hnutí v ČSSR', *Tvorba*, 42 (1970) and editorial articles (possibly also written by Ondrouch) in *Předvoj*, 4 and 11 June 1970.

invitation from Charles University to Polish scholars, victimised at home, to come and work in Czechoslovakia. Some students suggested that the invitation ought to be extended to Polish students as well. Peaceful demonstrations in support of Dubček and the new policy spontaneously erupted in mid-March, prior to Novotný's resignation from the presidency, in Prešov, Nitra, Banská Bystrica, České Budějovice, Košice and Olomouc. Several protest marches against the war in Vietnam took place, e.g. from Košice ('a drive'), Strakonice, Brno, Ústí and Prague. (Early in the year these protests offered a welcome opportunity to the Party leadership to counterbalance the stream of student criticism directed against internal grievances. On 9 February some forty marchers from Brno and elsewhere first demonstrated in front of the U.S. Embassy, then got a friendly reception at the North Vietnamese Embassy, went to call on Novotný at the Prague Castle and finally accepted badges and diplomas from the Youth Union and the International Union of Students.) In this connection one should note another remarkable document of the Prague Spring, namely an announcement by the Ministry of Education of 25 April. It stated that the Ministry had learned that on 26–7 April American students would stage a strike against the Vietnam war, racialism and drafting. 'The Ministry is convinced that the Czech and Slovak students too will show solidarity with the demands of the American students, and that they too will stage a protest strike on the above-mentioned days to support their action.' Having done this, the Czechoslovak students were then asked to write to the Student Mobilisation Committee, National Office, 17 East 17th St, New York.[1] On the day when the Ministry was drafting this unique exhortation, some thirty Prague students were reported to have demonstrated in front of the Foreign Ministry against the delivery of Czechoslovak arms to the Nigerian Federal Government 'which is waging a genocidal war against the nation of the Ibos'. (Czechoslovak aid to Federal Nigeria became increasingly unpopular in 1968 and public opinion in fact forced the government to discontinue supplying arms to Lagos.)

Of special significance was the effort to bring about a worker–student alliance. All reformers, from the extremely radical to

[1] *Rudé právo*, 25 April 1968, p. 6.

the extremely moderate, considered a joint stand and concerted action by the workers and intellectuals a crucial concept of the Prague Spring. While a full-bodied coalition of this nature did not come into being before the invasion, there was nothing to suggest that it would be impossible to achieve in the long run, even if not in an ideal form. The fact that the students repeatedly addressed themselves to workers teams (or the working class in general) and that they initiated frequent visits to the shopfloor, indicated a high measure of social democratic awareness among the students and, at the same time, an absence of élitist theories in the crude political sense. Some documents merit quotation.

'We are very disquieted by assertions that students seek to revert Czechoslovakia to capitalism, unemployment, hunger and poverty. We particularly regret the fact that sometimes it is the workers who say so. This could lead to a serious misunderstanding and we are afraid that some people, who are concerned about their own private status rather than the destiny of our country, could deliberately isolate the workers from the students and, by provoking such misunderstanding, distract attention from problems which call for solution if the life of workers, farmers and all the other citizens of this country is to be improved.' (Academic Council of Students of the Faculty of Philosophy, Charles University, 12 March 1968.)[1]

'A progressive policy . . . cannot be accomplished as long as the working class does not accept it as its own. We believe that the workers will repudiate the false "friends of the people" who insinuate themselves into their favour, and that they will reject a biased approach towards the intelligentsia.' (University conference of the Communist Party, Prague, 15–16 March 1968.)[2]

'We appeal to workers, co-operative farmers and university students and staffs to join forces in formulating our common aims . . . Comrades from Party committees in factories, delegate members of your organisations to plenary sessions at the universities! Comrades from the Party University Committee and the Faculty Committees, let the Borough and District Committees in your place of activity have lists of your comrades

[1] *Rudé právo*, 13 March 1968, p. 1.
[2] *Rudé právo*, 16 March 1968, p. 2.

who will be at the disposal of factory organisations! A solid
unity of workers, Communist intellectuals and agricultural
workers is a safeguard which will make Czechoslovakia one of
the first countries to accomplish the age-old dream of mankind –
a socially just and economically efficient order.' (Communists
from the Faculty of Natural Sciences, Charles University,
15 March 1968.)[1]

Some contacts were clumsy and ineffective. More students
than workers would turn up at a factory meeting. Confusion
would prevail after the awkward attempts of students to
'instruct' workers ran into a barrier of uneasy silence or
ridicule.[2] But on the whole the endeavour was undoubtedly
honest. After the students and the workers offered joint and
separate resistance to the invasion, the way seemed to have been
paved for unity in opposition to capitulation. The three-day
sit-in students' strike (18–20 November 1968) enjoyed the
support of many factories who sent money, food and words of
encouragement. On 19 December 1968 the Students' Union
and the Trade Union of Metalworkers concluded an agreement
of co-operation which must be considered a highlight of the
rapprochement between workers and intellectuals. In it both
parties rejected the policy of retreat before external pressure.
Protesting against a renewed concentration of power, they
demanded the convocation of a Czech Communist Party
Congress, repudiated attacks on the cultural community and
on press freedom and reiterated the need for an economic
reform and enterprise independence. A team of workers'
delegates and economists should be called together to work out
an economic policy to suit Czechoslovak conditions. Both
parties insisted on an immediate restoration of sovereignty
and the withdrawal of foreign troops. New elections should be
held as soon as possible and principles of human rights should
be incorporated into the country's Constitution. This was the
time, the agreement stated, to establish the widest possible
popular front. The two parties would regularly exchange
delegations and inform each other of their views and approaches
to new problems. They would strive for broad publicity,

[1] Ibid.
[2] For a sarcastic description of one such abortive meeting see Vladimír
Blažek's feuilleton in *Literární listy*, 4 April 1968, p. 13.

enlarge worker–student personal contacts and support the fulfilment of their demands by emphatic action.[1]

Under the circumstances the agreement could no longer be a positive step in pushing forward the reform. Neither could Jan Palach's self-immolation on 16 January 1969. Both tried to arrest the retreat from certain principles of the Prague Spring and to uplift the morale which had begun to sag. Dubček had included the *Student* weekly among the anti-Communist forces in his speech at the November 1969 Party Central Committee plenum. The students tried to publish another paper, *Studentské listy* (only ten numbers of which were issued between 25 February and 6 May 1969), and they voted not to join the National Front in April 1969 after Husák's ascendance. Then a group of trainees from the Military Political Academy formed an embryonic organisation willing to accept the new government's conditions and Husák's policies. This was all the authorities needed to let the axe fall, and on 20 June 1969 the Czech Ministry of the Interior dissolved the Union of University Students of Bohemia and Moravia on the grounds that it had engaged in politics while remaining outside the National Front. The union initiated by the military students ultimately merged with the Socialist Union of Youth in October 1970 and thus in fact ceased to exist. Once again the students found themselves without an organisation and slipping into indifference. The Czechoslovak counter-reformation tends to have a very unpleasant – and sad – look of *déjà vu*.

[1] *Dějiny a současnost*, 1 (1969), pp. 45–6.

CHAPTER FIVE

Nationalities

In a sense the entire Slovak nation comprised a political lobby. The feeling among Slovaks that they were being at once wronged, exploited and offended by the Czechs, even under Communism, grew acute long before 1968. Their aspiration was for greater autonomy in Slovak matters and for a greater say in the running of the country as a whole, a typical striving of a political group combining protection of its members' rights and promotion of a cause. Nonetheless, no specifically Slovak political party or organisation devoted to gaining a greater share of political power for its members came into being or was even contemplated. There was the Slovak Communist Party (discounting as we must the two minute non-Communist parties), but its subscription to 'democratic centralism' for long made it accept the curiously anomalous 'asymmetry' of the existing arrangements. The evolution of Slovak Communist thought from unitary statehood to federation has been extensively described elsewhere[1] and will be only briefly summarised here. As far as the place of federalisation within the reform was concerned, it is useful to reiterate the self-evident proposition which the majority of the Slovak political representation failed to accept, thus causing the official Slovak contribution to reform to lag behind the Czech.

The 'reform' (democratisation, renaissance, liberalisation, progress) was a matter of form and contents, while 'federalisation' was by definition a matter of form only.

While practically the entire Slovak community, including such political representation as it enjoyed, did not find it at all difficult to rally behind the federative idea, only a few Slovak groups and individuals went on record as saying that the

[1] See for example William Shawcross, *Dubček* (Weidenfeld and Nicolson, 1970).

substance of the system required an overhaul. And even many of those professing loyalty to reform, G. Husák being a prominent spokesman of this group, found it easy to switch roles not much later. No roll-call was taken and the strength of the various group attitudes is difficult to gauge; the course of events serves as the only yardstick and even this was distorted by the post-invasion anomaly. In broad terms, three Slovak standpoints seemed to crystallise.

First, there was the rapidly dwindling group of what we may call the 'Communist Unitarians', i.e. followers of lop-sided Czechoslovakianism or full government from Prague. Michal Chudík, chairman of the Slovak National Council and Party Praesidium member from 1963 and 1964 respectively to March–April 1968, would probably be cited by most observers as typifying this group. Some of the more discredited provincial henchmen, such as Rudolf Cvik, the Banská Bystrica Party Regional Secretary, would also easily qualify. On the whole, however, this was a dying breed in 1968, mainly because it was not difficult to switch loyalty from monocentric centralism to federation understood as bicentric centralism.

Neither was it apparently hard to switch away from federation in 1970 when the powers-that-be so decreed. By the same token the second, and largest, attitudinal Slovak group was heterogeneous; we may call it the 'Communist Federalists'. In it, avid centralisers of yesterday rubbed shoulders with genuine believers in federation as the one and only cure of the Slovak nation's malaise; passionate accusers, who charged the Czechs with a wide spectrum of anti-Slovak crimes, ranging from condescension and indifference to genocide, mixed with level-headed (and less so) economists trying to work out the best way of sharing out the common pie; emotional idealists who spent long hours discussing the details of a Slovak-only flag, anthem and State insignia mingled with shrewd politicians stubbornly pushing forward the principle of parity representation (and voting) in all federal agencies. No new organisation is known to have been set up in an attempt to unite or at least co-ordinate all these diverse and variable groups. Some *ad hoc* commissions of economists and jurists were in action, but they were rather consultative panels than political organisations.

The third group could be called the 'Reformist Federalists'

and largely recruited its followers from among the Slovak intellectuals. While agreeing that after the demonstrable failure of twenty years of 'asymmetry' a federative arrangement was the most likely to give the Slovak nation a sense of self-fulfilment, they were aware of its most dangerous pitfall: it was only a part of the overall political reform, not tantamount to reform in itself.

The Slovak Film and Television Artists' Union issued a statement on 29 March 1968: 'Both the Czech and the Slovak cultural communities feel that Slovakia's contribution to the current movement in this country is less than full.' The impression had arisen that the desire for federalisation was the only thing the Slovaks were aiming for. 'A kind of sentimental national conciliation has been achieved [in Slovakia] under the banner of federalisation. We declare that we are not at all indifferent to what measure of democracy will obtain under a federal arrangement. We reject the so-called minimum programme, i.e. federation without consistent democratisation. Quite the contrary, we maintain that federalisation is but a part of the principal objective, i.e. consistent democratisation.[1]

A day later the Slovak Economic Society stated: 'We are disquieted by the democratisation process in Slovakia being one-sidedly geared toward federation, without a clear-cut definition of the economic and political contents of the new statutory arrangement.'[2]

On 8 April 1968 a meeting of the 'young Slovak intelligentsia' convened in Bratislava on the initiative of the youth daily *Smena* and an 'eight-member working group' of young journalists, writers, artists and scholars. (Anton Hykisch, the writer, was the *spiritus movens*. The gathering agreed to launch a Club of Young Slovak Intelligentsia which, however, did not leave any marked imprint on the flow of events to come.) Many debaters were reported to be disconcerted by the uneven amount of energy expended on federalisation on the one hand and democratisation on the other.[3]

Most of the *Kultúrny Život* staff editors and writers thought it necessary to break off the alliance they had concluded in the

[1] *Rudé právo*, 30 March 1968, p. 6.
[2] *Rudé právo*, 31 March 1968, p. 11.
[3] *Rudé právo*, 9 April 1968, p. 6.

mid-1960s with federalists-only against Novotný. Pavol Števček wrote on 12 July that it was 'historically high time' for the Slovak political representation to crystallise and formulate its 'national programme', i.e. the aims which the Slovak nation would pursue after federalisation.[1] The resulting rift in the Slovak writers' community was described earlier in this book. This reform-oriented stream included Alexander Dubček and some other Slovak politicians.[2] Many, however, professed to follow the same line only to discard it lightly under conservative pressure of foreign and home provenance.[3]

The 'Communist Federalists' gained the upper hand in the wake of the Soviet invasion, as they probably would have done even without it. It seemed inevitable that political reform in Slovakia should gather strength only after federalisation. Husák and his supporters held the most influential posts in, and close to, the centre of power, and managed to make their concept of federation all-pervasive. In its primitive fashion, this concept appealed to the largest part of the Slovak nation, the Slovak 'populus', in whose midst the hurt feelings of genuine national grievance and desire for self-assertion went hand in hand with secessionist inclinations. Ideologically speaking, 'Communist Federalism' was, of course, easier to justify than 'Reformist Federalism': the federative arrangement, it could be argued, was but a new framework whose contents would remain the same, notably Communist. But Moscow's suspicion of everything that deviated from the Soviet Establishment, albeit in form only, proved insurmountable even for conservative Federalists. At the time of writing, the Federation – proclaimed on 28 October 1968 – remains little more than a useful training ground for indigenous administrators.

Matica slovenská, a Slovak national educative society, when

[1] *Kultúrny život*, 12 July 1968, p. 1.

[2] A statement by the Party Central Control and Auditing Commission, published in *Rudé právo* on 3 February 1971, p. 3, lists fifty-seven members of the so-called counter-revolutionary 'second centre', of whom ten are Slovaks. This is a rather mysterious list (Dubček is not in, but Černík and Smrkovský are) and the order of the names appears haphazard. The Slovaks are: S. Falťan, B. Graca, A. Ťažký, J. Turček, J. Zrak, V. Pavlenda, E. Löbl, E. Friš, H. Kočtúch and P. Števček.

[3] For example Ondrej Klokoč, Peter Colotka, Matej Lúčan, not to mention Laco Novomeský, Vojtech Mihálik, Miroslav Válek and others.

founded in 1863, aimed at 'uniting all lovers of the Slovak nation and life so that they may work together to raise the level of Slovak education and, in this way, the material well-being of the Slovak nation'. Under the conditions of Magyar rule its associative mission became tremendously popular and soon the nation projected into it all the cultural and political values which the people professed to cherish and strive for. The mushrooming communities of Slovak emigrés found the *Matica's* national commitment a stimulus to the preservation of their contact with the country they had left in search of employment. By 1949 the *Matica* had 1,200 local branches and 100,000 members all over Slovakia.[1] Its activity developed in four directions: research (mainly ethnical and historical); popular education; publishing; and contact with Slovaks residing abroad. The post-1948 *Gleichschaltung* of societal institutionalisation affected the *Matica* badly: research was taken away from it and allocated to State institutions (as opposed to the voluntary and democratic *Matica*) or abandoned altogether; publishing was curtailed; and local branches gradually dissolved. On 3 July 1953 the Slovak Commissioner for the Interior even decreed a total disbandment of the *Matica* but the ordinance was permitted to lapse, although activity remained close to nil. On 27 April 1954 the Slovak National Council put the *Matica* on a legitimate footing again, but not before pruning it still further: it was to be nothing more than a National Library with a limited amount of research in librarianship. (An official agency, *Československý ústav zahraniční*, subordinated to the Ministry for Foreign Affairs, took over all matters relating to contact with Czech and Slovak émigrés. This was met with suspicion by many expatriate Slovaks who reciprocated by setting up a *Matica slovenská* in America in 1962.) Degradation turned out to be conducive to the emergence of legends and a large part of the Slovak public identified their national plight with that of the *Matica*. Novotný could do no worse than when he offended the *Matica* during his visit to Turčanský Svätý Martin in the stormy year of 1967.[2] Thus it was not without political connotations when this essentially non-political institution sought to

---

[1] *Rudé právo*, 14 April 1968, p. 4.

[2] The episode is described in Shawcross, op. cit., pp. 126–7.

re-establish itself early in 1968. Nevertheless, not one of the proponents of the *Matica* cause (to my knowledge) intimated that a political lobby was intended. The *Matica* was to become 'a State institution of scholarship for the documentation of and research into Slovak national culture'[1] or, in other reformers' words, 'an ethnographic institute for research into Slovak national culture at home and abroad, in co-ordination with institutes of the Slovak Academy of Sciences'. In addition the *Matica* would hopefully 'associate friends of Slovak national culture and history' in a network of local branches.[2] Once again it would 'look after' the cultural life of expatriates. The *Matica* ceremoniously reconstituted itself on 10–11 August in the presence of President Svoboda. Invasion came ten days later.

One cannot help feeling, when looking at the development of Slovak aspirations in 1968, that they were largely motivated by national factors as opposed to the political reform sought by the Czechs. This is not meant to be disparaging. As practically everything, nationalism (used here in the non-pejorative sense) tends to become political in conditions of Communism and Slovak national dissension, which had especially crystallised after the inequitable Constitution of 1960, undoubtedly formed one of the factors which made the launching of an open reform movement possible. On the other hand, there was a certain historical and ideological incongruity between the Czech emphasis on political and economic changes and the Slovak preoccupation with national equity. In 1968 the Czechs were able to understand their nationalism more as a matter of content than form, notably as disentanglement from Soviet-type concepts and a return to Europeanism. Theirs was essentially a national philosophy, relying on a combination of the national heritage plus plans for social and democratic improvement. Kosík, Kundera and many others interpreted the Czech national predicament along these lines.[3] The Slovak version had to be much more rudimentary, and the

---

[1] *Rudé právo*, 14 April 1968, p. 4.

[2] *Rudé právo*, 21 April 1968, p. 3.

[3] See for example Karel Kosík, 'Naše nynější krize', *Literární listy*, Nos 7–12 (1968) and Milan Kundera, 'O nesamozřejmosti národa', in *IV. sjezd Svazu ceskoslovenských spisovatelů* (Prague, Čs. spisovatel, 1968) pp. 22–8

primary concern of reformers of all shades must have been with the institutional completion of the national self-realisation tendency which had begun in the nineteenth century, but was never brought to full fruition. Looking for a succinct description, we might call Czech nationalism 'political and philosophical' and Slovak 'institutional'. There is little point in damning the one and extolling the other. It is, however, easy to predict that the 'institutional' phase of Slovak nationalism, once accomplished, will be followed by roughly the same quest for conceptual transformation as that pursued by the Czechs in 1968.

It is perhaps paradoxical that of the two nations in Czechoslovakia the smaller and weaker one, the Slovaks, should be saddled with two minority problems of a considerably more explosive nature than the one which the Czechs had on their hands after the war. All four minorities in Czechoslovakia, the Hungarian, Ukrainian (Ruthenian), German and Polish, belong to the most recent type of minorities in Central and South-Eastern Europe which came into being some fifty years ago. They are border-land ethnic parts of important neighbouring nations. Three, excepting the Ukrainians, pertain to nations which have established their national States long ago. Thus the key question which must be posed if an inquiry into their political aspirations is to be attempted is whether they still comprise (and feel to comprise) only a segment of the neighbouring nation (or State) or whether they have already evolved into a separate ethnic entity. The events of 1968 offered a catalytic opportunity to provide an answer, especially because pent-up feelings were permitted to come into the open. The first thing that became obvious was that an identical description of all four was impossible. On the other hand, some general statements can safely be made. It seems that all the minorities in Czechoslovakia have passed into the intermediate stage between identification with their original nationality and acceptance of a self-fulfilling existence in the Czechoslovak community. They neither submit to full assimilation, nor do they yearn for a return to the 'homeland'. (The German case is somewhat equivocal although less than many would think.) They all appeared to harbour a dual sense of identification in 1968: they seemed to show preference for the

Czechoslovak social and economic system, but for their 'own' nations' language, culture and customs.

As the minority population is not scattered, the four mixed areas witness daily encounters of ethnically different groups. Except in relation to the Ukrainians (who were notoriously over-represented on the relevant Party and National Committees in Eastern Slovakia), political rule in the minority areas had been in the hands of the Slovaks or Czechs. The Hungarians had some influence in local government matters, but largely it was the cultural and educational sphere to which minority action remained relegated. (The Germans were for long a special case.) The three national societies (the Germans did not have one until 1968–9) were confined by statute to the pursuance of cultural enlightenment.

Statistical data on the numerical strength of the four minorities offer a widely discrepant picture, depending on their source. As it is not the purpose of this study to investigate the various claims to correct numerical representation, I shall quote official figures only and briefly point out the particularly gross deviations. The following table is in units of thousands.[1]

Nationality	1 March 1961	31 Dec. 1968	31 Dec. 1969	1961–9 (per cent)
Czech	9,070	9,301	9,317	+ 2·7
Slovak	3,836	4,236	4,275	+11·5
Ukrainian and Russian	55	59	60	+ 9·1
Polish	68	72	72	+ 5·9
Hungarian	534	565	569	+ 6·6
German	140	110	106	−24·3
Others and not given	43	46	46	+ 7·0

The Polish minority lives in two districts in north-eastern Moravia (Silesia); only one village has a Polish majority; the area had been ethnically unstable for centuries and it was always impossible to keep accurate records. To rely on what people themselves enter into census forms, which has been the official Communist policy, is notoriously misleading. This is, however, also true of other nationally mixed areas. A high-level

[1] *Demografie*, 2 (1970) p. 167.

Czechoslovak Communist Party report of August 1968 gave the number of Poles as 59,000.[1]

The same report spoke of 134,000 Germans, dispersed mainly over northern and western Bohemia;[2] twenty-one villages have more German than Czech inhabitants. A *Literární listy* writer put the number of Germans as high as 160,000.[3] Second generation assimilation does take place.

Hungarian minority spokesmen claimed over 700,000 compatriots in Czechoslovakia in 1968.[4] Political pressures obviously had affected census entries in 1946–7 (1946 in Slovakia, 1947 in the Czech Lands), 1950 and 1961. Over 450 villages in Southern Slovakia (451 according to one source,[5] 453 according to another[6]) had a Hungarian majority.

Discrepancies in the various estimates of the Ukrainian minority are the wildest, ranging from 58,000 to 1,400,000, and are too complicated to be gone into. Suffice it to say that Slovakisation, alternating pro- and anti-Sovietism and religion (Orthodoxy *v.* Greek Catholicism, to be mentioned later) have all been responsible for this fluidity. On a more sensible level, i.e. discounting the ridiculously high estimates, we discover a curious difference between official statistical evidence, which was running between 50,000 and 60,000 persons for many years, and the mention of 318,000 Ukrainians in the Party Praesidium report of 20 August 1968.[7] Hodnett and Potichnyj, who have done a detailed study of the subject, think that between 75,000 and 125,000 would probably be closest to the truth.[8] Ukrainian concentrations are to be found in two districts of Eastern Slovakia and Ukrainians constitute the majority in forty-five villages.

---

[1] 'Zpráva o současné politické situaci v ČSSR a podmínkách činnosti KSČ (srpen 1968)', *Rudé právo*, 2 July 1969, p. 10.

[2] Ibid.

[3] *Literární listy*, 1 August 1968, p. 2.

[4] *Uj szó*, 12 April 1968, quoted in RFE Czechoslovak Press Survey No. 2076, pp. 1–4.

[5] Juraj Zvara, 'Národnostné menšiny v etnickej štruktúre ČSSR', *Nová mysl*, 2 (1969).

[6] 'Zpráva o současné politické situaci . . .', p. 10.

[7] Ibid.

[8] G. Hodnett and P. J. Potichnyj, *The Ukraine and the Czechoslovak Crisis* (Canberra, Australian National University, 1970) pp. 31–2 and 136.

Taken together, minorities in pre-war Czechoslovakia represented 36 per cent of the population. By 1968 the percentage was down to 6 per cent, the substantial reduction having mainly been caused by large-scale emigration and the transfer of the Germans in 1945–6. In Slovakia the respective percentages were 24 per cent and 14 per cent.[1]

In addition, 369,000 Slovaks lived in the Czech Lands and 47,000 Czechs in Slovakia in 1968.[2] Such ethnic mixing led to demands for better cultural and educational facilities for the Slovaks who mainly came to find better-paid jobs in industry, notably in the Ostrava conurbation. Some complaints were also heard about the induced loss of national feeling among the Czech-based Slovaks who succumbed above all to linguistic assimilation. However, no substantial attempt to provide them with a political organisation was noted.

The post-1948 Communist régime did not understand the minorities as politico-ethnic entities and did not permit them a statutory constitution. Only the Ukrainians had their Ukrainian National Council (*Priashevshtina*) from 1945 to 1951–2. From then on, the Ukrainians, the Hungarians and the Poles had cultural organisations (actual dates of establishment varied and entailed different statutory stages) which were styled as follows: Cultural Union of the Ukrainian Working People (*Kulturny spilka ukrayinskykh trudyashchikh*), Cultural Union of the Hungarian Working People in Czechoslovakia (*Csehoslovákiai magyar dolgozók kultúregysülete*, CSEMADOK for short) and Polish Union for Culture and Public Education (*Polski zwiazek kulturalno-oswiatowy*). Their memberships in 1968 stood at 9,000, 40,000 and 20,000 respectively,[3] i.e. well below the actual strength of the minorities. They still claimed the right to speak on behalf of all minority inhabitants. With the growing strength of the reform-oriented community in the Czech and Slovak nations in the 1960s, the purely cultural nature of the minority organisations proved to be more and more elusive and the existing societies began to act as vicarious political pressure groups. The actual impact of their political desiderata is

[1] J. Zvara and J. Šindelka, 'Žijeme v jedné zemi', *Rudé právo*, 16 August 1968, p. 5.
[2] *Statistická ročenka ČSSR 1969* (Prague, SNTL, 1970) p. 87.
[3] *Hospodářsko-politická rukověť* (Prague, ČTK, 1968) pp. 1010–13.

difficult to measure, but the Party leadership must have been aware of the problem since it agreed to create a special inter-disciplinary commission before the thirteenth Congress (1966) to propose new legislation. The work of this commission was kept secret.

It did, however, produce a series of constructive suggestions: a nationality statute should be promulgated to give the minorities the status of politico-ethnic entities; the co-existence of nationalities in mixed areas should be regulated by law; a central body for minority problems should be set up; the cultural societies should have more rights and greater consultative powers; and further improvement in minority education should be pursued. (Czechoslovakia was the rare case of a country where minority schools offered all instruction in the respective minority language, with a relatively small part of the curricula devoted to the teaching of Slovak or Czech; this did not apply to the German minority.) Typically, the Novotný leadership backed out at the last moment, and the commission's conclusions were neither published nor indeed submitted to the thirteenth Congress.[1]

When the minority societies met to consider the 'new course' – in March 1968 at separate sessions – they based their deliberations and formulated their aims along much the same lines as the 1966 inter-disciplinary commission. Thus, for example, the CSEMADOK resolution called for political representation, an official statement setting right the wrongs of the past (forcible Slovakisation 1945–50), the establishment of minority agencies in the Slovak National Council and the National Assembly and of minority secretariats to be attached to the government and the Regional National Committees, improved representation on National Committees and in social organisations, and the administration of education by minority organisations. The Poles added demands for bilingualism on territory with a Polish minority and restitution of property (cultural premises, publishing houses, bookshops) formerly owned by Polish

---

[1] J. Zvara, 'Národnostné menšiny v etnickej štruktúre ČSSR', *Nová mysl*, 2 (1969). On the Hungarian minority from 1948 to 1954 see by the same author 'Mad'arská otázka v ČSR', *Příspěvky k dějinám KSČ*, 3 (1965) pp. 409–27. The book by J. Purgat, *Od Trianonu po Košice* (Bratislava, Epocha, 1970), deals with the Hungarian question from 1918 to 1944.

[2] *Rudé právo*, 16 August 1968, p. 5.

organisations.[1] The Ukrainians wanted the resignation of state and local officials responsible for injustices caused to the Ukrainian population.[2] All supported the policy of democratisation which, however, they mainly pledged to promote in terms of national freedom. To my knowledge there is no meaningful evidence of the minorities identifying themselves with the Soviet, Hungarian and Polish opposition to the Czechoslovak reforms. This is understandable: they were primarily seeking an enlargement of nationality rights, possibly with the eventual aim of political autonomy in mind, and these objectives coincided with the general trend of the Prague Spring. The leaderships of their 'original' countries, on the other hand, with a certain measure of exception in the case of Kadar's Hungary, stood for the same system of government which the minorities in Czechoslovakia saw as responsible for their pre-1968 grievances. (Admittedly, there is want of information on the undercurrents of the Polish minority movement. Hearsay reports from the time of the invasion speak of 'malicious' joy being expressed by some Poles in Czech Silesia who prophesied the annexation of the Těšín (Teschen, Cieszyn) area to Gomulka's Poland.)

On 14 August 1968 the three minority societies held a joint meeting in Bratislava, once again declared their support for democracy and 'factual and full' national equality and asked that the future Czechoslovak Constitution should recognise the minorities as constituent elements of the State.[3] After the invasion, together with the Law on Czech-Slovak Federation, the parliament passed a Nationality Act which gave the minorities 'full political and cultural rights' without, however, acknowledging the minority societies as their 'political and national' representation. Under this Act the Germans were granted a minority status for the first time since the war.

The Czechoslovak Germans merit separate attention. The main issues which they faced included official recognition, entailing such consequences as education, etc., emigration to West Germany and ageing. The Dubček leadership was prepared to grant them official recognition, realising that the

---

[1] 'Zpráva o současné politické situaci . . .', p. 10.
[2] *Rudé právo*, 20 March 1968, p. 2.
[3] *Rudé právo*, 15 August 1968, p. 2.

previous policy of pretending that a German minority did not exist was untenable anyway, let alone in the context of the Prague Spring. In practice this meant that a minority society, similar to the Hungarian, Polish and Ukrainian ones, would emerge and take over much of the agenda hitherto discharged by the so-called National Committee Commissions for Work with German Citizens, attached to local government agencies in the relevant areas.

Genuine active interest among the German population did not seem to be overwhelming. Thus we know about a meeting in the village of Jirkov in the Chomutov District at which 100 Germans (out of 360 in the village) deliberated over the setting up of a preparatory committee for such an organisation: 'We do not really know why we are founding this society. Only so that it may exist? But what is it to do? Organise an annual pilgrimage for our old folks? Aren't the existing societies good enough for this sort of thing? Never mind that they are Czech; they are ours as well.' No preparatory committee was set up in Jirkov. The village had only thirteen subscribers to the Prague-based *Volkszeitung*. More people would be interested in the 'foreign' German press and books, the visiting reporter was told, but only if they came from West Germany, Austria and Switzerland, not from the DDR.[1] On the other hand, a meeting in May of German citizens in Varnsdorf was reported eager to set up an organisation. The participants expressed full support for the 'democratisation process' and said that the Constitution should guarantee the right of the Germans to their 'own cultural life', similar to the arrangement pertaining to the Lusatian Serbs in East Germany. A German Cultural Institute ought to be established in Prague (!) and the Germans should be allowed to delegate their representative to the Central Trades Union Council. Also, a Nationality Committee with German representation should be attached to the National Assembly and the Slovak National Council.[2] Other demands, summed up in the Party Praesidium report of 20 August, called for German-language publishing, the transformation of *Volkszeitung* into a daily, the teaching of German as a mandatory subject in ethnically mixed areas and authority to use both the

[1] P. Pokorný, 'Zákon s mnoha přívlastky', *Reportér*, 41 (1968) pp. 10–11.
[2] *Rudé právo*, 24 May 1968, p. 3.

Czech and German languages at local government level in the relevant National Committees. Eventually – on 28 April 1969 – the Ministry of the Interior sanctioned a German minority organisation in accordance with the Nationality Act of October 1968. It is called the Cultural Association of Czechoslovak Citizens of German Origin (*Kulturní sdružení československých občanů německého původu*), its chairman is Herbert Panster, a forester and member of the Federal National Assembly, and the scope of its activity is confined to cultural enlightenment.

The German minority in Czechoslovakia has for some time been steadily diminished by emigration to West Germany and ageing. (The death-rate is higher than the birth-rate.[1] In addition, individual case histories known to the writer suggest a fading national awareness in the younger generation of Germans. No statistical evidence is available, but there are young people from established German families, bearing foolproof German names, who do not speak German.) Estimates of emigration, authorised as reunification or 'completion' of families and concerning mainly women, gave the number of German emigrés (approximately) 2,500 in 1965, 5,000 in 1966 and 10,000 in 1967, compared to the total emigration from Czechoslovakia of 5,676, 8,086 and 13,824 in the respective years. No figures for 1968 are available, except the preliminary total of 9,507 for the whole of the country, of which 4,210 were from Western Bohemia and 1,706 from Northern Bohemia (the 'German' areas); well above the numbers for the other regions.[2]

Unlike the German minority, which has not produced an intelligentsia after the war, the Ukrainians of Eastern Slovakia became known well beyond the Czechoslovak border precisely because of their scholarship and literary merit. The Ukrainian language and literature sections at the two Prešov faculties (of philosophy and education) of the P. J. Šafárik University in Košice, the Ukrainian section of the Czechoslovak (Slovak) Writers' Union, the four Ukrainian-language newsapers and periodicals with their supplements and the Radio Prešov

---

[1] *Rudé právo*, 6 February 1968, p. 5.

[2] For German emigration figures see *Rudé právo*, 6 February 1968, p. 5; for the total emigration from Czechoslovakia and the 1968 estimates see *Statistická ročenka ČSSR 1969* (Prague, SNTL, 1970) pp. 110–11.

Ukrainian broadcasting have all been actively promoting the Ukrainian cause and gave wholehearted support to the Prague Spring. These developments have been discussed at length in the monograph by Hodnett and Potichnyj.

Not long after January 1968 groups of villagers in the north-easternmost reaches of Eastern Slovakia started an action which soon reverberated throughout the Party and local government secretariats in the region and eventually had repercussions in Prague. They drove a number of Orthodox priests from their parish offices and took possession of church buildings which they proclaimed reconverted to the Greek Catholic (Uniate) faith. The origin of their move dated back to 1948–50. At that time the Uniates had 305,645 believers, 280 priests, seven monasteries and five nunneries and were the second largest church in Eastern Slovakia after the Roman Catholic.[1] The newly formed Communist régime then found itself locked in struggle with the Roman Catholic Church and the Vatican – to the point of contemplating the foundation of a special 'national' Catholic Church under the aegis of St Cyril and Methodius – and ordered the forcible dissolution of the Uniate Church. The campaign was abetted by the Moscow Metropolitan Nikolai[2] and termed the 'return to Orthodoxy'. When it met with local resistance, the police were sent in. Uniate monks, nuns and priests as well as Bishop Goidich were interned and some removed to work as farm hands in the Czech frontier areas, while newly recruited and crash-trained 'priests' and Orthodox *pops* were installed in the forcibly vacated offices. Greek Catholic believers were automatically listed as Orthodox. There was a remarkable measure of passive and not so passive resistance even after the coercive campaign had been brought to a seemingly successful end. Believers boycotted the imposed clergy: when an Orthodox priest arrived in the church, they left, and when he was gone, they held the service themselves, passing in defiant silence the part of the liturgic chant normally intoned by the priest. Funerals without a priest and secret baptisms were known to take place.[3]

[1] Jaroslava Radouchová, 'Návrat k pravoslaví', *Dějiny a současnost*, 1 (1969) pp. 29–31.
[2] Ibid.
[3] Ondrej R. Halata, 'Byla též akce P', *Literární listy*, 20 June 1968, pp. 6–7.

The whole affair had national connotations. The majority of the Uniates were in fact Slovaks and they opposed the pro-Ukrainian (and *ad implicite* pro-Soviet) overtones of the campaign. On the other hand, for Ukrainian Uniates to declare themselves Slovak meant more freedom to practise rites in hiding. Being a Slovak, one was supposed to be an atheist; being a Ukrainian, one was considered Orthodox.

One writer estimated that in 1968 some 200,000 Slovaks and Ukrainians still felt themselves of the Uniate faith.[1] In April 135 Greek Catholic priests met in Košice to set up an Action Committee and called for the annulment of the so-called Prešov Sobor of 28 April 1950, the legalisation of their Church and the restitution of its property.[2] Even before any official action, the authorities had to condone the resumption of Uniate religious services if they wished to preserve peace in the area. There were feverish negotiations with the Orthodox dignitaries and talks with Roman Catholic officials (who viewed the revival of Uniatism favourably), until the government decided on 13 June 1968 to give its blessing to the revival of Greek Catholicism. A touch of piquancy was added by the fact that this government session was chaired by Gustav Husák, who, as chairman of the Slovak Board of Commissioners and head of the Slovak Office for Church Affairs, had been partly responsible for paving the way for the suppression of the Uniates in 1949–50. (To do him justice, at least one writer says that he had reservations about the amount of coercion used in 1950.[3] In April 1950 the Slovak Office for Church Affairs was taken over by Laco Holdoš, although presumably not because of Husák's opposition to the campaign. Husák remained his own free agent until 6 February 1951.)

Gypsies in Czechoslovakia numbered over 220,000 in 1968 and their birth-rate was 20 per cent p.a. The majority (165,000) lived in Slovakia.[4] Detailed discussion is outside the scope of this study, but note should be taken of the successful attempt by a group of Gypsy intelligentsia from Bratislava and Brno to in-

[1] Ibid.
[2] *Rudé právo*, 12 April 1968, p. 5.
[3] J. Radouchová, op. cit., pp. 29–31.
[4] *Ročenka Reportéra 1968*, pp. 33–9, and RFE Situation Report, 29 April 1969.

itiate the foundation of a Gypsy Union (*Romàno Jekhetàniben*) on 27 April 1968. In a letter to the government they asked to be recognised as a separate nationality, to be allowed to have a permanent performing ensemble and to publish their own paper. Official policy towards the Gypsies has for long been vacillating between assimilation and forcible concentration in closely watched self-contained communities. Both the government and the public have been repeatedly embarrassed by the apparent absence of any suitable 'solution'.

A group of Moravian 'patriots' conducted a vigorous campaign in 1968 to have Moravia, possibly in conjunction with Silesia, recognised as a separate administrative entity and even as an autonomous 'Republic' equal to Bohemia and Slovakia. Campaigners for a tripartite federation came mainly from Southern Moravia in general and Brno in particular, and succeeded in winning the Brno Regional National Committee to their side.[1] Less unequivocal support to the idea was forthcoming from some regional officers of the Party. The movement could base its demands on genuine grievances which any small (and even not so small) country knows well: an excessive concentration of political decision-making and cultural facilities in the capital leaves the provinces thirsting for self-assertion. At the same time, the proponents of an autonomous Moravia did not hesitate to draw on history, emphasising that there had been Greater Moravia a thousand years ago and that the Moravian Margraviate existed throughout the Middle Ages (often playing the same part as, for example, Wales; while his father was still alive, Charles IV had the title of Moravian Margrave) and well into modern times, giving birth to a separate Moravian nation. Historians generally refused to take this argument seriously, although all reformers were united in their commitment to give greater powers to provincial bodies. This would probably have taken the form of abolishing Regional National Committees – which actually occurred in Slovakia, where they were reconstituted in 1970 – and introducing a three-tier administration, locality-district-centre. Not even some revived form of the traditional *Länder* (Bohemia,

---

[1] Of the 125 members of the Brno Regional National Committee ten were against and one vote was invalid when the motion on a tripartite federation was put to the vote. *Rudé právo*, 6 June 1968, p. 3.

Moravia, Silesia had territorial self-government in the past and later Moravia and Silesia were joined together) was considered entirely out of the question. The reorganisation would not, however, be carried out on national lines, and the Slovaks were saying that it was none of their business how the Czechs, including Moravians and Silesians, would arrange their internal affairs.

The most zealous core of Moravians formed a Society for Moravia and Silesia (*Společnost pro Moravu a Slezsko*) and claimed 140,000 members on 6 July and 250,000 on 17 August.[1] The figures must be considered fictitious, possibly the product of over-enthusiastic estimates, even though a sizeable following was evidently in the making. The society was campaigning for a plebiscite which the government was unwilling to concede. Many District National Committees in Moravia, especially in the Northern part, were less than convinced that a tripartite federation would not merely inflate the bureaucratic apparatus.

When the National Assembly got down to voting on the establishment of the Czech National Council – to be a partner of the Slovak National Council in the prospective bipartite federation – only one member from Moravia abstained. Nobody voted against.[2] Later the National Assembly Praesidium appealed for reason and self-discipline; it would be foolish to hastily create administrative patterns only to find them unworkable soon afterwards. The public should be patient and support an unhurried resolution of outstanding problems and just demands.[3]

The Silesians generally showed more circumspection and confined their promotion campaign to cultural and educational matters. They resolved to seek the re-establishment of the *Matice opavská* (an institution devoted to Silesian enlightenment, not unlike the *Matica slovenská*; first set up in 1877, it was disbanded by the Nazis in 1938, reformed in 1945 and once again liquidated in 1949) and to demand the rearrangement of district boundaries so as not to run counter to traditional Silesian ethnic distribution. The *Matice* would also campaign for at least one university in Silesia. The only Silesian institute

[1] *Rudé právo*, 7 July 1968, p. 1 and 18 August 1968, p. 2.
[2] *Rudé právo*, 25 June 1968, pp. 1, 3.
[3] *Rudé právo*, 9 August 1968, p. 1.

of higher learning, the Pedagogical Faculty in Opava, had been moved elsewhere by government decision in 1959.

A number of large municipalities showed interest in founding a Union of Cities (*Svaz měst*) to give weight to their requests for government assistance and to exchange views on administrative practices and technical problems. Eight such towns of secondary size and importance (after Prague, Brno, Bratislava, Ostrava, Pilsen and Košice) sent delegates to Žilina in May and demanded the speedy abolition of Regional National Committees which would give them greater powers and put them, as municipalities, on a par with the District National Committees.

All in all, the non-national 'territorial' movement within the reform can be summarised as an endeavour to achieve meaningful devolution of administrative powers from the centre to the provinces and localities. While impatient in some respects, especially where a search for territorial autonomy was combined with traditional 'patriotism', it coincided with the general commitment of 'central' reformers to democratisation. Speaking in broad terms, the result would probably have been a transformation of the National Committees from the position of officially decreed 'organs of State power' into genuine local government. The invasion, of course, put a stop to this.

CHAPTER SIX

Political Organisations

PARTIES

Unlimited political pluralism in Czechoslovakia died when the government of the day accepted the Munich Agreement of 1938. Since then, the emergence, existence and disappearance of political parties has been governed by other principles than simply the desire of groups of people to achieve political representation or promote political causes. Unlike the totalitarianism of the Occupation and the one-party Communism of post-1948, the overwhelming majority of the public appeared to welcome the arrangement which came into life from 1945 to 1948. The existing parties (Communist, Social Democratic, National Socialist, People's Party, Slovak Democratic Party and Freedom Party) struck up an alliance around a national programme and formed a coalition, termed National Front, to the exclusion of newcomers. The spectrum seemed wide enough to accommodate all the major groups and persuasions. The full seizure of power by the Communists in February 1948 cancelled this arrangement. The Social Democrats were merged with the Communists in June 1948. The Slovak Democratic Party virtually disintegrated and for all practical purposes ceased to exist. Its successor, the Party of Slovak Revival (*Strana slovenské obrody*), had little more than a ludicrous name and a handful of utterly uninfluential functionaries. The Freedom Party (*Strana slobody*), originally founded in 1946 as a splinter group, has never become anything more than an object of curiosity, with one or two names of its leaders outstanding. Almost total dissolution befell the Czechoslovak National Socialist Party, now renamed the Czechoslovak Socialist Party (*Československá strana socialistická*), in the whirl of 'purging' by the so-called Action Committees. Over 100,000 of its nearly 600,000 members joined the Communist Party, and the paralysed structure, endured by the post-1948 régime, sustained another 10,000 to 15,000 fellow travellers.[1] Fewer members of the 500,000-strong People's Party (about 25,000) acceded to the Communists after February 1948 because the Party (*Československá strana lidová*) had been fairly homogenously held together by Catholic ideology and professed non-Socialist premises. The remnants, whose organisational survival was tolerated for tactical reasons, were estimated at about 20,000.[2] None of the non-Communist Parties was permitted to retain any influence or authority, let alone power. Their functionaries were carefully screened before being nominated for public office, and a ceiling was imposed on their membership. Neither did any meaningful move towards greater independence emerge from within these parties themselves.

The only important contact between them and the general public (though not between them and the centre of power) lay in their publishing activities. Their dailies (*Svobodné slovo* and *Lidová demokracie* in Prague, and *L'ud* in Bratislava, belonging to the Socialist, People's and Revival Parties respectively) far surpassed the Communist papers in popularity, even if not in centrally regulated circulation, and demand for them consistently exceeded supply which depended on allocated newsprint quotas. The same was true about their publishing houses. The popularity did not arise from any political dissent let alone alternative political solutions offered in the non-Communist press, but simply because they could afford to be less political and more attentive to the everyday problems of a reader who was increasingly disaffected by political clichés. For all practical

[1] Figures giving post-February transfers from the other parties into the Communist Party have often been quoted. See for example Václav Pavlíček, *Politické strany po Únoru*, Part One (Prague, Svobodné slovo, 1966) and Jan Kašpar, 'Členská základna KSČ v letech 1945–49', *Československý časopis historický*, I (1971), pp. 1–25. Numerical data on the strength of the post-February non-Communist parties are much more difficult to come by. For the Socialist Party, see Heinrich Kuhn, *Handbuch der Tschechoslowakei* (Munich, Robert Lerche, 1966) p. 209, who gives an estimate for 1964 of 15,000. Bohuslav Kučera, the Socialist Party secretary-general and subsequently its chairman, said at a press conference on 27 March 1968 that the party had 11,000 members. See *Svobodné slovo*, 28 March 1968, p. 1.

[2] Kuhn, op. cit., p. 206, estimates People's Party membership in 1964 at 25,000. Jan Pauly, secretary-general of the People's Party, said on 31 May 1968 that the party had 32,978 members as of 15 May 1968, i.e. 55 per cent more than on 1 January 1968. See *Lidová demokracie*, 1 June 1968, p. 1.

purposes, however, the non-Communist parties were assigned the same transmission-belt role as the 'voluntary social organisations'. It is even dubious whether they could be of much use in this respect because of the limited radius of action earmarked for them.

The evolving theories of political pluralism have been mentioned in the Introduction and described at greater length elsewhere.[1] To objectively evaluate the participation explosion of 1968, one should realise that traditional disposition to political organisation and the requisite level of political sophistication in the Czech Lands has always been much greater than in any of the other Eastern European countries. The Czechoslovak situation was in this sense almost certainly unique. In February 1948 card-carrying membership of the then existing parties (excluding Slovakia, where conditions had been different, more along the lines of traditional Eastern European patterns) stood at something like 2,750,000 persons, i.e. every second to third adult was a party member.

It is perhaps surprising that no clear-cut legal stipulations have ever existed to define all the practical implications: before the war political parties were considered as loose associations which did not constitute 'legal entities' and could therefore not possess property, etc. (Such property as they administered was entered in the books under the name of individual functionaries.) Neither did the law provide for the founding of parties, which was left free, although it gave the government the power to disband them or 'suspend their activity'. In 1945 only some parties were explicitly sanctioned and others explicitly prohibited, but no legal regulation on the establishment and status of new ones was adopted. The norms on disbandment and suspension lost their validity. Gradually, as a matter of fact rather than written law, the confinement of political parties to the framework of the National Front, i.e. under Communist dominance, became consuetudinary and found its way into electoral legislation. The Constitution of 1960 mentioned only the Communist Party (as the leading force), to the neglect of any others, let alone those which might (inconceiv-

---

[1] See for example Radoslav Selucký, *Czechoslovakia: The Plan That Failed* (Thomas Nelson, 1970) and Vladimir V. Kusin, *The Intellectual Origins of the Prague Spring* (Cambridge University Press, 1971).

ably, at that time) spring into future existence. All this gave rise to a curious legal position in 1968: no one had the legal power to forbid the foundation of a new political party. However, only National Front parties were legally entitled to enter any election contest and, by the same token, the National Front could bar a new political party from putting up candidates. While allowed to exist, a new political party would not be permitted to compete for its share in political power (unless endorsed by the National Front) and would thus lose (not acquire) one of the essential attributes which make a political party what it is. Taken still further, only such a political party would make sense as would disavow parliamentary democracy and preach outright revolution. This, in turn, would be a punishable offence and a party of this kind would be banned.

Let us hasten to say that legal intricacies, though the subject of some argument in connection with the Club of Committed Non-Party People (KAN, *Klub angažovaných nestraníků*), were not foremost on the Party leaders' minds when they spoke out against a multi-party system. This was true of known reformists as well. Goldstücker was quoted as telling the Party's Ideological Commission in March 1968 that 'we must work out guarantees of socialist democracy while having only one leading party'.[1] Špaček said, 'The Czechoslovak road is not a classically pure road to socialism which entails the existence of more than one political party in the State. And it most likely will never be. History usually proves that what has been done cannot be undone. This is why we must accept the existence of a single leading party as a fact, base our deliberations on it and work out guarantees which would genuinely ensure socialist democracy . . .'[2] Gustav Husák rated among the top five reformers in the first months of 1968. His interview of 21 March, closely preceding Novotný's abdication and probably marking the culminating point in Husák's personal vendetta, was full of exhortation to democracy and lament over the pre-1968 system. ('We have lost twenty years . . . We have liquidated the classical forms of parliamentarism . . .') According to him, pluralism of political parties 'cannot be considered today'. Without going into detail, he did, however, accept the idea of

---

[1] Quoted by Josef Špaček, 'Jde o novou politiku', *Rudé právo*, 16 March 1968, pp. 1, 3.   [2] Ibid.

'control from the outside' over the Communist Party which he would like to see coupled with democratic control 'from within'. The former could be obtained from activated autonomous 'mass organisations' and from the 'vast State and economic apparatus' which ought to enjoy 'inner autonomy'.[1] Čestmír Císař could not have been more explicit when speaking on the subject at the Party Regional Conference in Pilsen on 28 April: 'The birth of an opposition party with an anti-socialist programme would mean an end of the Czechoslovak experiment to bring about a model of democratic socialism.'[2]

Much of the indigenous Party apparat must have considered political pluralism anathema no less than Moscow. The reformist Marie Miková put it this way, 'Primary Party branches and Party District Committees take badly to growing admission of members in these [non-Communist] political parties. They have often called us at the Regional Committee of the National Front: forbid it, don't permit them to do this, they have again recruited two or three members! Well, now they must get used to this thing going on without our endorsement.'[3] L. Hofman from South Bohemia, addressing the same Central Committee session as Miková, raised a warning finger when quoting from a mimeographed letter, allegedly received by a sports club (*sic*) in Tábor, which advocated separate candidacy of the various political parties in the next elections.[4]

Warning signals from local Communists came from other parts of the country as well. Thus, for example, the Czech Socialist Party had had a single member, a Mr Karel Chovanec, in Rožnov since 1960. By mid-July 1968 there were about fifty of them. In the same town, the People's Party grew from fifteen in March 1948 to nearly 150, and about 1,000 people were reported to frequent the local church.[5] In the Hodonín District of South Moravia the People's Party grew from 442 to 2,410 members and the Socialist Party from 304 to 612 members in 1968. (After the 1970 purge their membership in some villages was actually higher than that of the Communist Party.)[6]

[1] *Rudé právo*, 21 March 1968, pp. 1, 3.
[2] *Rudé právo*, 29 April 1968, p. 1.
[3] *Rudé právo*, 13 April 1968, p. 9.   [4] *Rudé právo*, 9 April 1968, p. 3.
[5] *Rudé právo*, 26 July 1968, p. 5.   [6] *Život strany*, 5 (1971) p. 17.

Thus, in spite of the two Czech non-Communist Parties having lost their programme, membership and credit since 1948, the issue of political pluralism in 1968 appeared to centre around the question whether its emergence should be expected as the result of completely new organisations coming to life, or whether a renaissance of the Czech Socialists and the People's Party should be attempted? In his well-known article advocating a two-party system, Václav Havel, the playwright, said he did not believe in the regenerating powers of the extant organisations. His solution would be to have a coalition between the Communist Party and a newly formed Democratic Party based on a framework agreement on their common goal, namely democratic socialism.[1] Jiří Lederer, on the other hand, was more optimistic about the Czech Socialists and the People's Party. We have three parties, he wrote; how can we introduce a model embracing only two? At the same time he would not exclude the possibility of the 'two inner currents' in the Communist Party evolving into factions and, eventually, two parties, the democratically socialist and the bolshevist.[2] Michal Reiman saw the emergence of new and activation of old parties as not mutually exclusive. For him, political pluralism was a *sine qua non* of normal development, and he thought that a stabilisation of democratic socialism would anyway, sooner or later, lead to the emergence of a number of political groupings.[3] Zdeněk Jičínský endorsed both alternatives equally, but suggested that all parties should proclaim their adherence to a socialist programme which should be stipulated by law.[4] Zdeněk Mlynář is reputed to have proposed the adoption by the National Assembly in July of a constitutional amendment whereby political parties or organisations acting as political parties could exist and come into existence only within the National Front. The National Front Central Committee would have the authority to accept or evict them, and they would have recourse to a special bench of the Supreme Court if not admitted. At the last minute the Party Praesidium resolved not to put this proposal on the parliament's agenda. After the invasion

---

[1] Václav Havel, 'Na téma opozice', *Literární listy*, 4 April 1968, p. 4.
[2] *Literární listy*, 25 April 1968, p. 3.
[3] *Rudé právo*, 4 May 1968, p. 3.
[4] *Rudé právo*, 30 May 1968, p. 3.

Mlynář allegedly reproached his comrades: the National Front limitation would have pleased the Russians.[1]

This, then, was the less than clear attitude of Dubček's Party leadership. The non-Communist parties already in existence would be considered 'partners' with the Communists within the National Front at all levels. As such, they would exercise an influence on policy making. They would also be free to enlarge their memberships and conduct their business independently. No explicit pronouncement on possible newcomers to the political arena was made, possibly for fear of losing the newly acquired democratic appearance. One can, however, deduce from specific behaviour, especially *vis-à-vis* the Social Democrats and KAN, that the odds in the Party leadership of the day, even with its reformist majority, were against the endorsement of new parties. This seemed to be the result of foreign disapproval as much as of a built-in ideological barrier and a genuine fear of a return to 'capitalist' parliamentarism. The crystallising philosophy of political pluralism largely arose from Mlynář's theory of a policy-making 'inner circle' within the National Front (Communist Party and other major groups and organisations) and his blueprint for combined general and group representation in a multi-chamber parliament.

What did the two non-Communist parties do during the Prague Spring? The answer of a detached observer with the benefit of some inside knowledge would probably be: not too much in terms of real contribution to the shaping of fundamental political decisions, but enough in the less visible sphere of internal build-up and preparation for meaningful independence.

They both changed their leaderships, but not too radically. The man who became chairman of the Socialist Party had been its secretary-general, and the new chairman of the People's Party had served as its deputy chairman. They both issued several proclamations of support to the idea of 'partnership' within the National Front, while at the same time acknowledging the leading rôle of the Communist Party. They both entered into some round-table discussions with the Communists in pre-1948 National Front-style. They both slightly repaired the image of their history, hitherto largely taboo, while not

---

[1] 'Jak jsme v Praze jednali: fakta a mýty', *Svědectví*, 38 (1970) pp. 171–88.

reclaiming personalities, periods and action of explicit anti-Communist nature. They both admitted new members of unspecified numbers, presumably more modest than the outcry of local Communist invigilators would indicate, mainly as a result of public interest rather than determined recruitment campaigning. The Socialist Party even tried, rather timidly, to set up some branches in factories (e.g. *Škoda*, Pilsen), which earned it a particularly irritated rebuff by the established guardians of working-class preferences. Both non-Communist parties consolidated their publishing enterprises (staff changes in *Svobodné slovo* and *Lidová demokracie*; improvement of professional standards of reporting and feature writing; new, more liberal plans for their publishing houses; launching, after the occupation, of new periodicals *Zítřek* and *Obroda*) and to some extent strengthened the theoretical element in their educational and research institutions (Party schools). In some instances, the local committees turned more militant in demanding independence than the centre, such as the Brno branch of the Socialist Party. The People's Party gave support to the Cause for Council Revival (*Dílo koncilové obrody*), a more independent association of Catholic clergy than the discredited *Mírové hnutí katolického duchovenstva*, and, more hesitantly, to the awakening school of modern Catholic philosophy. Finally, both parties issued new provisional programmes. The People's Party did so on 1 April 1968 in the form of a declaration of intent. The People's Party, it said, would like to develop 'independent activity' within the National Front and pursue the rôle of 'a factor of social control' relying on principles of Christian morality and supporting a favourable relation between the State and the Churches. The People's Party was not anti-socialist and would not permit itself to be misused for anti-socialist aims, the programme concluded.[1] On a later occasion, the People's Party expressed itself against the founding of new parties. As a more specific concern, it pronounced itself in favour of encouraging the work of artisans and craftsmen and of competition between producer co-operatives.[2] The Socialist

[1] *Lidová demokracie*, 2 April 1968, p. 1.

[2] People's Party officials stated this during their talks with the Communists and the Socialist Party at municipal level in Prague on 25 May 1968. See *Rudé právo*, 26 May 1968, p. 1.

Party's programme (*Nástin ideových zásad Čs. strany socialistické*), presented for public discussion on 14 April, pledged a constructive approach to co-operation with 'the other partners', notably the Communist Party, in the National Front. While rejecting anti-Communism, the Socialist Party recognised, right from 1918, the merits of the Communists in striving for a socialist transformation of Czechoslovakia. In the National Front, 'effective co-existence' and creative co-operation ought to prevail. Economy, too, needed a plural arrangement whereby different 'forms of ownership' could engage in wholesome competition. The programme singled out 'small private enterprise', based on individual labour, as the best element to operate in conditions unsuitable for large State or co-operative units. The Socialist Party expressed itself in favour of socialism and of alliance with the Soviet Union.[1]

Once again the length of time available to the reformers did not suffice to test the devised arrangements in practice. I would venture to guess that once a reformed system was established fewer people than many expected would probably seek membership in political parties. In a telegraph-style poll, conducted by the Institute for Public Opinion Research from 24 to 26 May 1968, two-thirds of the respondents, all non-affiliated to any party, stated that they would not want to be members. Only one-tenth would join a party if the conditions were right.[2] Be that as it may, the touchstone of democratisation and the tactical skill of the Communist reformers must be seen in their handling of the attempts to re-establish the Social Democratic Party.

SOCIAL DEMOCRATS

The merger which dispensed with the Social Democratic Party took place on 27 June 1948. Between 45,000 and 160,000 Social Democrats entered the 1·4 million-strong Communist Party. The lowest estimate is attributed to Blažej Vilím, formerly secretary-general of the Social Democratic Party, the highest to a Communist Party apparatchik who quoted, in 1971, 118,104 entrants in the fusion and another 48,962

[1] *Svobodné slovo*, 14 April 1968, pp. 1, 3.
[2] Incompletely quoted in *Rudé právo*, 30 May 1968, p. 2.

individuals.[1] With the Social Democratic membership standing at some 363,000 in 1948, the unmerged numbered between 200,000 and 300,000. In the Communist Party, the former Social Democrats were given 14 per cent of the seats on the Central Committee and 20 per cent in the Praesidium.[2] It should be noted, however, that the amalgamation was engineered by a group of Communist-oriented members under Zdeněk Fierlinger with the help of several wavering middle-of-the-roaders.

Twenty years later a few better-known former Social Democrats joined the reformist current in the Communist Party.[3] Many of the lesser-known probably did the same, although there is of course no exact way of telling how many. But the majority of the leaders who had marched into the Communist embrace in 1948 remained on the sidelines and, perhaps characteristically, were not missing in the set-up which once again rose to power after the fall of Dubček.[4]

The Dubček leadership in the conditions of reinvigorated political life in 1968 soon became aware that the Social Democratic question could not easily be swept under the table. They hoped to be able to settle the outstanding debts without actually allowing the re-establishment of the party, knowing that this, more than most issues, would antagonise the Russians. Thus, Social Democratic victims figured high on the rehabilitation lists and the ninetieth anniversary of the founding of Czechoslovak Social Democracy was to be commemorated at a number of celebrations, including the reopening of a museum in the house where the constituent meeting had taken place in 1878. (The museum had been closed in 1962.) More than once a willingness was expressed to accommodate in the Communist Party those Social Democratic functionaries and members who had chosen not to go through the merger in 1948, and even to give them prominent posts. Appealing to the sentimental attachment of many Social Democrats to their party and its history, a promise was given that their entry date into that party would be marked on Communist Party membership

---

[1] Jan Kašpar, op. cit., pp. 15–16.
[2] *Dějiny Československa v datech* (Prague, Svoboda, 1968) p. 381.
[3] For example Jiří Hájek, the Foreign Minister, and Ludmila Jankovcová.
[4] For example Zdeněk Fierlinger and Evžen Erban.

cards. A number of former Social Democrats opposed the resumption of independent activities. Some of them genuinely believed the move to be ill-timed and unnecessary. For other people, the Communist sense of obedience outgrew former loyalties. They issued a statement on 9 May to the effect that re-establishment of the Party would be a step backwards and could in fact contribute significantly to a reversal of the entire reform movement. Not much later the government informed the chief editors of all papers that they should not publish anything about Social Democratic restoration attempts. (This, incidentally, was an example of censorship without censorship.) The double standard – a much publicised statement by the one party to the conflict and a ban on all publicity for the other – irritated many people, including those who had not seriously thought of taking any action. (The three main newspapers which disobeyed the government's 'D-notice' were *Student, Svobodné slovo* and *Literární listy*.)

Not all who were against restoration deferred to the ideological attitudes. Their opposition was mainly based on a rational rejection of maximalism as an ill-advised approach to reform. Let's get our priorities right, they were saying. Both the Russians and their domestic assistants are worried by the progress of reform which, if it is to succeed, must be wrested from them even at the expense of some recognised objectives. More than that, let's be honest with ourselves, is there really such a compelling need for the Social Democratic Party to re-emerge in this specific situation, twenty years after its (unfortunate and unjust) demise, right in the middle of an effort to cleanse the all-pervading structure of Communism? Are the workers really so impatient and eager to join the Social Democratic organisation? Or is it only an urge in a group of people who cannot come to terms with the deep injustice done to them and their comrades, some dead by the executioner's hand? Do they just want to re-establish the balance of things and thus prove that, after all, they were right while the others were wrong? This kind of reasoning appeared for example in a commentary by Dalimil in *Literární listy*, a by no means insignificant and uninformed advocate of consistent reform. 'The haste with which they [proponents of Social Democratic revival] wish at this moment to revive their party complicates the situation considerably and enhances the tendency to return to pre-January methods as well as the danger of full-scale political reversal. Fine words to the effect that they would rather go to prison than abstain from a public proclamation of their party's reconstitution are a help to nobody, except the conservatives. The post-January régime is not yet sufficiently stable to afford such a trial of strength . . . This country needs no martyrs, either Communist or Social Democratic.'[1]

A leading pre-war Social Democratic functionary (not one of the few who profited from the merger) found three good and rational reasons why the constitution of his party should not be attempted 'in the given situation and at the present moment': (1) No programme had been prepared for the party to suit its new mission. A party ought not to be set up simply because it was possible and because some people wanted it. (2) The party would not have enough able and experienced functionaries; those active before 1948 were generally too old. (3) The step could wreck the entire reform process.[2]

The five-member committee which was behind all the efforts comprised four members of the Central Committee of the Social Democratic Party elected in November 1947 (Zdeněk Bechyně, František Čoupek, Josef Munzar and Josef Veverka) and a former functionary of the party's Youth Section (Přemysl Janýr). They called on National Assembly chairman Josef Smrkovský on 18 May and told him they had decided to revive the Social Democratic Party. On the same day they delivered a letter to the National Front Central Committee announcing the resumption of activity. They argued that the amalgamation in 1948 had happened against the will of the majority and that the statutes of the party had been broken in

---

[1] *Literární listy*, 27 June 1968, p. 4. Ludvík Vaculík, the writer, received a letter from a reader as early as in March 1968 exhorting him to start a Social Democratic Party. Should he do so, the reader had no doubt that 95 per cent of the nation would join him. Vaculík replied that he had given some thought to the idea, but had come to the conclusion that March was still too cold a month to launch an opposition party. And anyway, *it* would certainly obtain 95 per cent majority because as soon as *it* would get over 50 per cent everybody would want to join in. Then he, Ludvík Vaculík, would once again be in a party with *everybody* else, which as it was he did not like. *Literární listy*, 14 March 1968, p. 5.

[2] Josef Novotný in *Rudé právo*, 9 July 1968, p. 3.

the process. Consequently, the merger had been invalid and the party that would be reborn now, in 1968, had never really ceased to exist. As it was not a new party, no formal or legal procedure needed to be invoked to allow it to break out of the state of suspended animation. For three and a half hours on 23 May the five Social Democrats talked their case over with Smrkovský, Kriegel, Indra and Pošusta whose unequivocal opposition contained all the ideological arguments about working class unity, which must have sounded hollow, as well as all the very clear-cut warnings about how dangerous it was to rock the boat. Smrkovský especially was insistent in his plea for reason.

Similar discussions, night-long, took place a month later (21 June) between officials of the Communist Party Municipal Committee in Prague and the Prague preparatory committee of the Social Democrats. On 5 July Bechyně and Janýr were called to see Smrkovský again. He told them that official endorsement of their party was out of the question, and again repeated the offer of posts for any number of formerly victimised Social Democrats they cared to name. By then Soviet pressure was rapidly becoming unbearable and the very continuation of the Prague Spring was at stake, yet the Communist reformists had to plead almost daily with the central and the municipal preparatory committees of the Social Democrats to hold at least in abeyance the public proclamations they threatened to make. On 18 July, after difficult negotiations, the Social Democrats promised to suspend, until further notice, the holding of members' meetings, public gatherings, sending of letters to the National Front and publication of statements in the press. After Čierna and Bratislava the central preparatory committee was split between a majority advising caution and a sizeable minority calling for open action.

On 17 August, four days before the invasion, a three-member Social Democratic delegation talked to F. Kriegel. They again pressed for recognition and called the restoration of Social Democracy 'the crucial question of democratisation'. They would not wait any longer before stepping into the open. The Social Democratic membership would consider it a betrayal if they backed out. Finally Kriegel elicited a promise from them that they would wait until the Fourteenth Communist

Party Congress, scheduled for 9 September. In the meantime the Communist Party Secretariat confidentially instructed Communist functionaries to recruit prospective Social Democrats for membership in the Communist Party.

Unfortunately, the key information which would assist an objective judgement is missing, notably information about the numerical strength of the Social Democratic movement in 1968. Both the Social Democratic and Communist (1968 and post-Dubček) sources are very inconclusive on this point. Two sources (from opposite ends of the political spectrum) agree on the figure of 230 'organisations' allegedly prepared to come into the open in June–July 1968.[1] Another source speaks of 300 such organisations,[2] and yet another mentions 150 'cells' with 1,700 prospective members.[3] We also know from several sources, which however may have copied one another, about an unspecified number of factory branches which were actually constituted and about an equally unspecified number of Communist Party branches waiting 'for the suitable moment' to stand up and declare themselves Social Democratic.[4] Also imputed to the preparatory committee is the estimate, allegedly made on 19 August 1968, that after its proclamation the Social Democratic Party would be joined by about one-third of the members of the Communist Party (about 600,000) and another 600,000 of non-partisans.[5] What are we to make of it all? Maybe that hard undisputable evidence has been tucked away in order not to incriminate people who must live with, and under, orthodox Communism in post-Dubček Czechoslovakia. Nevertheless, on the strength of what is known and admittedly with the benefit of hindsight, the movement to restore Social Democracy to life will most likely be counted among those errors of the Prague Spring which could have been avoided.

[1] 'Jak jsme v Praze jednali: fakta a mýty', *Svědectví*, 38 (1970) pp. 171–88, and Václav Příhoda-Vilím Netrefa, 'Sociální demokracienástroj kontrarevoluce v Československu', *Život strany*, 3 December 1969, p. 12.

[2] F. D. Pór, 'Nezapomínat na poučení historie i dneška', *Tribuna*, 51–2 (1970) p. 14.

[3] 'Zpráva o současné politické situaci v ČSSR a podmínkách činnosti KSČ (srpen 1968)', *Rudé právo*, 2 July 1969, p. 3.

[4] Příhoda and Netrefa, op. cit., *Život strany*, 26 November 1969, p. 12.

[5] Příhoda and Netrefa, op. cit., *Život strany*, 3 December 1969, p. 12.

Even if pressure from below on the five protagonists was overwhelming, they should have known better than to force the issue themselves. More and more people agree that good politics is the art of the possible. Where principle and compromise clash it is not always the principle that is right. Even less so in an Eastern European reform movement.

KAN

How does one go about preaching that it is tactically inadvisable to have any non-Communist party to people who, rightly or wrongly, emerged from long years of political frustration clinging to the idea that institutionalised opposition is the only remedy? Dissent had been found much too intangible and checks by apparats much too inadequate. In the Czech context, the Prague Spring inevitably gave birth to the desire for 'the real thing'. At the same time, a high measure of circumspection in most reformers militated against radical revolutionary action. Gradualism marked the reform.

Semantically, pre-1968 political participation had been marked by the positive-negative dichotomy: the adult population divided into sub-classes of Party and non-Party members (*straník-nestraník*). Over four-fifths of the public did not have a name of their own and had to derive it from that of the one-fifth of Party members: Communists as opposed to non-Communists. The 'nameless', writer Alexander Kliment called the latter.[1]

According to the Communist doctrine, political parties are organised representatives of social classes and their existence in a classless society would constitute a *contradictio in adjecto*. The continuing survival of non-Communist parties in Czechoslovakia and some other Eastern European countries belied them. Moreover, many reformers argued that the very substance of the theory was false: while some political parties had indeed come to life as instruments of a class or group in the socio-economic sense and even though in some societies this distinction persisted to date, it was equally true that other parties had emerged and developed as attitudinal, rather than

[1] A. Kliment, 'Aktivita nepojmenovaných', *Literární listy*, 14 March 1968, p. 4.

sectional, organisations. The absence of classes (in the Marxist sense) in Czechoslovakia in 1968 should not have been in itself a reason against the setting up of a multi-party system. Kliment suggested that, rather than from class motives, opposition would emerge from 'moral, political and cultural civil interests'.

Karel Kaplan admitted that the Prague Spring gave some room for action to non-Party people within the social organisations and even in the State machinery, previously blocked by Communist predominance. He thought, however, that institutional safeguards were one of the key issues in socialist democracy. Should it decline to offer such safeguards, it would pull the carpet from under its own feet.[1]

Just about everybody agreed that 'opposition' ought to be permitted, even though there was no unanimity as to its form. Kliment warned lest this 'opposition' was established by decree; in Bohemia this could well happen, he said, and we would all have to be ashamed. In fact, the sarcasm was not so completely beside the point. In April Jan Piller had to face a public meeting in Mariánské Lázně, and the audience fired no fewer than 163 questions at him: 'They applauded his statement to the effect that the Party Central Committee wished to see the non-Party people represented in the government. At the moment able non-Party technicians and experts are being selected and trained to take up jobs of first deputy ministers, and later even ministers.'[2] This little newspaper report, surely one of the cameos of Prague Spring chronicling, stimulates one's imagination in the best dadaistic manner.

KAN was one attempt, unguided by the benign hand of power-holders, to provide a point of departure for a new non-Communist political unit. The initials stand for *Klub angažovaných nestraníků* (Club of Committed Non-Party People) and the emphasis was on the word Club, to indicate that the organisational ties were looser than those of a fully fledged party. Throughout its not quite real existence, KAN appeared to be poised to do something which it in fact never did. Its initiators freely admitted that their creation was provisional in addition to being only half complete. The philosophy behind

[1] K. Kaplan, 'O výsledcích lednového pléna ÚV KSČ', *Rudé právo*, 13 April 1968, p. 3.
[2] *Rudé právo*, 14 April 1968, p. 1.

it was minimal since it defined membership in the negative sense, i.e. non-Party people, with a slight positive modification in the vague adjective 'committed'. The traditional attributes of a Central European political party, such as a standing order of behaviour or membership cards, were missing.

Public interest in KAN cannot be easily assessed, but it was certainly very uneven. Local clubs were said to have been established in all districts in northern Bohemia, while elsewhere there may have been only one or two sporadic attempts. Enthusiasts in Kutná hora, Most, Prague and Ústí sought to build up branches in factories, whereas other saw KAN as an explicitly intellectual organisation. To my knowledge no factual evidence has been published on KAN's numerical strength or social composition. From very incomplete first-hand and second-hand accounts, it seems that members were mostly recruited from among the technical intelligentsia and teachers, and that the average age was below and around thirty. They were not agreed on any detailed political programme other than the most general profession of adherence to socialism, democracy and freedom of the individual. They stressed the intention to build their club 'next to' rather than 'against' the Communist Party, whose reformist policy they welcomed.

We have at our disposal three 'programmatic statements' by KAN; the first from the constituent *aktiv* of 144 persons on 5 April at which they formed the central preparatory committee,[1] the second from this committee issued on 14 May,[2] and the third from the first Prague meeting of KAN supporters on 18 May attended by 3,000 people.[3] These documents were moderately worded and seemed to indicate a certain degree of political naïvety. As declarations of intent, couched in not too specific terms, they offer a valuable testimony to the circumspection with which the founders and leaders of KAN trod their delicate ground. Above all they lay emphasis on their 'feeling of co-responsibility' for the future development of the country. Socialism was for them 'a reality from which they arose' and they understood it as linked with democracy. In the long run they hoped to achieve for their members 'an equal

---

[1] *Literární listy*, 11 April 1968, p. 2.

[2] *Rudé právo*, 15 May 1968, p. 3.

[3] *Rudé právo*, 19 May 1968, p. 2, and *Literární listy*, 30 May 1968, p. 2.

status' to that enjoyed by the Communists. They were willing to co-operate and possibly even integrate with organisations similar to their own, i.e. they did not see themselves as an exclusive non-Communist political group. On more specific issues, they wished to see the National Front become 'an open forum of co-operation' which would put no obstacles in the way of 'new political forces'. For their members they demanded 'the opportunity to take an active part in political life'. In the forthcoming parliamentary and local government elections (which eventually did not take place) KAN would want to nominate its own candidates. It would also organise public debates and uphold the United Nations Declaration of Human Rights.

In spite of all its wariness, KAN did not meet with the Communist Party leaders' approval. Neither was it, however, flatly repudiated. Reporting the by now legendary May Day parade, *Rudé právo* mentioned 'the apprehensiveness of the organisers' when they learned that KAN members planned to form a separate section within the march-past. The overseers felt a little relieved when the multitudes spontaneously swept away all detailed schedules and simply flooded the streets in a human mass. But pockets of KAN members still paraded their banners and handed a bouquet of red and white carnations to Svoboda. Not all the slogans they chanted were correct, suggested *Rudé právo*, but the one declaring that opposition should never again be sent behind bars was. (*Opozice nikdy více nesmí patřit do věznice!*)[1]

On 7 April the preparatory committee asked the Prague Municipal National Committee for registration (indicating its local sphere of activity; KAN existed as a series of local clubs only loosely connected in some districts, but a central network did not come into being), and the request was repeated on 16 May with the Ministry of the Interior, but in vain. This meant that only 'preparatory' activity was permitted. The authorities were obviously under pressure from the Russians, who must have complained bitterly about anything that smacked of political opposition. The Post Office even refused to deliver letters addressed to KAN (a P.O. Box was hired) and the organisers had to appeal to the public to use the name

[1] *Rudé právo*, 2 May 1968, pp. 1 and 2.

of a private individual as the addressee.[1] Retreating before this pressure, KAN representatives in northern Bohemia declared on 10 July that they did not want to evolve into a political party, that they supported the progressive policy of the Communist Party, that they wished to help overcome economic difficulties and that they publicly condemned anti-socialist manifestations. They would still want to see KAN legalised.[2]

It is difficult to pass a judgement. KAN was obviously very much the product of Czechoslovak conditions (very little is known about the Slovak counterpart of KAN, the *Združenie aktívnych nestraníkov*), and an attempt to respond quickly to the overwhelming public desire for a non-Communist political outlet. It was neither radically conceived nor radically brought to life. In the long run it may have evolved into a proper organisation or even a political party, although one source mentions decreasing interest among the supporters when some branches of KAN decided to impose stricter organisational rules on their members.[3] The Prague Spring was inducive to *ad hoc* meetings and statements, but less so to real organisation which many thought ran contrary to the general striving for more freedom and less limitations. In any case, a new political party would have to formulate its programme differently. Everyone, including the Communists, subscribed to the main tenets of 'democratic socialism' and 'humanism' around which the KAN proclamations were built. As a programme, non-Communism may have been attractive in the context of a general dissociation from die-hard practices and dogmas, but would be found totally lacking in terms of a practical contest.

Nevertheless, Moscow took KAN more than seriously and after the invasion it figured high on every list of counter-revolutionary sins committed during the Prague Spring. It had to be sacrificed almost immediately: on 4 September its eastern Bohemian branch was said to have disbanded itself 'due to the current interpretation of the law governing association' and on 5 September the Ministry of the Interior announced its definite disapproval of KAN's request for legalisa-

---

[1] *Literární listy*, 20 June 1968, p. 20 and 27 June 1968, p. 2.
[2] *Rudé právo*, 11 July 1968, p. 2.
[3] 'Zpráva o současné politické situaci v ČSSR a podmínkách činnosti KSČ (srpen 1968)', *Rudé právo*, 2 July 1969.

tion. On 14 November Dubček named KAN as one of the 'anti-Communist forces' whose existence prompted foreign intervention.

K231

Exactly the same fate as that described in the preceding paragraph befell the extraordinary organisation, the one and only of its kind in the world so far, which went by the name of Club 231 or, more commonly, K231. There was, however, more than a little difference between the two and they were condemned for different reasons, although lumped together under the joint label of counter-revolution.

K231 derived its name from Law No. 231 passed by the National Assembly on 6 October 1948 and styled 'For the Protection of the People's Democratic Republic'. Under it, large-scale prosecution of political offenders took place, non-Communist and Communist alike (e.g. Slánský's 'conspiratorial centre').

How many former political prisoners survived, rehabilitated partly or fully or not at all, to welcome the Prague Spring we may never accurately know. The estimates vary. The literary scholar Bedřich Fučík, himself a former political prisoner, spoke about a 30,000-strong 'army' of persons who, in 1968, were still largely living 'on the periphery of civil life'.[1] The Anti-Fascist Fighters' Union thought that about 30,000 to 40,000 were still waiting for rehabilitation (not counting people victimised outside the courts, and relatives).[2] The Supreme Court allegedly put the number at 40,000, this including 'genuine culprits'.[3] Václav Havel, the writer, wrote about 'perhaps' 80,000 former political prisoners.[4] And an editorial note in *Literární listy*, introducing a round-table discussion on rehabilitations and legal guarantees, referred to 'cases from 1948 to 1967 whose numbers are in the order of a six-digit figure'.[5] We have other indications to go by. A *Rudé právo* writer (in 1970) made a puzzling reference to 201 cases of

[1] *Literární listy*, 4 April 1968, p. 6.
[2] Interview with J. Hušek, *Rudé právo*, 15 March 1968, pp. 1, 3.
[3] Ibid.
[4] V. Havel, 'Na téma opozice', *Literární listy*, 4 April 1968, p. 4.
[5] *Literární listy*, 23 May 1968, p. 4.

anti-State activity allegedly heard before the courts 'in five Czech Regions' between February and December 1948 (in fact 'regions' as administrative units were started only on 1 January 1949 with nine Czech, including Prague, five Moravian and seven Slovak, including Bratislava). In these 201 cases, 1,614 persons were said to have been ordered to prison, including 703 for espionage, 256 for carrying arms and launching terrorism, 244 for organising escapes abroad and 411 for disseminating anti-State leaflets.[1] These were, indeed, typical offences. A scholar who had access to some archives wrote that nearly 27,000 had been sentenced to imprisonment between October 1949 and the end of 1952. He added, quoting Vasil Bilak from the Party Central Committee session of April 1956, that more than 24,000 criminal proceedings [presumably for 'political' offences, such as religious activity and resistance to collectivisation] had been started in the Prešov Region alone in 1952–3.[2] The Piller Report, rather surprisingly, does not give systematic figures, but its says that political prisoners in the Czech Lands numbered 6,136 as of 1 November 1949, 8,491 as of 1 March 1950 and 9,765 as of 1 May 1950. 'In the middle of 1950' in the whole of Czechoslovakia 11,026 persons were in jail for political offences. Persons arrested by the State Secret Police (STB) numbered 2,977 individuals and 3,112 groups in 1951, and a total of 16,010 persons in 1952. (Of them 5,962 were workers, 3,162 employees, 1,080 farmers, 554 kulaks and thirty-two large estate-holders and aristocrats.) From October 1948 to the end of 1952, the State Court (for political crime) pronounced 233 death sentences, of which 178 were carried out. Supreme Party organs confirmed 148 capital sentences between 1951 and 1954.[3] As yet another indication, 335 penal institutions and 107 forced labour camps existed in 1952, the peak year of persecution.[4] It is not known to me how many people were summarily sent to forced labour camps by special National Committee panels, for which no judicial proceedings were required, but the number of these

---

[1] *Rudé právo*, 25 June 1970, p. 3.

[2] V. Brabec, 'Vztah KSČ a veřejnosti k politickým procesům na počátku padesátých let', *Revue dějin socialismu*, 3 (1969) p. 374.

[3] *Das unterdrückte Dossier*, ed. J. Pelikán (Vienna, Europa Verlag, 1970) pp. 67–8.   [4] *Rudé právo*, 11 June 1968, p. 3.

camps suggests a fairly high figure. In addition, tens of thousands of young, and not so young, 'unreliables' were drafted into penal battalions in the army where conditions did not differ from those in labour camps.[1] All in all (and taking into account the estimated membership of K231, to be discussed later) there were probably around 80,000 former political prisoners in Czechoslovakia in 1968, not counting those victimised by the loss of their jobs, deportations, demotions, frustrated careers, etc. This represented about 0·8 per cent of the adult population.[2]

The law under which most were sentenced was an unusually wide-ranging and thorough, even if elastic, legal document. Not

[1] The so-called PTP (*Pomocné technické prapory*) or Auxiliary Technical Battalions existed from 1950 to 1954. Those drafted into them, often outside normal conscription, were not issued any weapons, but had to go through the usual training. In addition they did heavy work, especially in pits and at building sites. Victimisation continued after release with the entry in their reference books: 'Does not reveal the profile of a socialist citizen.' Estimates of numbers vary from 25,000 to 100,000. Among them only 1 per cent were said to have been non-political 'parasites', 'habitual offenders', etc. The PTP men held a gathering in Prague on 25 May 1968. Between 3,000 (*Rudé právo*) and 6,000 (*Literární listy*) of them attended to demand rehabilitation and establish a PTP-Club. See *Literární listy*, 23 May 1968, p. 12, 30 May 1968, p. 12 and 27 June 1968, p. 12, and *Rudé právo*, 26 May 1968, p. 2 and 6 July 1968, p. 2.

[2] A jurist divided the former political prisoners into five main groups which suffered most: former resistance fighters (including members of the International Brigades in Spain), farmers, small artisans, functionaries of political parties and social organisations (including the Communist Party) and ecclesiastical persons. *Rudé právo*, 30 April 1968, p. 3. A pre-war law (1931) distinguished between the treatment of political and ordinary prisoners, on condition that the political offence had not been 'specially condemnable' and that the perpetrator's motive had not been 'lowly and dishonourable'. This law, revoked in 1950, gave a *bona fide* political prisoner the right to have his own cell, to use his own clothes and bedding, to refuse to work or clean the premises of the prison, to accept food, books and newspapers, etc., from outside, to spend four hour a day in the open, to use writing utensils, to smoke and to receive visitors unless otherwise stated. There was some talk in 1968 suggesting that a line should once again be drawn in this respect, but others (e.g. Jiří Hochman, *Rudé právo*, 26 April 1968, p. 3) objected, saying that the term political prisoner should disappear altogether. To recognise them and guarantee them special treatment could have been considered progressive fifteen years ago, but now only warmongering and preaching of racial or other hatred should be considered offences. All the other 'political offences' ought to be exposed to public

counting formal and procedural paragraphs, it listed thirty-nine political offences. They were: high treason; association against the State; sedition; slandering the Republic; espionage; intelligence work against an ally; negligent keeping of State secrets; endangering the defence of the Republic; potential espionage; harmful activity in time of war and emergency; war-time treason; use of unauthorised information; accessory to military crime or offence; assault on constitutional personages; bodily harm to constitutional personages; conspiracy to assault constitutional personages; violence against constitutional personages; arrogation of powers pertaining to constitutional personages; rebellion; violence against public agencies; defamation of the President; slander of some constitutional personages; support to and promotion of fascism and similar movements; instigation; defamation of a nation or a race; misuse of an ecclesiastical or similar office; unauthorised possession of arms; co-operation with unauthorised armed or military-type group; spreading of information liable to cause a disturbance; instigation to crime and civil disobedience; approval of crime; failure to interrupt or report a crime; sabotage; jeopardising economic plans through negligence; treachery; unlawful departure from the country and refusal to return; causing harm to the interests of the Republic while abroad; slandering an allied country; instigation to aggressive war.

It may be interesting to note that Law No. 231/1948, as a major piece of legislation, bears the signatures of all members

polemics only. Hochman demanded to know how many political prisoners still remained in jail. Not much later, on 3 May, J. Zvara, chairman of the National Assembly commission for civic control over penal servitude, reported the following: As on 3 May 1968 there were 20,930 persons in jail in Czechoslovakia, including 732 sentenced according to Part One of the Criminal Law, i.e. for 'crimes against the Republic'. The remaining inmates had been convicted as follows: 6,016 for economic offences, mostly misappropriation of State property; 1,367 for offences against public order; 5,066 for gross violations of civic coexistence, including 3,022 for parasitism and 1,436 for hooliganism; 1,722 for offences against the family and juveniles, including 1,507 for failure to pay alimony; 3,058 for offences against the life and health of others, including 809 for murder and 1,935 for causing bodily harm; 3,539 for offences against the freedom and dignity of others, including 1,182 for burglary, 941 for rape and 1,194 for sexual abuse; and 5,533 for theft. They worked in mining, building, agriculture and industry and earned roughly the same wages as free workers. *Rudé právo*, 4 May 1968, p. 6.

of the government of the day, including the then Minister of National Defence, Ludvík Svoboda.

Law No. 247 of 25 October 1948, which stipulated the establishment of forced labour camps, stated that both persons sentenced under Law 231 and certain other legal categories, as well as otherwise un-tried persons, could be ordered into these camps for a period of from three months to two years by special three-member commissions set up by the Regional National Committees. The charge could be work evasion, menace to the people's democratic order or to the economy, and assistance in any of these. In addition, labour camp inmates could have their flats confiscated, businesses expropriated and, on release, could be banished from or to certain places.

The main concern of former political prisoners was rehabilitation, legal and moral, both of which could have had some very practical consequences, for example, for the future careers of their children. Not long after the policy change in January 1968, all political institutions and organisations became committed to a full-scale rehabilitation. The process itself was obviously bound to be cumbersome after so many years had elapsed, and would have to entail such practical things as financial compensation. With the question of the resignation of discredited persons from Party and government bodies still hovering in the air, and the consistency of the rehabilitation process therefore not quite certain, the idea was born at the beginning of March to set up an organisation which would protect the interests of former political prisoners and watch over ethical genuineness of the rehabilitations.

The initiative came from Jaroslav Brodský, a teacher and veteran of political jails, and a small group of his friends. They contemplated the organisation as 'a non-political club'. Brodský later wrote that he had believed the club would carry considerable moral weight because its membership would comprise the cream of non-Communist and Communist leaderships smitten in the wake of the 1948 takeover.[1] On

[1] J. Brodský, *Řešení Gama* (Amsterdam, Nederlandse Stichting Comenius, 1970) 4th edition, p. 132. This book, a literary self-biography, is a source for much that remained unpublished in 1968, but accurate information, such as dates, names and numbers, is hard to find. It was not, of course, written to provide it.

26 March, i.e. prior to any public action, Brodský informed the Party Central Committee and the Ministry of the Interior about his intention and in fact asked them 'to formulate the rules of the game themselves until the Club is legalised'.[1] This circumspect conduct was typical of many reformist actions, and the two authorities showed no displeasure at this stage. The constituent meeting, after only a few days of inconspicuous publicity, convened in Prague on 31 March (Sunday) in the presence of 3,500 to 4,000 people.[2] As it could not be otherwise, a gathering of this nature was an emotion-laden affair but at the same time surprisingly orderly. The many speakers emphasised that they were free of any vindictive complex and renounced hate as a policy. They would not discriminate between people of different political colouring; they wished to help the new order of things, called by Dubček 'socialism with a human face'; they had confidence in the new leadership. By a show of hands they elected Professor Karel Nigrin, a historian, as chairman of the club, General Václav Paleček as first and Jan Šmíd as second vice-chairmen, Jaroslav Brodský as secretary-general and Zdeněk Mráz as his deputy. Also elected was an eighty-member central committee with several seats left vacant for future members. Shortly the club was able to open offices in Prague and began to accept donations, not only for the running of its agenda (which was overwhelmingly done on a voluntary basis), but mainly for aid to next-of-kin and sick members. Local branches and district committees were being set up all over the Czech Lands. (In Slovakia the function of K231 was to be performed by the Society for the Protection of Human Rights, but some offshoots of the club did come into being.)

---

[1] Ibid., p. 135.
[2] Eye-witness accounts. The motto of the meeting was taken from Comenius, who had spoken about the Thirty Years War, 'May It Never Happen Again!' (*Aby se to už nikdy neopakovalo*). A small table, draped in black, with empty chairs around it, reminded the audience of those who had not survived. Two books lay on it, the Bible and a volume of Palacký's *History of the Czech Nation*. The hall filled up after 7 a.m., hundreds had to remain outside and loudspeakers were hastily installed for them. The meeting was followed by a press conference, but coverage in the main papers was not extensive. At one moment a journalist asked whether there were any workers among the participants; about a hundred men offered to speak immediately, others raised their hands on the floor.

Registration of members with the headquarters, including social and age composition breakdowns, was never completed, so that we have to rely on estimates once again. They come from three sources: *Literární listy* wrote of 30,000 preliminary applications for membership as of mid-June,[1] Bohumil Šimon, the Communist Party municipal secretary in Prague, spoke of 48,000 members 'with a considerable intellectual potential' as of mid-May,[2] and Jaroslav Brodský later concurred with Šimon's estimate, while indicating that the figure rose to 'over 60,000' by the beginning of August. He added that the average age was well over fifty.[3]

Who ought to have been admitted as members? This question aroused one of the major controversies connected with K231. The organisers firmly declared that, while carefully vetting applications to weed out people guided by 'lowly and dishonourable motives' (all applications were 'preliminary' and subject to endorsement), they would not distinguish between entirely innocent victims of judicial frame-ups and those culpable under extant regulations.[4] The Communist leadership, including many reformers, soon became visibly embarrassed by the growth of K231 and the public response to it. They would not object to an interest organisation of former political prisoners, they seemed to suggest, if it included only the demonstrably innocent, and not the victims of 'revolutionary justice'. Seeking to counter the success of K231, they initiated a press campaign (possibly conducted from the Ministry of the Interior if one can judge by such elusive signs as linguistic style and idiom) to discredit K231 leaders by reminding the public of their past 'crimes'.[5] Someone had fled to West Germany in 1948, was contacted by U.S. intelligence, returned to Czechoslovakia on a mission, was caught red-handed and sent to jail for twenty years: did he possess the moral right in 1968 to claim rehabilitation for himself and others at public rallies, or should he confine himself at the most

[1] *Literární listy*, 27 June 1968, p. 6 gave the figure as 80,000 which was corrected on 4 July 1968, p. 14, to 30,000.

[2] J. Brodský, op. cit., p. 163.

[3] Ibid., p. 180.

[4] *Literární listy*, 27 June 1968, p. 13, *Rudé právo*, 8 June 1968, p. 3.

[5] See for example *Rudé právo*, 28 May 1968, p. 3, 1 June 1968, p. 3; 3, 19 and 26 June 1968, all p. 2; 12 July 1968, p. 6.

to complaining about the severity of the sentence and the manhandling he had to go through while in jail?

Similarly, no agreement existed on whether rehabilitation (to which everybody subscribed in principle) ought to take the form of individual retrials, often very laborious in view of the time span between the original proceedings and 1968, or whether it should be proclaimed *ex lege*. Even some of the more radical reformers advocated the former, pointing out that a sweeping rescission of all political sentences would make it impossible to put one's finger on those individually responsible for miscarriages of justice. K231 suggested that all sentences should be quashed at a stroke with the government retaining the right to reprosecute where it deemed necessary. This solution, K231 leaders believed, would be in keeping with the basic philosophy they thought necessary to preach, namely that of 'national conciliation'. The infamous past would be considered closed and the door would be open to joint work without prejudice and recrimination. (People directly responsible for maltreatment of prisoners would still be brought to justice.) To promote this aim, K231 was working on the draft of a Law on General Conciliation (*Zákon o obecném smíru*), hoping that it would be possible to promulgate it on 28 October 1968, the fiftieth anniversary of the birth of independent Czechoslovakia. Such an approach, defying class criteria, must have been unacceptable to the guardians of ideological purity.

Finally, K231 came under attack during the Prague Spring and especially afterwards for allegedly being nothing other than a cover, to be discarded later, under which the class enemy was organising a political party whose programme would lie in wreaking vengeance on all and sundry. It was from the dark corners of K231 that the Hydra of counter-revolution was about to spring into action, cutting the throats of honest Communists. There is little evidence, if any, to support such an allegation. Of course, it would be wrong to pretend that K231 was a pro-Communist organisation. One must not forget that its members had often been exposed to protracted inhuman and humiliating suffering under the banner and on behalf of Communism. They addressed hundreds of meetings and, accusing, as many others did, the neo-Stalinist system of responsibility for the many social and human ills, did not always choose their words carefully. But on the whole the leaders of the club showed unmistakable preference for reform and renounced retribution. They repeatedly asked not to be attributed views and policies which they did not adhere to. At a press conference on 3 June they assured the audience that K231 did not follow any other goals than to achieve the rehabilitation of its members, to enable them to return to normal life and to help uncover those guilty of crimes against humanity. They did not propose to transform the diverse community of K231 into a political party. They would disperse as soon as their objectives were achieved.[1] (Later Brodský indicated that they were aiming at the adoption of the Law on General Conciliation on 28 October 1968 as the culminating and final point of their activity.[2] They gave credit to the Communist Party for having embarked on the process of reform. 'Socialism is for us an obvious and undoubted reality, while democracy we take as an absolutely vital necessity.'[3] The temporary nature of the club's existence also arose from practical considerations: most members were ageing people; past their prime, sick and disabled, affected by severe mental strain (nearly 70 per cent of their marriages had foundered as a result of prolonged incarceration).[4] It would be foolish to strive for political power which, ideally, should be in the hands of healthy people. After all, even if having been a political prisoner could not help but shape a person's outlook, it did not automatically engender identical programmes, indispensable for a political party. Having been incarcerated for political beliefs or deeds was a personal experience and a state of mind, not a political platform.

Essentially, K231 directed most of its activity in 1968 towards its own members and their concerns, while its very existence of course influenced other groups and individuals. Among its extroverted action, the club inspired the celebration of a Requiem Mass in St Vitus Cathedral, appealed to the public to commemorate the 'victims of war and violence' with two minutes of silence on Holy Saturday (as had been customary before 1948), suggested the resumption of friendly contacts

[1] J. Brodský, op. cit., pp. 180–1.   [2] Ibid.
[3] *Rudé právo*, 5 June 1968, p. 6.   [4] J. Brodský, op. cit., p. 181.

with Yugoslavs who had been jailed in Czechoslovakia for Titoism, interceded with the Greek Embassy on behalf of a girl student who went on public hunger strike in Prague to demand the release of her mother, a political prisoner in Greece, and spoke in favour of abolishing capital punishment.

There is also a not very clear history of co-operation between K231 and the government. Many members of K231 were a little suspicious of Josef Pavel, Dubček's Minister of the Interior, because they remembered his role as chief of the People's Militia in February 1948, head of the Party's Security Department and Deputy Minister of the Interior prior to his arrest in 1951. He met two representatives of the club not long after his appointment in April 1968, heard their case and presented them with his views on how rehabilitation should proceed. No specific conclusion was apparently reached other than Pavel's agreement to accept evidence on maltreatment of political prisoners in the past.[1] However, not much later, the spokesman for the Ministry of the Interior let it be known that neither the Ministry nor any of its departments had co-operated with K231 or intended to do so.[2] K231 replied by publicly stating that Dr Rezek, head of one of these departments (for inquiry into defects in penal establishments), had already received at his own request some (unspecified) documentation from the club.[3] Writing on the subject later, Brodský said: 'I submitted to the Party Central Committee and the General Procuracy documentary material on the first sixty-one murders in fields, woods, cells and camps.'[4] More talks have been hinted at, allegedly taking place between K231 and Prime Minister Černík's aides. 'A final meeting' is said to have been held with Černík and Colotka 'two days before departure for Čierna'. An unspecified 'agreement' was allegedly worked out and approved by the government on the same day.[5] Even if the shroud of mystery is frustrating (justified as it may be), one thing is almost certain, notably that no sinister collusion subservient to imperialism could have been going on. I suspect that the talks were prompted by Soviet threats, that the government sought to dispel Moscow's displeasure by explicitly

---

[1] Ibid., pp. 155–8.
[2] *Rudé právo*, 6 June 1968, p. 2.   [3] Ibid.
[4] J. Brodský, op. cit., p. 170.   [5] Ibid., p. 176.

limiting in scope and time the club's activity, and that the club yielded and decided to play the game with the new rules. It is not conceivable that the government should have entered into any other agreement at the end of July.

Invasion caught K231 by surprise. On 21 August Brodský should have attended an election meeting in Litoměřice to accept nomination in a constituency vacated by General Šejna, the escapee. There had been no plans, and no activity was undertaken in the invasion week. The praesidium of the club met briefly, burned some papers (including material allegedly convicting Alois Indra of pro-Nazi collaboration in the Second World War)[1] and dispersed. Brodský fled to Austria, climbing through the barbed wire and drawing sub-machine gun fire from the frontier guards – at a time when others calmly and simply walked out and continued to do so for almost another year. But then, prosecution and persecution was always close to members of K231, and they knew it.

NEW LEFT

The Czechoslovak reform movement started from different premises and aimed at different objectives from those which were being pursued almost simultaneously by that aggregative political force known in the Western world as the New Left. Not only was the parlance of the New Left felt to be similar to the discredited phraseology of the Czechoslovak conservatives; the reformers were above all concerned with a positive alternative to the system which had been imposed on their country and which they considered alien and demonstrably unsuitable. They were all aware of the need to go beyond this system, and the reform can be understood as a constant search for new institutions, new structures, new relationships. The methods of achieving this alternative state of affairs were generally recognised as having to be reformist. To that extent the reality of twenty years of Stalinism and neo-Stalinism at home and the looming presence of Soviet Russia abroad were acknowledged as constraints. Rudi Dutschke came to Prague and failed to establish communication: What is he talking about? Is that all he has to offer? Does he not realise that

[1] Ibid., pp. 164–5 and 185.

every revolution must have its after-life and that it is precisely this 'after' that we are grappling with?

Thus it is not surprising that New Left objectives and formulas did not strike roots and remained confined to a handful of people and a few theoretical debates. The student community, elsewhere the primary supplier of revolutionary socialists, Maoists, Guevarists, Marcuseites, Trotskyites, syndicalists and other radicals, in Czechoslovakia remained committed to democracy and freedom rather than 'permanent revolution'. Admittedly, they were more radical than most, spearheading action and debate on issues which the less outspoken would have liked to evade, forget or even suppress. Suffice it to say that it was the students who pressed hardest for the restoration of Social Democracy, i.e. a party which is the object of scorn for many New Left protagonists in the West. Let us have genuine non-Communist political parties and let us have freedom of non-Marxist thought, the Czech students were saying in direct contrast to their Western colleagues who held parliamentary democracy in contempt and could not pride themselves on tolerance towards non-Marxist philosophy. Perhaps it was all wrong and the Czechoslovak reformers placed their bets on a losing horse. But it certainly was consistent with the intellectual origins of the Czechoslovak reform movement and with the politico-economic configuration from which it arose.

The following is a quotation from two statements published in May 1968 by a small group of persons (typically: most were middle-aged) who believed that a combination of New Leftism and the Czechoslovak reform was possible and necessary:

'We expect that within our society there is a numerous group of those who . . . wish to adhere to a genuine revolutionary left wing, a label which was unjustly misused by the conservative leaders of the Party, and who are seriously interested in achieving genuine socialist democracy, such as would not degenerate into formalism, opportunism and compromise. We are of the opinion that . . . it is useful to create a platform for discussion and co-operation between both the Marxist-Leninist and the non-Marxist left wing. . . . We shall start without the slightest material and organisational support from any of the existing institutions . . .'[1]

[1] See reports in *Rudé právo*, 11 May 1968, p. 2, and *Literární listy*, 16 May 1968, p. 12 and 13 June 1968, p. 12.

The eleven signatories (including one former editor of *Rudé právo*) appealed to the public to join them and proceeded to prepare for the establishment of an Association of the Marxist and Non-Marxist Left (*Sdružení marxistické i nemarxistické levice*). The constituent rally they convened on 7 June could not in fact constitute anything because they had only been able to hire a hall on condition that no new organisation would be formed there. (This was not directed against left-wingers in particular; many landlords insured themselves in this way against falling out with the law.) More importantly, the gathering numbered only some 100 people who were later described as workers, technicians, intellectuals, Communists and Catholics. The proclamation they issued laid emphasis on the principles of socialism and suggested that the economic reform should be conceived so as to remove economic inequality. Democracy should not be understood as a narrowly institutional affair because as such it did not ensure equal opportunities for all. The workers' councils must not be a mere appendix to the management, but ought to wield decisive influence over enterprise decision-making and the distribution of the products of society. One man in the assembly got up to repudiate any Maoist tendencies, but the majority thought there was no reason to be afraid and recommended that Chinese, Cuban and Albanian experiences should be studied, as well as those of radical movements in Western Europe. Another participant declared that no one wished to form a Maoist party today or tomorrow, but that it would be wrong to reject Mao *a priori*.

That was about as far as the theoretical preparation for a New Left movement went. Some articles on radical socialist theorists and practitioners appeared in *Literární listy, Student* and *Nová mysl*, and there was increased interest in Isaac Deutscher, mainly in his criticism of Stalinism. On the whole there is no doubt that it all remained the intellectual exercise of a few. The group of young people (Petr Uhl *et al.*) who were put on trial for conspiracy and Trotskyism in 1971 had been later prompted into action by the fate of the reform more than the reform itself.

CHAPTER SEVEN

Societies and Churches

Diversity of association must be one of the indications of the citizen's interest in running his multifarious microcosms, sometimes as a springboard to the macrocosm of politics. In 1948 Czechoslovakia had between 60,000 and 70,000 societies, clubs and other associations. In 1967 the number was down to 700–800.[1] Of them, the political parties and thirty-one other 'voluntary social organisations' were members of the National Front. The organisational infrastructure had been affected and, to a large extent, devoured by the political structure: it had to subscribe to the overall ideology and, with the exception of its small and unimportant components, to the principle of democratic centralism. This arrangement still offered a certain leeway for the assertion of an innocuous group interest or the pursuit of a pastime, but the suspicion with which the authorities viewed any kind of horizontal identification outside the official pyramid hindered truly voluntary association. In fact, only two things among those affecting the relationship between citizen and authority were left by the law entirely at the discretion of a government agency, which did not have to state its reasons when turning down an application: the issuance of passports and the permission to set up an organisation. In both instances the agency in question was the Ministry of the Interior, meaning the police.

It had not always been so. Freedom of association was granted to the public as one of the achievements of the revolution in 1848. It was revoked in 1849 and, until reintroduced in 1867, an official licence had to be obtained before a new organisation could emerge. The grounds on which an application for a

[1] Z. Mlynář and V. Pavlíček, 'Politická organizace ve vztahu k vývoji sociální struktury socialistické společnosti', in *Sociální struktura socialistické společnosti* (Prague, Svoboda, 1967) pp. 653 ff.

licence could be rejected were then enumerated by law. From 1867 to 1948, with the exception of the period of Nazi Occupation, the founders could simply announce that an association was being formed. Law No. 68/1951 on Voluntary Organisations and Assemblies and the related procedural ordinance No. 320/1951 put at end to all this libertarianism. Both statutes remained valid in 1968 (and to this date) and the reformers considered it imperative that they should be changed. 'As we can see,' F. Kriegel said, 'uniformity of social and political life evidently does not suit us. We need active citizens and it is quite natural that their activity should find expression above all in those fields which are of interest to them. Besides, the activity of the various associations is of considerable material value.'[1] And so, while a new Bill was being drafted (and pre-1968 draft amendments to the old Bill criticised), the Ministry of the Interior, as the licensing agency, adopted a more lenient attitude towards applications.

An 'organisation-to-be' was required to submit to the Ministry a brief definition of its purpose in the form of a declaration of intent and a draft of its statutes. Until these documents were returned to the applicants with the Ministry's endorsement, only a preparatory committee was allowed to exist and pursue 'preliminary' activities. In practice this was difficult to enforce because it was almost impossible to draw a strict line between preliminary and proper action. Generally the authorities tended to be tolerant and, where delicate or uncertain ground was broken, such as with the K 231, KAN or the Social Democratic Party, the Ministry preferred to procrastinate. It might seem, if one goes by the various general descriptions of the Prague Spring, that hundreds of new organisations queued up for legalisation or simply set up shop without asking anybody. In fact only seventy applications for registration had been received by the Ministry by mid-June 1968, of which thirty-one submitted draft statutes while the others merely wished to conduct tentative talks about procedural matters.[2] At that time the Ministry had sanctioned only one organisation, the Society for Human Rights. On several occasions, spokesmen for the

[1] *Rudé právo*, 19 June 1968, p. 1.
[2] J. Pavel speaking in the National Assembly Committee for National Committees. *Rudé právo*, 19 June 1968, p. 2.

government emphasised (or other Establishment speakers warned) that new organisations must not expect to be susidised from public funds (in A. Indra's words), or that only the 'important and publicly beneficial' ones (as Minister Pavel put it) could hope for government grants.[1] The several versions of the new Bill on Association were never publicised and information on its provisions remains scarce. It seems that while reverting to the principle of simple notification of the authorities by the founders of a new organisation and while laying down reasons which might entitle the government (local government) to step in, the Bill explicitly did not apply to political parties, trade unions, co-operative organisations and churches.

In conditions of Communism the distinction between a sectional interest organisation and a promotional (attitudinal) organisation is considered false because the unity of social and particular interests appears beyond doubt and because the promotion of Communism as the single all-embracing cause is taken for granted. Among other things, the latter assumption does not preclude the existence of organisations officially consecrated to active campaigning for ideologically wholesome causes, most notably for friendship with the Soviet Union and peace. Compared to the newly emergent associations, the Czechoslovak–Soviet Friendship Union (SČSP) and the Peace Defenders' Committee (ČSVOM) faced a different set of problems in the context of the Prague Spring, notably that of a redefinition of aims and methods.

Since the 1950s, SČSP ranked second in size, after the trade unions: its official membership in 1968 was given as 2,500,000.[2] This was a thoroughly inflated and formal figure, including collective members, i.e. other organisations. Factory branches were abolished in 1965 and the entire Union suffered from a chronic lack of public interest. Perhaps, paradoxically, the conditions of the Prague Spring could have breathed new life into it, even if on a more realistic basis as far as size of membership and scope of activity were concerned. Although it was not easy to relinquish the formal notion of its own greatness and

[1] A. Indra addressing the Northern Moravian regional conference of the Party, *Rudé právo*, 20 April 1968, p. 3. J. Pavel, op. cit.

[2] *Hospodářsko-politická rukověť*, *II. díl* (Prague, ČTK, 1968) p. 1005.

strength, the union took steps to work out a more modest programme of action: it still wished to remain 'an explicitly political organisation with a firm place in the National Front', but its attention would be turned to the exploration of specialised fields of interest related to the Soviet Union, and to the satisfaction of its members' personal hobbies. It hoped to expand private contacts between Czechoslovak and Soviet citizens, establish its own travel bureau, hold courses in Russian, keep in touch with sister organisations in other countries, lobby the authorities to relax passport formalities, extend its information service for Soviet citizens, etc. Other proposals included the establishment of a permanent Czechoslovak–Soviet museum in Prague (in the subterranean halls on Letná Hill under the plateau which had supported the notorious giant statue of Stalin) and in Bratislava, and of a standing exhibition of Russian and Soviet fine art. It was suggested that special attention should be paid to those Soviet Republics in which Czechoslovak citizens were particularly interested, such as the Baltic Republics and Armenia, and that, in addition to Russian, language courses of Ukrainian, Belorussian, Lithuanian, Latvian, Armenian and Georgian should be offered to the public. Organisationally, the union contemplated going over to a federative structure which would include a Union of Individual Members, a Union of Collective Members, several Societies of Friends of Russian (Ukrainian, etc.) Culture, several societies promoting group interests related to the Soviet economy, a publishing house (which had existed under the name *Svět sovětů* and was renamed *Lidové nakladatelství*) and a travel agency. Plans for the future were accompanied by fairly extensive activity along the traditional lines, such as the holding of Days of Ukrainian Culture and Art (from April to August), which comprised exhibitions on Shevchenko, Kassian, applied art, books and illustrations, and visits by ensembles, etc. Twenty-nine summer camps (as against twenty in 1967) for students of Russian were held or about to be opened, and several summer seminars on foreign policy, the cinema and the theatre were either in progress or being prepared.[1]

Soviet pressure against reform naturally had an adverse effect on public interest in all these activities and plans, although

[1] *Rudé právo*, 23 April 1968, p. 6.

some very sensible ideas about what ought to be done to preserve and enhance such friendship as still existed date from the very tense first days of August. What would happen if the Czechoslovak experiment had been permitted to go on must remain a matter of conjecture. The realistically subdued thinking about the future programme of the union looked promising. On the other hand, freedom of inquiry and discussion, newly enjoyed by the Czechoslovaks, would probably be a constant source of friction. For example the Shevchenko discussion in Prague offered an opportunity to probe into the problem of Ukrainian nationalism. Sore spots, such as Solzhenitsyn, Pasternak, the Kronstadt rebellion and Trotsky, could not remain taboo for the inquisitive mind freed from artificial barriers. Michal Reiman's book on the 1917 Revolution, for example, drew bitter criticism from the Soviet side. Unless officially decreed and enforced, to be friendly while at the same time turning a blind eye to every issue which the other side automatically considered offensive was out of the question. As far as Czechoslovakia is concerned, the dilemma disappeared (at least for some considerable time) with the entry of Soviet tanks into the country. For all practical purposes the Union of Czechoslovak–Soviet Friendship ceased to operate. After painstaking revival, it is said to have numbered half-a-million members by the end of 1970.[1] There is no means of verifying this figure. Nevertheless, every reform movement in Eastern Europe has and will have to face the dilemma: either a genuine quest for personalised contact and free exploration of values is permitted and the reform movement immediately faces the lethal danger of invoking Soviet wrath, or 'friendship' is officially dispensed and regulated. The sensible will choose the latter, if they can.

The case for the Peace Movement was difficult to present to the public and, against the backdrop of the Prague Spring, all sporadic attempts to this effect looked pale and unreal. The ČSVOM functionaries seemed to indulge in an exercise of self-justification, again and again going on record to emphasise how important and useful their organisation was. At the same time they themselves were at a loss as to what kind of activity to pursue. Their 'action programme' (in draft form) of early

[1] Radio Free Europe, *Situation Report*, 4 February 1971.

April was painfully vague: the movement, it said, would develop various initiatives, closely co-operate with young people, prominent personalities and social organisations with the aim of cementing the unity of views and action in their struggle for peace, promote the scientific study of questions of peace and internationally co-operate with sister organisations. A fortnight later the Praesidium addressed a press appeal to the public to send in proposals of what they thought the movement should do. At the same time the Praesidium 'demanded' that the movement should be considered 'one of the main political organisations in the National Front'.

The cause of 'peace' or 'the preservation of peace' must have appeared much too broad to merit the existence of a special organisation, although anti-war feelings in connection with specific conflicts, such as Vietnam and Biafra, were manifested publicly. Similarly, even if on a different plane, to promote a better deal for women on the lines of the largely formal structure of the Czechoslovak Women's Union must have seemed a fairly fruitless exercise. One had the feeling, however, that a women's lobby would have eventually found a meaningful place among the genuine pressure groups. A suitable organisational form, however, was not discovered during the short-lived existence of the Prague Spring.

A vigorous search for newly defined (and revived) aims occurred in the Union of Anti-Fascist Fighters (SPB – *Svaz protifašistických bojovníků*) which, within an orthodox organisational network, had been deflated to the dimensions of a charity. In 1951 the numerous resistance groups, hitherto enjoying separate existences and a much respected status on the strength of their recent war exploits, were forced to merge in a single centralised union. As memories of war and anti-Nazi resistance receded and as new generations began to assert themselves in tackling entirely new problems, the 100,000-strong union became more and more orientated towards the past. Moreover, for ideological reasons the Party leadership imposed restrictions on contacts within the union between members of resistance movements who had been active in the West and in the East. An atmosphere of suspicion surrounded the dwindling group of First World War legionaries (some of whom 'had fought against the Bolsheviks') as well as members of the

International Brigades in Spain (dubbed Trotskyites in the post-February purges) and the former soldiers and airmen from Britain. Many former partisans, fighters in the Slovak National Rising of 1944 and those who had manned barricades in Prague in May 1945, were viewed with only slightly less vigilant eyes.

The Prague Spring offered all these groups, and the union as a whole, a new common denominator behind which they could rally and shake off the image of retrospective brooding. The new cause was rehabilitation, conceived both as a rehabilitation of tradition and a rehabilitation of the victims of Communist persecution. The Union hoped to achieve the former by attaining a permanent and influential place among the major political organisations of the reformed National Front, as well as by promoting respect for anti-fascist traditions through co-operation with history teachers, cultural organisations, etc. As far as the rehabilitation of political prisoners (i.e. victims of Stalinism) was concerned, the picture was somewhat less clear, unless one wished to consider this activity 'anti-fascist' as well. Nevertheless, there was a certain overlapping of interest, because an unusually high percentage of the victims had belonged to one or another component of SPB.

At an *aktiv* in the middle of March, members of the union were among the first to go on record as demanding general rehabilitation (*ex lege*) and, almost with the same breath, the resignation of Novotný and Defence Minister Lomský.[1] The union established a rehabilitation commission, chaired by Mrs M. Trojanová, and asked the President of the Supreme Court to appoint SPB representatives to rehabilitation 'senates'. Taking an unprecedented step, Trojanová and another member of her commission (himself a former political prisoner) secured permission from the Ministry of the Interior to visit the Valdice penitentiary. There they found out (on 30 April) that fifty of the inmates had been incarcerated for political delicts, including fifteen convicted before a military court. Trojanová and Rohlena told them that the Anti-Fascist Fighters' Union was trying to have their sentences 'interrupted' so that they could plead for rehabilitation as free men. (Unfortunately, I have no information on the outcome of this remarkable episode.)

[1] *Rudé právo*, 17 March 1968, p. 11.

The union also demanded freedom of publication, including a completely independent publishing house and authority to issue its newspaper *Hlas revoluce* as a weekly and later to revive its one-time daily *Národní osvobození*. It hoped to reacquire its health and recreational facilities, which had been transferred to the State and to other organisations, i.e. the trade unions.

Similar to the other unitary organisations, SPB planned to transform its centralised structure into a kind of federation, thus giving a much coveted autonomy to its constituent parts while preserving the advantages of a state-wide lobby. Four basic associations were to be formed within the Czech Union (to be subdivided further): of political prisoners (war-time) and their next-of-kin, of partisans and members of the internal resistance, of participants in the Czech Rising of 1945 and of members of the resistance on foreign soil in both wars. The diversity of interests was still greater, and had the process not been halted the fragmentation would have continued.[1] This need not have been detrimental because the very nature of association of former comrades-in-arms called for small groups of people linked by common memories, while the overall issues, such as rehabilitation, could have been left to the federal committee. On the whole the Union of Anti-Fascist Fighters seemed to have found both sufficient zeal among its members and a worthy cause to reassert itself as a viable and meaningful organisation carrying a good amount of political weight.[2]

Foremost among the newly emerging promotional organisations was the Society for Human Rights (*Společnost pro lidská práva*), whose statute was authorised by the Ministry of the Interior and which was constituted in Prague on 17 May 1968. Milan Machovec, the philosopher, became chairman, and

---

[1] As a matter of interest, the Czech Partisans' Association counted among its collective members 2,000 Czech and Slovak guerrillas who had fought in Yugoslavia, and some 8,000 members of the Union of Greek Partisans who had emigrated to Czechoslovakia in 1948–9.

[2] For example, on 27 April Josef Smrkovský characterised the resistance movements in the First and Second World Wars as 'prominent expressions of Czechoslovak statehood'. *Rudé právo*, 28 April 1968, p. 1. Ludvík Svoboda met an SPB delegation in Lány on 28 June and told them that 'resistance and anti-fascist fighters carry great moral weight because they have stood in the front ranks of the struggle for freedom, democracy and socialism in this country.' *Rudé právo*, 29 June 1968, pp. 1, 3.

Emil Ludvík was elected secretary-general. (In Slovakia the title was *Spoločnosť pre ochranu ľudských práv*.)

In the preparatory stages, the society formulated its aims in general terms: 'The time has come for our nations, faithful to their traditions, to recognise the necessity of fully restoring the principles of democracy and humanism in this state . . . Aware of the historic nature of this struggle for democracy in our country, we have resolved to establish the Society for Human Rights whose purpose it will be to assist in the renascent process, so important for the very existence of our people.'[1] Seventy-three well-known and not so well-known signatories affixed their names to this resoundingly noble appeal, among them the chairmen of both non-Communist parties. Although many of the founding fathers (including Machovec) were members of the Communist Party, no Communist dignitary deemed it possible to sign in his official capacity. In less lofty but equally general statements, the society promised to encourage the process of democratisation, to watch over the observance of human rights and liberties and to press the government to ratify the U.N. General Declaration of Human Rights of 1948.

Considering the several practical occasions on which the society chose to intercede with the authorities, one feels that this was meant to be an ethical lobby, and certainly not an embryonic political party whose aim it would be to strive for political power or a share of it. Thus, for example, the Society circulated National Assembly members (in June) with a letter, imploring them not to let 'crimes against humanity committed in the name of socialism and Communism' lapse on statutory grounds. Rehabilitation cannot be approached on solely legal premises, the society said; it must be considered primarily an ethical question. The period whereby offences against humanity become statute-bound should be stipulated to begin only on 5 January 1968, the day on which the era of arbitrary power had come to an end (Dubček's ascendance). Later in the same month the society published a protest against the release from custody of a former police officer who had been suspected of having caused the death of a Catholic priest in the early

[1] *Kulturní noviny*, 26 April 1968, p. 1. Machovec was the author of a very good book *Tomáš G. Masaryk* (Prague, Melantrich, 1968).

1950s. The society also planned to publish a weekly (*Občanské noviny*) and some preliminary selection of staff was made. Observers, however, felt that in this respect enthusiasm ran ahead of practical expertise and a rational evaluation of the situation.

Advocacy of civil rights and liberties on ethical grounds is undoubtedly pertinent to the reform of a system which claims to be based on the class struggle and which relies on the bureaucratic arrangement of the power structure. Whether the Czechoslovak Society for Human Rights represented a viable model of an organisation devoted to this task is difficult to say. It was certainly quite popular and the misgivings of detached observers may have arisen from the fact that it was not given enough time to crystallise properly. It did not long survive its first anniversary: the Ministry of the Interior banned it on 28 May 1969 'because it had engaged in functions of a political nature' for which it had not been licensed.

Among the several professional organisations which sought to re-establish their status by insisting on separation from the trade unions, one should name the Union of Czech and Slovak Physicians (*Svaz českých a slovenských lékařů*). Its constituent congress in Brno on 8 June 1968 claimed to represent 21,000 doctors.[1] (Another report gave the number as 23,127.[2] Official statistics say that Czechoslovakia had 32,179 doctors at the end of 1968, including 22,801 in the Czech Lands and 9,378 in Slovakia.)[3] The Central Committee of the Trade Union of Workers in Public Health almost pathetically protested, saying that the congress had taken place 'without its approval' and that the doctors should have been content with the newly established physicians' sub-section of the union. The new Union of Physicians responded by asking its members not to cease working along trade union lines, but declared that the profession could not content itself with representation in a large organisation devoted to general trade unionism, whose membership included less qualified health service personnel and even administrative staff. Later, in 1970, the doctors were accused of acting as a splinter group, not unlike the Federation of

[1] *Rudé právo*, 9 June 1968, p. 2.
[2] *Literární listy*, 25 July 1968, p. 2.
[3] *Statistická ročenka 1969* (Prague, SNTL, 1969) p. 505.

Engine Crews. On 11 February 1970 the Physicians' Union was disbanded.

A simple enumeration of some other new and renewed organisations will illustrate the 1968 situation which was very conducive to sectionalism. The Union of Professional Pilots, abolished in 1951, reconstituted itself on 30 April. The Union of Czechoslovak Divers was formed on 26 May. Artistes and entertainers founded their Union on 27 May. The Union of Czechoslovak Musicians, first founded in 1908 and wound up in the 1950s, announced its reconstitution. The Union of Prague Folk Musicians dissociated itself from the Prague Cultural Centre. The preparatory committee of the Czech Union of Small-Scale Production and Service Industries hoped to foster private enterprise on a small scale and at the same time represent small socialised and co-operative shops. General managers of manufacturing enterprises and their deputies intended to set up a Union of Managers. Also planned was the establishment of an Association of Economists and a Union of Architects and Builders, both technical rather than creative organisations, while the Union of Civil Engineers held its constituent congress on 28 June. A group of old-age pensioners in Brno formed a preparatory committee of a Union of Retired Workers and collected 600 applications for membership by the beginning of August.

A host of societies planning to promote co-operation with other countries on an unofficial basis came into existence, such as the Czechoslovak–French Society, the Czechoslovak–British Society, the Society of Friends of Yugoslavia, the Society of Czechoslovak–Rumanian Friendship, the Society of Friends of Polish Culture and the Society of Friends of the German Democratic Republic. A Club of Friends of China was set up in Slovakia.

New Slovak organisations included the Economic Movement of the Intelligentsia and Students, the Slovak Union for Adjustment of Land Holdings, the Reform Movement, the Republican Society and several religious organisations.

A brief announcement at the end of April spoke of the beginning of activity by the T. G. Masaryk Society which intended to popularise the first Czechoslovak President's legacy and to campaign for the erection of his statue in Prague.

Thirteen young people formed a Dubček Club in Pilsen on 9 August.

The main points at issue in para-military and sports organisations were connected with the separation of the Automobile Club from the tutelage of Svazarm (Union of Co-operation with the Army); the dispute over the revival of the physical training organisation Sokol – should it be within the Czechoslovak Union of Physical Training and Sport or separately; and the bickering between the Czech and Slovak officials in the Football Union over the way the union was to be run and national competitions organised.

As a point of interest, the first 'genuinely voluntary' organisation founded after 1948 was the Club of Akin Souls (*Klub spřízněných duší*), the brain-child of Jiří Suchý, the actor, poet and singer. It was begun in 1966 and by March 1968 its membership numbered 1,136. A meticulous breakdown stated that most of its members were students, clerks, teachers, workers, doctors, librarians, housewives and old-age pensioners.

Neither religion in itself nor the Churches played any significant part in the reform movement. The Czechs are not devoutly religious, and a lukewarm attitude to matters of faith goes hand-in-hand with tolerance. The overwhelming majority of the reformers were atheists, but they recognised both the uselessness and idiocy of officially mounted campaigns of militant religion-baiting. Since the first half of the 1960s a number of 'authentic Marxists' from among the reformist community of philosophers and social scientists participated in the then fashionable Christian–Marxist dialogues. One such encounter was even held in Mariánské Lázně in April 1967 under the joint sponsorship of a West German society and the Sociological Institute of the Czechoslovak Academy of Sciences. Emerging from these meetings and their aftermath was a modern and sympathetic recognition that religion did offer man one way of coping with existential questions, especially those affecting him as an individual. Belatedly, a new generation of non-Marxist thinkers also aspired for recognition. Some of the young philosophising Catholics or catholicised philosophers were associated with *Tvář* literary magazine, whose

<hr>

[1] *Literární listy*, 7 March 1968, p. 10.

preoccupation was with spiritual values. On the whole, however, this trend did not show the same strength as, for example, in Poland. Neither was it always associated with the Catholic Church, which, one must bear in mind, most certainly did not constitute a reformist point of reference, let alone a political force outside the official structure which had to be given a place in the reformist plans. Thus, while not being religious, the reform movement was neither pro- nor anti-religious. It did, however, bode well for both the Churches and non-institutionalised believers precisely because of its emphasis on freedom of thought and association.

In 1968, eighteen Churches and religious societies were legally in existence, including the newly authorised Greek Catholic (Uniate) Church.[1] Their numerical strength is impossible to estimate because official statistics and censi had long ceased to register religious affiliation. They were: Roman Catholic, Greek Catholic (Uniate), Czechoslovak Church, Religious Society of Czechoslovak Unitarians, Evangelical Church of Czech Brethren, Evangelic Methodist Church, Brotherly Unity of Baptists, Seventh Day Adventists, Unity of Czech Brethren, Unity of Brethren, Silesian Evangelical Church of the Augsburg Confession, New Apostolic Church, Old Catholic Church, Christian Congregations in Czechoslovakia, Slovak Evangelical Church of the Augsburg Confession, Slovak Reformed Christian Church, Orthodox Church, Council of Jewish Religious Communities in the Czech Lands and Central Union of Jewish Religious Communities in Slovakia.

There were six theological faculties; namely, two Roman Catholic; one catering for the Czechoslovak Church and the Unitarians; one for the Evangelical Church of Czech Brethren, the Slovak Reformed Church, the Methodists, the Baptists and the Adventists; one for the Slovak and Silesian Augsburg Denomination Churches; and one for the Orthodox Church. Two publishing houses printed books with religious themes and issued twenty-nine religious papers and journals. The Czech Catholic Charity looked after retired clerics, nuns, priests and parish housemaids, maintained several recreation and health facilities, and was the sole producer and distributor of ecclesiastical objects.

[1] See Chap. 5 on *Nationalities*.

The first serious attempt to go beneath the surface of seemingly unruffled progress from religion to atheism is connected with the name of Dr Erika Kadlecová, the sociologist who was to replace Karel Hrůza as chief of the Church Office in the Ministry of Education on 25 March 1968. In 1962–3 she led a team of investigators who conducted a survey of religious beliefs and habits in five districts of the north Moravian Region. The findings caused something of a sensation when they were published in October 1964:[1] 30 per cent of the respondents were found to be clear-cut atheists; 40 per cent had lost some but kept other religious characteristics; and 30 per cent were classified as fully religious. Kadlecová also detected deviation from 'conformist faith' to 'individual religion': 55 per cent of the sample were persons for whom 'true Christianity' lay in compliance with moral commandments; 24·5 per cent gave priority to 'belief in the existence of Jesus Christ'; and 5·2 per cent saw both as equal in importance. Extrapolation of the north Moravian findings to the whole of the country is not reliable. Relative to a greater part of the Czech Lands, the region is known to be traditionally more religion-minded, while a comparison with Slovakia shows the contrary. The only other comparable survey was undertaken by the Sociological Institute of the Slovak Academy of Sciences in October and November 1968 and covered the whole of Slovakia.[2] Its results are shown in the following table juxtaposed to Kadlecová's inquiry (in per cent of respondents):

	Slovakia, 1968	North Moravia, 1963
Atheists	14·1	30·0
Believers	70·7	30·0
Undecided	15·2	40·0

The Slovak survey revealed other interesting information: 28·2 per cent of the respondents thought that the clergy should be allowed to carry out public-political activity; only 15·6 per cent of young people in the 18–24 age group were non-believers; percentages of atheists in the three main social groups were

[1] E. Kadlecová, 'Výzkum religiozity v severomoravském kraji', *Nová mysl*, 10 (1964).
[2] P. Prušák, 'K niektorym výsledkom prieskumu religiózity na Slovensku', *Sociológia*, 1 (1970).

10·1 per cent of workers, 28·0 per cent of employees and 8·3 per cent of farmers; and predominance of Roman and Greek Catholics was confirmed as follows:

Denomination	Percentage of total respondents	Percentage of total believers
Catholics	57·63	81·6
Protestants	12·72	18·0
Orthodox	0·08	0·1
Jews	0·08	0·1
Small Churches and Sects	0·15	0·2

While the Slovak figures were collected too late to be available to the reformers, the Dubček leadership must have been aware that the religious issue had not been completely swept away by twenty years of undivided Communist rule. One has the impression, however, that they approached the problem as a question of principle rather than a tactical political issue. Kadlecová put it thus: 'In a non-antagonistic society freedom is indivisible. If the law is broken *vis-à-vis* one group of citizens, no one can feel safe, not even those who misuse the law.'[1] She mapped out the reform which the new government proposed to follow in conjunction with the legitimate religious leaders. (This State–Church dialogue about practical reform steps was in itself a new element in the previous uneasy co-existence of unequal partners. Gustáv Husák took part in it as Deputy Prime Minister.) Essentially, both sides, with the Vatican apparently having given its backing to the idea, agreed on gradualism rather than radical change. Accordingly, several bishops received permission to take up their posts at the head of unoccupied dioceses. A number of priests and persons persecuted for religious beliefs were released from prison and others were 'rehabilitated'. Religious instruction was transferred from cumbersome official supervision to the sole responsibility of the Churches (as from the 1968–9 school-year). A green light was given to religious press, the total circulation of which increased from 31,000 copies in Bohemia and 42,000 in Slovakia in 1966 to 170,000 in Bohemia and 125,000 in Slovakia in 1969,[2] and to religious writers of home and foreign

[1] E. Kadlecová, 'Společnost a náboženství, *Rudé právo*, 18 May 1968, p. 3.
[2] K. Hrůza, 'Religiya i ideologicheskaya bor'ba v Chekhoslovakii', in *Ateizm i stroitel'stvo sotsializma* (Moscow, Znanie, 1970), pp. 26–32.

provenance (e.g. in the *Vyšehrad* publishing house). Favourable consideration was given to at least a partial revival of religious orders. Freedom was granted to religious gatherings, debates and recruitment of new priests. The discredited Peace Movement of Catholic Clergy (*Mírové hnutí katolického duchovenstva*) was allowed to expire; its notorious chairman, excommunicated priest Josef Plojhar, and most members of the praesidium resigned on 21 March 1968. The cautious and prudent Catholic leader, Bishop Josef Tomášek, Apostolic Administrator of Prague, took over the 'provisional action committee' with the aim of setting up a new organisation styled the Cause for Council Revival (*Dílo koncilové obnovy*). Not long after the invasion the Ministry of the Interior refused to register the Cause, and two years later a not entirely successful attempt was made to reimpose a State-controlled organisation on the clergy under the name *Pacem in Terris*.

Although the Catholic dignitaries were prominent in pursuing a circumspect move towards reform, many of the new measures applied to other denominations as well. Facing a somewhat different predicament, the spokesmen for the Jewish community (some 16,000 strong) hoped to obtain from the new State leadership an unequivocal proclamation denouncing the anti-Semitic features of the trials of the 1950s and condemning racial discrimination. In view of the delicate foreign political implications, notably Czechoslovak subscription to the Soviet stand in the Middle East, the Jewish Religious Community in the Czech Lands showed considerable circumspection in merely asking that its contacts with abroad should not be impeded and that international developments should not be allowed to influence the status of Jews in Czechoslovakia.[1]

The reformers certainly did not have a religious outburst on their hands. Bishop Tomášek, Chief Rabbi Feder and other religious leaders were more than willing to co-operate without much ado. Tomášek endorsed socialism, which he did not see as necessarily atheistic. If it is to give man more freedom than the previous forms of government, it must grant him full religious freedom, he wrote.[2] Feder stated that the Czech Jews regarded socialist Czechoslovakia as their home and that

[1] See *Rudé právo*, 9 May 1968, p. 2, and *Literární listy*, 30 May 1968, p. 2.
[2] *Literární listy*, 21 March 1968, p. 4.

even after the bitter experience of the 1950s they would do the utmost for a country headed by people who enjoyed popular confidence.

It is difficult to imagine what the forms and scope of religious organisation in reformed Communism would be and whether the promising Church–State co-operation would lead to a lasting *modus vivendi*. Full separation of the Churches from the State, including termination of the payment of clerical salaries from the government's coffers, was privately mentioned as a possibility. Most likely, the resulting state of affairs would be less than sensational (as indeed with many other reformist designs). The Church leaders, especially the Catholics, who commanded the largest following, were sensible enough not to seek political power. The reformists, on the other hand, were obviously willing to give up control over the internal life of the Churches and the consciences of individuals. This is not to say that the reformist future would be problem-free. Erika Kadlecová intimated the nature of a possible conflict in the following way: 'We shall face the fundamental problem . . . of how to incorporate into the structure of a democratic society an institution which itself is structured undemocratically and hierarchically and whose supreme leadership resides abroad. How do we incorporate an international institution with its own canon law into our community and legal order so as not to disrupt or permit the disruption of the indivisible sovereignty of a socialist country?'[1] She was speaking about the Catholic Church, not the Communist Party.

[1] E. Kadlecová, 'Společnost a nádboženství', *Rudé právo*, 18 May 1968, p. 3.

Conclusions

It is now recognised that the ideological and organisational monolith of a Communist society conceals divergent relationships and processes. An increasing number of students of Communism agree that this extends to the formulation and promotion of sectional interests and even advocacy of causes which do not tally with the central ideological postulates. Many are, however, prepared to look for group attitudes and action only at the top. For them, personal affection or animosity between Politburo members, with the associated formation of cliques and coteries, are the only meaningful division. At most, vested interests of huge immobile apparats such as the army, the police, the Party machinery, the planners and the managers, are recognised as another. On the opposite end of the spectrum, atomised dissenters among the intellectuals are seen to be desperately seeking horizontal association with like-minded colleagues.

I have no doubt that personal followings, checks and influences by apparats and dissent on the part of genuine opponents of the *status quo* are all present beneath the ostensibly singular dedication of the whole of society. Simultaneously, however, I seem to discern a more conventional group behaviour asserting itself as a corollary of that relatively recent phenomenon in Eastern Europe – the economic and political reform movement. It pertains to those sections of the societal machinery which normally play, or aspire to play, the part of a political infrastructure. Components of the 'united' trade union organisation, other workers' groups, farmers' unions, various groups of scientists, scholars, artists, creative intellectuals and journalists, segments of the technical intelligentsia, parts of the conglomerate of youth organisations, students, ethnic entities, religious groupings, territorial particularisms, sub-divisions in official

promotional organisations and various local and interest
societies and clubs – they all have begun to seek a life of their
own. Nowhere was the scene better set for an observation of
this budding assortment of political lobbies than in reform-
oriented Czechoslovakia.

The most frequent process during the Prague Spring whereby
a new organisation came into existence was *disintegration* of old
monopoly structures. This was true about the Party, the trade
unions, the Youth Union, the Anti-Fascist Fighters' Union, and
others. Not always was the divisive process consummated; what
used to be the central committee changed into a 'roof' representation, while the constituent parts ceded to it a certain amount
of their newly won powers. It seems that protection of sectional
interests acted as a factor conducive to separation, whereas
promotion of overall political reform blanketed group divergencies. There were few particular causes to promote, other than
those subsumed under the crystallising plan for a general repair
of the system.

Some organisations came into life as a result of *associative
processes*. In the case of the Co-ordinating Committee of the
Creative Unions the motivation lay in an endeavour to unite
the reformist strivings of numerically fairly small groups of
intellectuals, who were simultaneously shifting away from the
traditional organisational pattern of democratic centralism in
their internal structures. In other cases obvious gaps in the
sub-governmental set-up were being filled, as with the constitution of the Co-operative Farmers' Union or the Union of
Scientific Workers.

Several organisations emerged in response to *newly felt
requirements*, which had been unthinkable in orthodox conditions; for instance, the workers' councils, the Society for
Human Rights, the Club of Committed Non-Party People
and the K231.

Straightforward *replacement* was another type of formative
action, observed, for example, in the case of the Cause for
Council Revival superseding the Peace Movement of Catholic
Clergy. The Boy Scouts and the Social Democratic Party could
be considered examples of simple *revival* of organisations
defunct since before the advent of full Communist rule.

Some existing organisations sought to meet the challenge of

reform by *redefining their aims and methods*. In a way, every part of the political structure and infrastructure had to undertake an introverted inspection, but as the main self-preservation exercise this process occurred especially in the non-Communist parties, the quasi-promotional associations, such as the Peace Defenders and the Czechoslovak–Soviet Friendship Union, and the less reform-oriented apparats such as the secret police and the People's Militia.

Certain elements of *ad hoc group formation* of the once-and-for-all type were present, as in the holding of rallies to help enforce a certain policy or, say, a resignation, in petition-type collecting of signatures, and in insistence on direct communication between the leaders and the masses; for example, when a crowd demanded to be addressed on a certain issue by a certain politician at a certain moment.

Conclusions which transpire from the findings described in this book can be summarised as follows:

(1) Emancipation was sought above all by distinctive socio-economic units which had been incorporated into large, ideologically determined wholes or had been denied representation altogether.

(2) Autonomous or fully independent organisations, carved out of old agencies or established via a take-over by new leaders with new ideas, did not go beyond the initial institutional phase, that is, declaration of a general programme and preparatory steps towards full constitution.

(3) Typically, the new and renewed organisations combined sectional and promotional elements. While professing to advocate the interests of their members better than was possible under the old set-up, they aspired to promote a cause. Invariably, advocacy of interests was directed against pressure from the State more than against other sections of society or organisations, and cause promotion centred around political and professional freedom and general reform.

(4) The key aim of group action was to achieve participation in political decision-making. Most organisations accepted the curtailing principle of National Front and even the leading role of the Party, albeit understood in a reformed way. They hoped to launch a pluralistic system, but did not concur in what its crucial characteristics were to be.

(5) Group action was overwhelmingly constitutional and circumspect, with the exception of some *ad hoc* behaviour. It largely gave support to the new government as a whole, prompted it into a certain kind of action, and criticised some of its policies. There was no expression of overall opposition to the reform cause and the elementary socialist principles. Advocates of *status quo ante* formed no organisation, but did show signs of opportunistic grouping.

(6) The newly emergent groups and organisations had a considerable effect on the government of the day. It took their existence and many of their demands into account when formulating such crucial policies as the Action Programme, the establishment of workers' councils, the new understanding of the trade unions, abolition of censorship, continuation of economic reform, the new Party Statutes, its stand against Warsaw Pact pressure, etc., as well as many lesser measures. In this sense the emerging organisational infrastructure belonged to the most successful political lobbies ever to exist. The various groups among the intelligentsia exerted the greatest influence.

(7) At the same time the political leadership of the country sought to develop counter-influence, mainly in three directions: to preserve a certain measure of organisational unity; to push workers' organisations to the fore in order to enhance the working-class character of its policies; and to curb various excesses, especially the institution of a multi-party parliamentary system and, by the same token, the formation of organisations totally unacceptable to the guardians of orthodoxy.

Much as the Czechoslovak experience is determined by unique conditions, it would appear that group activity seeking self-assertion as well as a share of political power constitutes one of the major driving forces concomitant to every movement which is designed to reform a system based on false pretences of singularity.

Index of Names and Subjects

Names which do not bear direct relevance to the developments described in this book are not included in the index although they may appear in the text or, more often, in footnotes, e.g. as authors of books or articles.

Index of Organisations

This index includes non-governmental organisations discussed in the book. In the first list the Czech or Slovak titles are in alphabetical order. The second list comprises translated titles grouped for easier reference under thirteen headings.